William T. Harris

Psychologic Foundations of Education

An Attempt to Show the Genesis of the Higher Faculties of the Mind

William T. Harris

Psychologic Foundations of Education
An Attempt to Show the Genesis of the Higher Faculties of the Mind

ISBN/EAN: 9783337158811

Printed in Europe, USA, Canada, Australia, Japan

Cover: Foto ©Andreas Hilbeck / pixelio.de

More available books at **www.hansebooks.com**

International Education Series

EDITED BY

WILLIAM T. HARRIS, A. M., LL. D.

———

VOLUME XXXVII

INTERNATIONAL EDUCATION SERIES.

12mo, cloth, uniform binding.

THE INTERNATIONAL EDUCATION SERIES was projected for the purpose of bringing together in orderly arrangement the best writings, new and old, upon educational subjects, and presenting a complete course of reading and training for teachers generally. It is edited by WILLIAM T. HARRIS, LL. D., United States Commissioner of Education, who has contributed for the different volumes in the way of introduction, analysis, and commentary. The volumes are tastefully and substantially bound in uniform style.

VOLUMES NOW READY.

1. **The Philosophy of Education.** By JOHANN K. F. ROSENKRANZ, Doctor of Theology and Professor of Philosophy, University of Königsberg. Translated by ANNA C. BRACKETT. Second edition, revised, with Commentary and complete Analysis. $1.50.

2. **A History of Education.** By F. V. N. PAINTER, A. M., Professor of Modern Languages and Literature, Roanoke College, Va. $1.50.

3. **The Rise and Early Constitution of Universities.** WITH A SURVEY OF MEDIÆVAL EDUCATION. By S. S. LAURIE, LL. D., Professor of the Institutes and History of Education, University of Edinburgh. $1.50.

4. **The Ventilation and Warming of School Buildings.** By GILBERT B. MORRISON, Teacher of Physics and Chemistry, Kansas City High School. $1.00.

5. **The Education of Man.** By FRIEDRICH FROEBEL. Translated and annotated by W. N. HAILMANN, A. M., Superintendent of Public Schools, La Porte, Ind. $1.50.

6. **Elementary Psychology and Education.** By JOSEPH BALDWIN, A. M., LL. D., author of "The Art of School Management." $1.50.

7. **The Senses and the Will.** (Part I of "THE MIND OF THE CHILD.") By W. PREYER, Professor of Physiology in Jena. Translated by H. W. BROWN, Teacher in the State Normal School at Worcester, Mass. $1.50.

8. **Memory: What it is and How to Improve it.** By DAVID KAY, F. R. G. S., author of "Education and Educators," etc. $1.50.

9. **The Development of the Intellect.** (Part II of "THE MIND OF THE CHILD.") By W. PREYER, Professor of Physiology in Jena. Translated by H. W. BROWN. $1.50.

10. **How to Study Geography.** A Practical Exposition of Methods and Devices in Teaching Geography which apply the Principles and Plans of Ritter and Guyot. By FRANCIS W. PARKER, Principal of the Cook County (Illinois) Normal School. $1.50.

11. **Education in the United States: Its History from the Earliest Settlements.** By RICHARD G. BOONE, A. M., Professor of Pedagogy, Indiana University. $1.50.

12. **European Schools; OR, WHAT I SAW IN THE SCHOOLS OF GERMANY, FRANCE, AUSTRIA, AND SWITZERLAND.** By L. R. KLEMM, Ph. D., Principal of the Cincinnati Technical School. Fully illustrated. $2.00.

13. **Practical Hints for the Teachers of Public Schools.** By GEORGE HOWLAND, Superintendent of the Chicago Public Schools. $1.00.

14. **Pestalozzi: His Life and Work.** By ROGER DE GUIMPS. Authorized Translation from the second French edition, by J. RUSSELL, B. A. With an Introduction by Rev. R. H. QUICK, M. A. $1.50.

15. **School Supervision.** By J. L. PICKARD, LL. D. $1.00.

16. **Higher Education of Women in Europe.** By HELENE LANGE, Berlin. Translated and accompanied by comparative statistics by L. R. KLEMM. $1.00.

17. **Essays on Educational Reformers.** By ROBERT HERBERT QUICK, M. A., Trinity College, Cambridge. Only authorized edition of the work as rewritten in 1890. $1.50.

18. **A Text-Book in Psychology.** By JOHANN FRIEDRICH HERBART. Translated by MARGARET K. SMITH. $1.00.

OTHER VOLUMES IN PREPARATION.

D. APPLETON AND COMPANY, NEW YORK.

INTERNATIONAL EDUCATION SERIES

PSYCHOLOGIC FOUNDATIONS OF EDUCATION

AN ATTEMPT TO SHOW THE GENESIS OF THE HIGHER FACULTIES OF THE MIND

BY

W. T. HARRIS

NEW YORK
D. APPLETON AND COMPANY
1898

PREFACE.

In offering this book to the educational public, I feel it necessary to explain its point of view. Psychology is too frequently only an inventory of certain so-called "faculties of the mind," such as the five senses, imagination, conception, reasoning, etc. And teachers have been offered such an inventory under the name of "educational psychology." It has been assumed that education has to do with "cultivating the faculties." Perhaps the analogy of the body has been taken as valid for the soul, and, inasmuch as we can train this or that muscle, it is inferred that we can cultivate this or that faculty. The defect of this mode of view is that it leaves out of sight the genesis of the higher faculties from the lower ones. Muscles are not consecutive, the one growing out of another and taking its place, but they are co-ordinate and side by side in space, whereas in mind the higher faculties take the place of the lower faculties and in some sort absorb them. Conception, instead of existing side by side with perception, like the wheels of a clock, contains the latter in a more complete form of activity. Sense-perception, according to the definition, should apprehend individual things, and conception should take note of classes or species. But conception really transforms perception into a seeing of each object as a member of a class, so that the line between perception and conception has vanished, and we can not find in consciousness a mere perception of an individual object, but only that kind of perception which sees the object in its process of production.

Moreover, this inventory-psychology misapprehends the nature of classification and generalization. It believes it to be a result of analysis and abstraction, whereas it is really a synthesis; to the object there is added its cause; the idea of the individual is enlarged by thinking it in the process that has produced it and others like it. For we connect one object with another by going back to the common process that originated both. This is the most radical error of the inventory-psychology. It is the source of a long train of other evils, for it arrests the investigation at the stage of isolated details, and makes impossible any insight into the genesis of the higher faculties of the mind. The doctrine of nominalism—and the so-called conceptualism of Hamilton and others is practically nominalism—is the only logical result from its theory of generalization. Universals are only *flatus vocis*—mere names or mouthfuls of spoken wind: only individuals exist. It has never occurred to such psychologists to inquire whether the processes in which individuals are generated are not real too, and real in a higher sense than the individual things and events that they originate, modify, and destroy.

Education has use for psychology only in so far as it shows the development of mind into higher activities and the method of such development. What if the psychologist happens to know and recognise only the lower faculties, and to be ignorant of all but the names of the higher ones? It is evident that he will conceive under those names only the lower activities with which he is acquainted. This has, in fact, happened often. Perception of individuals is all that inventory-psychology thinks under conception and generalization. The understanding with its relativity doctrine is all that some followers of Kant think under the name reason.

Again, it has happened that psychology recommended for teachers has been mostly of an individualistic character, the principle of participation * in spiritual life being ignored. Hence all allusion to the psychology of society, of nations, of institutions, and especially of art and religion, has been omitted.

Education can not be wisely administered except from the high ground of the spirit of civilization. The child is to be brought most expeditiously into a correct understanding of his relation to the race, and into a helpful activity within civilization. Unless the psychology of civilization is understood by the teacher, he will quite likely be harmed by learning a list of the so-called faculties. He will suppose, for example, that his business is to bring about a " harmony among these faculties," and develop them all symmetrically. Being ignorant of the way in which higher faculties re-enforce the lower, he will attempt to cultivate them isolatedly, and he will generally produce arrested development of the mind in the lower stages of its activities or faculties, and prevent the further intellectual growth of his pupils during their lives; for it happens that the fundamental categories of the different faculties or activities are radically opposed, and to harmonize them is to stultify

---

* There is lately much activity among the deeper sort of thinkers on psychology in this province of social participation. See Chapter XXXV for some mention of it.

the mind. The first stage of the understanding, for example (Chapter XXVII), holds an atomic view of the universe, while the second stage holds a pantheistic view; the former believes that all reality is an aggregate of individual independent things and events, while the latter thinks the reality is a one substance out of which things and events arise and into which they again disappear, like waves of the sea.

The view of the reason is theistic and opposed to both views of the understanding, holding to individuality, like the first or atomic stage of the understanding, but limiting its atomic existence to personal beings; like the second or negative-unity stage, in holding that there is one institutional person in whom all persons unite socially and find their freedom.

The attempt to harmonize these fundamental categories, which preside over the activities called faculties, is, of course, worse than useless. The highest faculty contains the solution of the contradictions of the lower ones. The solution of immature activities is to be found in growth out of immaturity.

Education needs a psychology that will show how all activities, whether individual or social, react on children and men so as to develop them. The educative influences should be shown not only of each branch in the course of study, or each discipline in the school, but also of each institution—family, industrial vocation, state, and Church; also of art and religion, of play and work, of each national life from China to western Europe and America. Each object and each situation, every act of man or every refusal to act causes a reaction in the soul, educative in its effect; it has its mental factor or subjective coefficient, and hence an educative result.

This indicates sufficiently the point of view of this book. It is an attempt to show the psychological foundations of the more important educational factors in civilization and its schools. Special stress is laid on the evolution of the higher activities or faculties, and on the method of it.

In my attempt to make a ladder of explanation from each new phase of life or thought to the principle of self-activity, which is invoked as the ultimate principle, I have, as I am aware, seemed to make endless repetitions. But I hope that the candid reader will patiently try to justify me by seeing that the iteration is necessary for the connection of the new matter with the old principle of self-activity, and to save that reader from the burden of carrying in his memory what he has already read earlier in the book.

W. T. HARRIS.

WASHINGTON, D. C., *February 3, 1898.*

ANALYSIS OF CONTENTS.

xi

furnish clews to psychology and reveal its method of investigation; the insight into self-activity as the key to the explanation of life and mind.

§ 8. All activities of man have an internal or mental side; hence there is a psychology to all that man feels, knows, and wills; the business of psychology to show this; moreover, this inner reaction is educational; hence educational psychology must investigate the inner reaction that accompanies the manifold activities of man.

§ 9. Consciousness of the inward activity of the mind is a necessary factor in observation of the world in so far as self-activity is recognised in the life of plants and animals; or activity according to design in any objects. § 10. Theory of evolution sees everywhere development from mechanical aggregates toward vital organisms; Clifford's "ejects." § 11. Hence evolution recognises introspection in the objective world as the goal of its progress; Plotinus said, "Nature is greedy of beholding itself."

§ 12. The great central fact in psychology is self-activity; denied by Herbert Spencer in his First Principles; also by Mansell. § 13. Mental pictures of self-activity impossible, but also motion, change, and energy unpicturable. § 14. Assimilation, sensation, volition, thought, are forms of self-activity, and its denial makes both physiology and psychology impossible. § 15. Phenomena that involve self-activity; plants have assimilation. § 16. Animals have assimilation, locomotion, and sensation. § 17. Feeling. § 18. Sensation. This chapter (III) to be expanded into Part II of this work.

§ 19. Plato discovered the third stage and described all three; the atomic stage, or "common sense." § 20. The category of relativity; Isaac Newton a perpetual schoolmaster; ancient scepticism; Buddhism; correlation of forces. § 21. Relativity presupposes self-relation. § 22. Each of the three stages a view of the world; the third stage of knowing sees all in each or each in the light of all.

§ 23. Current doctrine of percepts and concepts not true; a concept not a mental image, but a definition of the process that produces the individual object. § 24. Mental image a specimen illustrative of the definition or concept; concepts correspond to deeper realities than mere percepts; Hume and nominalism.

§ 25. Kant's doctrine of the structure of mind; how its *a priori* forms or categories make experience possible. § 26. Synthetic activity of the mind, using time, space, and causality; reaction of mind upon its sense-impressions. § 27. Space thought as infinite. § 28. Infinite space a positive idea and not a negative idea as Hamilton supposed, for we see the necessity of space beyond any limit to space; a limit to space requires space to exist in. § 29. Again, in order to know that a mental picture does not include all space, we must see that the boundaries of the picture require space to exist in, and therefore continue space rather than terminate it. § 30. Time also infinite, because a supposed beginning presupposes time before it. Importance to psychology of this fact—that we know the infinitude of space and time in an affirmative manner instead of negatively as Sir William Hamilton supposed.

§ 31. Causality makes experience possible. If we had no idea of causality, we could not recognise ourselves as producers of our own deeds, nor recognise objects as causing our sense-impressions; we should not distinguish what is subjective from what is objective; and yet Hamilton supposed the idea of cause to be a "negative impotence" of the mind; but it really is the basis of all our positive or affirmative knowledge of the not-me, the objective world. § 32. Cause involves the idea of producing something new; it is the unity of identity and difference in a deeper idea—that of energy; without it we should deny the possibility of origination of anything new. § 33. Analysis of the idea of cause finds that it consists in the production of a distinction within itself and the transfer of it to another, which is the effect; self-separation accordingly is the basis of causality; this is self-activity; this can not be imaged; Kant's third antinomy solved; causality the basis of the ideas of God and moral responsibility. § 34. Distinction between human and divine personalities; potential and real.

CHAPTER VIII.—*The Psychological Meaning of the Infinite and Absolute* . . . . Pp. 58–62.

§ 35. The true ideas of infinitude and first cause lie at the basis of educational psychology, because they make possible the higher orders of knowing; without them the ideas of education (God, freedom, and immortality) are not possible; Herbert Spencer's self-contradiction in denying ultimate religious ideas while affirming the doctrine of the persistence of force. § 36. True insight into causality as originating distinctions and differences—as producing variations and modifications is necessary for any progress in understanding psychology; Herbert Spencer's denial of free will.

CHAPTER IX.—*The Logic of Sense-perception. What Figure of the Syllogism Apperception uses* . . . . Pp. 62–70.

§ 37. The logical structure of the intellect an important part of rational psychology; the syllogistic activity of the mind used not only in conscious reasoning, but also in the lower activities, such as sense-perception and even feeling. § 38. Sense-perception uses the second figure of the syllogism in recognising its object; it is identified by perceiving some mark or quality in it that is remembered as belonging to an object formerly perceived, the common mark being the middle term. § 39. The four valid modes of the second figure; the technical terms of logic; definitions of figures.

CHAPTER X.—*How Sense-perception uses the First Figure to re-enforce its first act which takes place in the Second Figure.*
Pp. 70–77.

§ 40. The class or species of the object having been identified by the second figure, the first figure is used to anticipate other features of the object known to belong to the class, and these are identified one after another in the object, or, if not found, lead to a correction of the first act of recognition and a new classification. § 41. It is important to note that the so-called valid modes are not used in sense-perception; certainty is reached by multiplied acts of verification. § 42. School instruction gives the pupil the stored-up results of human experience, and prepares him to anticipate experience by using the first figure to test the results of the second figure and revise its conclusions; hence, quick perception is taught not so much by repeated perceiving as by ap-

2

brain are instruments for learning and controlling the external world; the body organic, but the soul something higher—namely, a builder of organisms; knowing and willing not biological but psychological.

§ 72. What physiological psychology may be expected to discover, in view of its methods and means—namely, a stock of pathological knowledge regarding the proper care of the nervous system and the cure of its diseases; the study of special organs can not reach metaphysical or moral results, because these relate to universal conditions of being and therefore transcend all organs; the conclusions of physiological psychology would therefore be only negative; unless organism can be transcended, there can be no universal conclusions, or, indeed, conclusions of any sort; for each conclusion is a subsumption of a particular under a universal. § 73. The will lies entirely within the field of introspection; its existence is a fact of consciousness; its inconceivability is simply unpicturability; the difference between the consciousness of the child or savage and that of the man cultured in reflection. § 74. Freedom of will seems impossible to minds on the first stage of reflection, or in the doctrine of relativity; the two difficulties: first, to see beyond the doctrine of relativity; secondly, to explain the fatalistic doctrine of the strongest motive and its alleged constraint over the will.

§ 75. Psychology must show why a false doctrine seems to be true, by the three stages of knowing; the motive seems to control the will only when it is regarded as an external reality existing independently of the will; but a motive is not an existing thing any more than is a mental image; it is a purpose or ideal of something that does not yet exist, but will require an act of will to make it exist; to say that a motive constrains the will is to say that something acts before it exists; I must think away the conditions of existence in order to conceive a motive, for a motive is an ideal of a state of existence different from the actuality. § 76. The will is thus creative in two ways in acting according to motive: First, it makes the motive by thinking an ideal that may

.

possibly exist in place of the actual; secondly, it realizes the
motive or ideal and annuls the actuality that was; here it proves
its freedom and superiority over the actuality, because it can conceive an ideal in place of the actual, and then proceed to make it
take the place of the actual. § 77. The moral motive contains
the ideal self—the perfectly independent ego—as its object, or end
and aim; it is therefore transcendent of all reality and outweighs
death; the moral motive is therefore the strongest and at the
same time the arrival at perfect freedom of the will, because
the will makes its independent self the sole object in willing according to the moral motive; in sacrificing its life for another,
it weighs in the balances all the motives of empirical reality and
outbalances them with its transcendent self; the moral is the
form of consistent self-activity; that self-activity which would
deny its own independence by nullifying the freedom of others
is immoral. § 78. Spontaneity distinguished from moral freedom; co-operation of the individual will with the will of the
social whole; Kant's "categorical imperative": act so that the
deed will not contradict itself if it is made the universal act of all
intelligent beings; act so that if the social whole acted as you do,
it would not reduce your action to a zero. § 79. The moral the
highest motive, because it re-enforces the individual will by the
will of the community, and thereby consolidates all intelligent
will power into one; Hegel's thought on this point.

§ 80. Self-activity is presupposed as belonging to independent
being; dependent beings therefore presuppose it also. § 81. Freedom does not presuppose fate as its ground, but, on the contrary,
fate presupposes freedom as more fundamental; fate is phenomenal and freedom is noumenal. § 82. Dialectic of fate or necessity
shows it to be a part or side of the more comprehensive category
of self-activity or freedom; assuming that all things are necessitated to be just as they are by the totality of conditions, it follows
that each thing is derivative from the environment or totality,
and hence there has been change; in change something new begins and something old ceases to be; but the old was necessitated
to be as it was by the totality of conditions. § 83. The new also
is necessitated by the totality; hence there must be two totalities
of conditions, one for the old and one for the new, and therefore

the totality must have changed; but there is nothing outside the totality to necessitate it; if it is necessitated it necessitates itself; if it changes it changes itself; hence the totality must be self-active. § 85. Necessity, therefore, must be of a part and never of the whole; fate is partial, self-activity total; necessity belongs to the realm of effects, to dependent beings, self-activity and freedom to independent being. § 86. Fatalistic necessity is a different thing from logical necessity, which is an internal necessity of being and not an external necessity; a dialectic circle in which necessity is used in two senses.

§ 87. The so-called "new psychology" taken to include physiological psychology and "child study." § 88. The "old psychology" had discovered and described the rational structure of the soul, (*a*) its syllogisms in three figures, (*b*) its stages of ascent; (1) nutritive as plant, (2) sensation and locomotion as animal, (3) rational in man who has sense-perception, imagination, memory, reflection, and pure thought; the active and passive intellects were discriminated and the doctrines of theism, freedom of will, and immortality were demonstrated by it. § 89. New explication of self-activity as object of introspection. § 90. German (Kantian) distinction of universality and necessity as the criterion of *a priori* knowledge which transcends experience; space, time, causality, and many other ideas transcend experience and yet make experience possible. § 91. Bodily conditions and how to rise out of the lower stages of mind to the higher, need physiological psychology and child study for their elucidation, and here is a great field for new psychology. § 92. The long period of helpless infancy. § 93. Arrested development occasioned by overcultivation and too "thorough" drill in mechanical studies at this epoch. § 94. The *gamin* of Victor Hugo.

§ 95. System arises from the application of method; method is the mode of activity of a principle; its activity produces an organic whole or system. § 97. Part I gave glimpses of the method, discussing self-activity, the infinite, the absolute, mental pictures and concepts, figures of the syllogism as showing mental structures, the physiological psychology as counterpart to logic, the freedom of the will as the acme of self-activity. § 98. Method now applied to produce a system; a growth or progressive realization of the principle (self-activity) through its method; all facts should be seen as illustrations of the principle, or else the science is not yet perfect.

perception not only receptive of impressions but an act of introspection; the scale of the senses; touch, taste, smell, a more or less violent attack on the individuality of the environment; hearing and seeing, ideal senses in that they do not involve the destruction of the object perceived.

§ 115. Feeling a sort of digestive activity not directed on its food but turned inward and acting upon itself and for itself; touch, taste, smell, hearing, and seeing considered more in detail.

§ 116. Recollection can recall at pleasure the ideal object formed in the act of perception; memory is systematized recollection; it generates the faculty of perceiving things and events as individuals of species or members of classes, and this makes possible language and the specially human form of mind; it looks behind the object to its producing causes; it sees in each object many other possibilities, a sort of halo of potentiality. § 117. This is a further activity of introspection; it is an attention to the activity of recollection; for it re-enforces the present perception of the object by adding to it its past perceptions, hence completing the present object by adding to it its variations and thus seeing it in the perspective of its history; it thus transmutes the transient into the permanent and sees each individual in its universal; the act of attention here makes its appearance, since the mind in collecting its experience around one individual must needs neglect other objects. § 118. Generalization thus goes on in the swift unnoticed process of sense-perception and memory. § 119. Mnemonic systems usually attempt to strengthen the memory by attention to accidental associations instead of essential relations; cultivate the memory directly where it is weak, but do not train the mind to notice accidental relations, for this weakens the power of thought. § 120. The scale of ascent from limitation of the subject by the object in sense-perception to free reproduction of the object in memory. § 121. Memory a double self-activity as compared with sense-perception. § 122. Overcultivation of sense-perception arrests development in memory and thought; overcultivation of memory likewise arrests or deadens the power of thought and also of imagination; the will also settles into passive obedience through too much cultivation of the memory. § 124. Cases in which memory

the individuals which it absorbs again into itself, and cause them through its own energy or self-activity; hence self-activity is the basis of a negative unity. § 154. Self-activity is therefore presupposed by pantheism to make its negative unity possible; but self-activity establishes theism rather than pantheism; analysis of self-determination finds in it the substance or negative unity of pantheism, and, besides it, also the causal creative energy of theism. § 155. *Causa sui;* the negative unity the ultimatum of analysis and the beginning of synthesis. § 156. The affirmative function of the understanding; the significance of naming things for the child. § 157. Language makes both phases of the understanding possible, for it is a process of taking up into consciousness the results of the unconscious action of the concept-forming stage, which have been preserved by words. § 158. The doctrine of persistent force as negative unity of things and forces when grasped fully reveals personality underlying it as the true form of being; the four forms of ideas—(1) sensuous, (2) abstract, (3) concrete, (4) absolute —correspond to four views of the world (*Weltanschauungen*).

§ 159. Explanation of the style of this book, its repetitions and incessant return to the beginning. There are many lines of result that lead out from each new principle, and hence it is necessary to trace out one after another, and a new statement of the first step becomes necessary; how a method grows to a system; if its principle is self-activity it is also a method, for we have only to ask what a self-activity will do or produce to discover its method; Hegel's Begriff as the identity of principle and method; review of the systematic unfolding of self-activity from plant to the rational soul in the light of immortality. § 160. The study of the higher faculties reveals the destiny of the lower faculties; it shows what is positive or affirmative in them and what is negative (this is the most valuable service of psychology for the educator); where permanent individuality begins; the memory of the self necessary to immortality; memory dies only when replaced by a higher activity, which is memory and a great deal more. § 161. The arrival at this higher activity a matter of education and the goal of human existence; man's bodily and spiritual individualities; significance of death.

§ 162. Still another review of the ascent from sense-perception to reason, but this time from the standpoint of the will; with the view of the world given by reason we see that complete self-determination, such as is found in conscious personality, is the ground of the objective world and its innermost cause; personality is not only intellect but will, not only subjective but objective. § 163. How the will turns the passivity of mere sensation into *attention*. § 164. Attention the beginning of culture or education; it turns the chaos of sense-impressions into a system by selecting one object and neglecting all others. § 165. Attention produces analysis or discrimination in the object (use of the third figure of the syllogism, the object being the middle term, new qualities discovered in it furnish subclasses); through analysis we discover the influence of other objects, and hence we see how the object belongs to a larger whole, including it and other objects which influence or modify it; this is synthesis. § 166. Synthesis is the discoverer of relativity, of essential relation; two kinds of attention—critical alertness in the observation of the things and events going on around one, and absorption in a train of thought following out the logical presuppositions of an object (compare Herbart's Besinnung and Vertiefung). § 167. The continued use of analysis and synthesis arrives at the discovery of interrelations and dependence, and the doctrine of universal relativity makes its appearance, for if each is dependent on the others there is only one whole. Here we have found again the negative unity as the result of the action of the will on the intellect; further, the whole can not be dependent on another whole, and hence it is independent, and therefore again self-active. § 168. Illustration of the transition from the thought of negative unity to the thought of self-activity; correlation of forces shows each force as running down, but in so doing it winds up another force, hence perpetual motion; but perpetual motion logically presupposes self-activity, for it continually produces the tension (winding up) which, in restoring its equilibrium (running down), becomes change and movement (a tension is produced by the difference between an ideal and a real; a coiled spring has a shape in which it is at equilibrium, and then it exerts no force on its environment; wind it up and we make its real different from its ideal; we destroy its

equilibrium of ideal and real, and force exerted on its environment is the result; unless there is winding up by the separation
of the ideal from the real, all would stop with its running down.
Grasp together this winding up with its running down, and we
have the idea of self-activity; in exerting our wills by a volition
we create an ideal different from the real, and this results in force;
I will to raise my arm by making its ideal an elevated arm, whereas it is really by my side). § 169. The action of the will in inhibiting the lower and relatively passive orders of knowing; the five
intentions of the will producing successively attention, analysis,
synthesis, reflection, insight; Aristotle's nomenclature. § 170. Insight perceives personality or completed will as the truth of the
universe; but insight arises in us through the determination of
the intellect by the will; hence will causes the intellect to see
will as the universal reality. § 171. The feelings tend toward
intellect or toward will; hence they can be educated by the conscious will, as shown in Chapter XXVI. § 172. Not sense-perception but insight sees the concrete truth. § 173. Psychology
not necessary for the unfolding of the higher orders of knowing,
any more than physiology and hygiene are necessary for the performance of digestion and breathing; but it explains them, and
is necessary for a correct theory of them or for any just criticism
of them; if something is wrong, psychology is necessary to correct it.

THIRD PART. PSYCHOLOGIC FOUNDATIONS . Pp. 253–400.

§ 174. Part I illustrates the method. Part II deduces systematically the phases of the intellect. § 175. Part III applies the
doctrines unfolded in Parts I and II to the explanation of problems of human culture or education, for there are psychological
foundations to each product of human activity; this psychologic
basis is to be shown for (1) society and its institutions; (2) the
history of nations; (3) art and literature; (4) science and philosophy; (5) the course of study in schools; (6) the grading of
schools as elementary, secondary, and higher.

CHAPTER XXXI.—*The Psychology of Social Science.*
Pp. 254–263.

§ 176. Participation produces the social whole; through it the
individual is elevated above savagery; vicarious living of the race
for the individual; Nature *versus* human nature; society a human

creation, and hence the ascent out of mere nature into human nature an act of freedom or self-determination. § 177. The institutions of civilization, family, civil society, the state, the Church. § 178. The family equalizes the differences of age, sex, strength, health and disease, maturity and immaturity, through mutual help. § 179. Civil society the realm of individual independence; each producer avails himself through his own production to lay tribute on all the other workers in the world; he makes all civil society serve him, but he in turn serves all. § 180. The state is the social whole become a person for itself, the will of the whole acting for itself, the intellect of the whole discovering its true interests; the principle of justice; the return to each man the fruits of his deed; the overt act; sin and crime; justice and mercy. § 181. The Church; worship and sacrifice the two elements of religion; the negative act of the intellect and the negative act of the will.

CHAPTER XXXII.—*The Institutions that educate.*

§ 182. The education of infancy by the family called nurture; personal habits, courtesy toward others, etiquette of life, self-control, mother tongue; play. § 183. Education of the school in the "conventionalities of human intelligence"; the technicalities of intercommunication, reading and writing; tools of thought; mathematics and science. § 184. Education of one's vocation; to limit himself to a specialty and acquire skill of production; the consciousness of his dependence on society, and of his discharge of his obligation by means of the product of his industry; division of labor increases indefinitely the quantity of production and improves its quality: the consciousness of his power to convert dependence and debt into independence and economic freedom by industry a high order of education. § 185. The education of the state a still higher influence; giving him the consciousness of his greater self, the personality of the social whole; his possession of its might and his pride in its deeds; his consciousness of justice and responsibility. § 186. Education of state contrasted with that of civil society. § 187. The education of religion highest of all; the absolute ideal, its influences on all other forms of education.

action against social order becomes crime when it fixes itself permanently and seriously; (*a*) crime attacks the social whole and tends to destroy the great process of re-enforcement of the individual by society; (*b*) sin and crime discriminated; (*c*) separation of Church and state; (*d*) the measurement of crime; the penalties as symbols of the effects of the deeds returned on the doers; (*e*) poetic justice; literature as teaching the nature of crime and sin and their reactions against the doers. § 195. Man's two selves (*a*) the psychology of Dante's Inferno: (1) the sins of incontinence, their effects on the soul to punish it; (2) the sins of envy take the form of fraud, and punish the doers by shutting them off from the blessings of social intercourse; (3) the sins of pride take the form of treachery; (*b*) the psychology of Dante's Purgatory; the consciousness of the nature of mortal sin makes the sinner desire purification, and he is glad of the pain which helps him rid himself of what obstructs his ascent to holiness.

CHAPTER XXXV.—*The Psychology of Infancy.* Pp. 295–321.

§ 196. What the child learns in his first four years; Preyer's observations on the infant; some of the epochs of the first year; holding up its head; standing alone; walking; recognition of the members of the family; imitation. § 197. The acquisition of language enables him to learn not only by his own senses, but, through the senses of all his acquaintances; his delight in discovering that each thing and event are links in a long causal series (the "house that Jack built" is a symbolic account of this discovery). § 198. The place of imitation in education; it is social in its very nature: (*a*) manners and customs are imitated forms of doing; fashion has a high meaning as a sort of emancipation from superstitious observances; (*b*) imitation as the basis of intellectual culture; hypnotic suggestion. § 199. Imitation is self-activity; it is an act of emancipation from heredity and natural impulse, for the imitator represses his own impulses to be himself alone, and puts on by an effort the habits or semblances of another person: (*a*) there is an element of originality in all imitation; (*b*) originality increases by progression from imitation of external details to imitation of the spirit in which the deed is done, when an insight is reached into the causes and motives of the thing imitated; (*c*) when the principles and methods are understood, the child is emancipated from imitation; (*d*) M. Tarde, Les lois de l'imitation;

(e) M. Tarde the anti-Rousseau. § 200. Parrotlike imitation is considered the lowest intellectual activity; to make it the basis of all education as well as the staple of it has something of raillery in it; to say that man is a symbol-making animal suggests art and literature, institutions, religion, civilization; the monads of Leibnitz; Wilhelm Meister and the theatre; to acquire culture, one must assume higher ideals and practise them until they become a second nature; Goethe intended to show how much this resembles the dramatic art. § 201. Language enables the child to see possibilities and form motives; it adds to the external seeing an internal seeing of possibilities in the shape of uses, adaptations, transformations and combinations, surrounding the object as a sort of halo; the animal has the external seeing, which beholds the real object, but man adds the internal seeing which beholds these long trails of adaptation. § 202. The symbolic stage of mind, wherein the child thinks in images or mental pictures, comes first; in the definition, which is non-picturable, the child arrives at thought; but the mental picture or symbol does not suffice for a definition; it has only one side of a definition, namely, the particular; the mind is to supply the universal by an unconscious effort; in the definition both the universal and the particular are expressed ("the proximate genus and the specific difference"). § 203. Consequently the symbolic phase is synthetic rather than analytic. § 204. (a) Personification places a soul in a particular thing, or a self-activity in a dead result; (b) metaphor transmutes a thing into soul by giving it a spiritual meaning; (c) play substitutes one thing for another or one activity for another, dealing with particulars like symbolism; it changes the fixed limits of actuality, and thus adds to the particular object a sort of universal adaptation; to play that a stick is a horse is to give the stick a universal being—the possibility of becoming horse and anything else that the fancy may dictate; (d) unconscious symbolism of poetry and mythology in which particular things become universal types ; fairy tales mould the real world to suit the caprice of the child; they give him a sense of freedom, a consciousness of the power of mind over matter. § 205. The symbolic passes over into the conventional when the mental picture is less considered and the idea it conveys more sharply accented; by and by the mind forgets the material image altogether; the rise of a myth out of symbols; the natural symbolism of regularity, symmetry, and circular movement; the sun myth; the poetic myth contains a view of the world; Egyptian symbols. § 206. The kindergarten occupations, songs, and games; the child's reproduction of the doings of society; his conscience; he outgrows his playthings; unmaking as useful as making; Wilhelm Meister's puppet show and arrested development. § 207. The conventional; what the child needs at the age of seven; reading and writing; play *versus* work; danger of arresting development by too much work in childhood.

CHAPTER XXXVI.—*Psychology of the Course of Study in Schools—Elementary, Secondary, and Higher.* Pp. 321–341.

§ 208. The psychological meaning of the course of study; the five windows of the soul: (1) mathematics, time, space, and mechanical relations; (2) organic nature, geography; (3) literature and art, human nature as feelings, convictions, aspirations; (4) grammar, logic, philosophy the intellectual structure; (5) history, the doings of the greater social self as reaction; five co-ordinate groups. § 209. Education for culture and education for one's vocation; general and special education; symmetry for culture studies and specialization for vocation studies. § 210. Psychological coefficient of each study; category of quantity in mathematics, of self-activity in language studies; introspection in grammar; symbol-making activity in literature: (a) will, history, (b) intellect, grammar, (c) heart, literature; these are categories of human nature, while the categories of Nature are quantity for the inorganic phase, and life for the organic stage; proof that these five divisions of studies are co-ordinate, and that no one of them is a substitute for any other, (a) to (e); other school studies or disciplines, drawing, manual training, music, gymnastics; their intellectual coefficient already found in the five groups (f); school education considered as the acquirement of techniques (g). § 211. Secondary instruction continues the five groups. § 212. Higher instruction continues the five lines into (a) higher mathematics and physics, (b) organic sciences (biology, geology, botany, etc.), (c) philology, logic, philosophy, (d) moral philosophy, political economy, and other social sciences, philosophy of history, constitutional history, (e) literature and art, their history and philosophy; the limits of elementary education (a);

3

how the secondary education corrects its defect by studying the grounds of the data given by it, (c) higher education is mostly comparative study, the view of each branch in the sight of all the others; hence it is practical or useful for directing one's actions: it is philosophical and ethical because it connects particular facts and events with the view of the world (d), (e); contrast between elementary and higher educations, the "self-made man" (f), (g); a general conspectus showing the five co-ordinate groups in each of the three classes of schools.

CHAPTER XXXVII.—*The Psychology of Quantity.* Pp. 341–350.

§ 213. Mathematics and literature the extremes of the five groups of study; special investigation of the psychologic basis of these extremes in this and the next chapters. § 214. Quantity as opposed to quality, indifference as opposed to difference; sameness necessary for enumeration; quantity a double thought, positing quality and negating it; a thing becomes a unit when it is thought as being a series of repetitions of itself, one of a multiple and itself a multiple of equal parts (a), (b). § 215. Quantity is therefore a ratio of two units, the constituent units being the first, and the whole or sum which they make being the second; seven is a unity of its ones, and each of its ones is a constituent unity; the elementary operations of arithmetic. § 216. Ratio not explicit in simple numbers, but becomes explicit in fractional forms; the psychology of the operations in thinking fractions (a), (b); decimal fractions (c), (d), (e); ratios in the form of powers and roots, logarithms, the calculus (f), (g), (h). § 217. Quality includes (1) affirmation; (2) negation; (3) limitation; in self-activity the self is the limited and also the limit; quantity lies between quality and self-activity; its limits, being similar units, continue as well as limit it; in quality the other is not a repetition of the thing which it limits, as is the case in quantity and self-activity. § 218. The idea of quantity.

CHAPTER XXXVIII.—*The Psychology of Art and Literature.* Pp. 351–375.

§ 219. Psychology of the beautiful; sensuous elements—regularity, symmetry, and harmony; symbolic, classic, and romantic epochs of art; architecture, sculpture, painting, music, and poetry; art not merely for amusement (a); art the manifestation of the divine to sense-perception; the true, the beautiful, and the good, as bases of philosophy, art, and religion (b); matter becomes a work of art when made to manifest self-activity (c), (d). § 220. Regularity beautiful because it suggests the repetition of the self in consciousness, self being subject and repeating itself as object (a); importance of return to self. § 221. Symmetry a more adequate symbol of the self. § 222. Harmony the correspondence of the outer to the inner, a still deeper identity under difference than regularity or symmetry; why the human form is beautiful in Greek statues (a); psychology of ungracefulness (b); gracefulness is the expression of freedom in the body (c). § 223. Is art the imitation of Nature? Nature does not reflect freedom in itself except in its forms of life, and even then does not reflect so high an order of freedom as is found in human action; but Nature is charming to us for a subjective reason—namely, it suggests a sense of relief from care and worry (a). § 224. Symbolic art does not create forms of free movement, but represents the crushing out of individuality; it indicates the soul struggling with matter to find free expression and not attaining it; symbolic art in India (b), Persia (c), the Euphrates Valley (d), Egypt (e), (f), (g). § 225. Classic art reaches the expression of complete bodily freedom, which is gracefulness; "classic repose"; the Greek religion one with art (a); the Olympian, Isthmian, Nemean, and Pythian games; the preservation of the shapes of the victors at these games in stone by the sculptors (c). § 226. Romantic art reveals the aspiration of the soul for the supersensual, and hence it contradicts art, for it shows the inadequacy of show; it manifests freedom *from* the body while classic art manifests freedom *in* the body. § 227. Romantic or Christian art the transition of art to religion; the perennial function of Greek art to portray man's conquest over Nature by means of science and mechanic inventions. § 229. Architecture symbolic (a), classic (b). (c), romantic (d). § 230. Christian not so successful as the Greek with sculpture. § 231. Painting better fitted for romantic art because it is able to show, by aid of colour, the feelings and emotions of the soul. § 232. Music not confined to a single moment in its portrayal of an action, like sculpture, but it can give its genesis and all the steps of complication and the *dénouement;* tones, chords, and counterpoint (c), (d); architecture and music do not deal with the human form. § 233. Poetry the form of art that unites in itself all the others; epic, lyric, and dramatic forms; comedy and tragedy; the personages of the great poems types of human character; the education of the people chiefly through the vicarious experiences of literary personages.

§ 235. Science systematized results of observation; particular objects having the form of time reveal only a portion of their potentialities at a given moment; experience gradually gathers all the phases together in the definition of the object: (a) science learns to see each thing in the perspective of its history; (b) education in science gives directive power to the labourer. § 236. The three stages of science: (1) inventorying; (2) study of interrelations; (3) comparative history of the science; (a) and (b) the nature of a fact; it is a relative synthesis, including less or more according to the intelligence of the thinker who thinks it; (c) the entire fact to Aristotle would be the entirety of all facts. § 237. Philosophy investigates the presuppositions of existence; it seeks a first principle. § 238. Natural science points toward philosophy as a sort of science of sciences. § 239. Philosophy finds the principle of causality transcendent—i. e., it contains as its nucleus origination or self-activity; philosophy does not inventory anything, it assumes the inventory already made, and tries to explain it by the first principle. § 240. Philosophy not a science of things in general, but a special kind of knowledge—namely, of the general forms found in the world by the several sciences, and the relation of these general forms of existence to the first principle. § 241. All philosophies imply the same first principle, no matter what name is given to it; call it X, and it is assumed as originating all that exists through its own activity, and hence must be self-active: (a) the evolution theory in its positive aspect; (b) in its negative aspect. § 242. To pass from intellect to will—i. e., from theory to practice—requires a philosophic activity of the mind, because deliberation must be arrested, the case must be closed before the will acts; the philosophic activity is one which closes the inventory and assumes that all the facts are in, and then passes judgment regarding their bearing on the question; if the mind kept always in the scientific attitude, it would never act; (a) the bearing of the facts as a whole is seen by a survey which is taken by the philosophic attitude of the mind ; (b), (c) science in its third stage becomes philosophical in its endeavour to discover the relation of each special science to the others; (d) the working scientific man has to resist the tendency to philosophize. § 243. Since philosophy endeavours to discover the bearing of all the conditioning circumstances on a situation, it is ethical. § 244. The first stage of science not practical, and its results not tending to action or ethics. § 245. As the mediator between the intellect and the will, the philosophical attitude always must have a place. § 246. The psychology of the history of philosophy; the five intentions of the mind: (I) the first intention the most rudimentary form of knowing—namely, sense-perception, seizing and holding the fleeting objects of sense by means of the universals. § 247. (II) The second intention contemplates the universals, classes, or genera, and is the second stage of the scientific mind. § 248. (III) The third intention is the philosophic stage of the mind; it looks to the unity of all universals in a first principle. § 249. (IV) The fourth intention is that of philosophical scepticism; it observes method and criticises the third intention by showing inadequacy in the demonstrations of the first principle. § 250. (V) The fifth intention refutes sceptical philosophy by showing method as a whole, and proving the first principle, not by ontological steps, but by finding one by one the presuppositions of each and every sceptical argument, these being psychological attitudes ; when every sceptical attitude is shown to presuppose the result of the ontological proof of the third intention, philosophy is re-established on a firm basis: (a) Fichte's version of Kant's criticism ; (b) Hegel's discovery of the presupposition of the ethical foundation of Kant's Practical Reason; (c) Hegel's logic.

Price, $1.50, postpaid.

D. APPLETON AND COMPANY, Publishers,
NEW YORK, ∴ BOSTON, ∴ CHICAGO.

PSYCHOLOGIC FOUNDATIONS OF EDUCATION.

INTRODUCTION.

§ 1. It is said that the teacher needs to know psychology because it is his business to educate the mind. And it is true that in his vocation he is constantly occupied with a critical observation of the mind in a few of its aspects. For this is necessary in order to manage a school successfully. The teacher must observe the pupil's grasp of the topic of his lesson. He must interpret the pupil's behaviour by such knowledge as he can attain of his disposition and the spirit of his intentions; he must assign lessons of a length suited to the mental capacities which he knows his pupils to possess; he must grade them in classes according to his knowledge of those capacities; he must arrange a course of study in accordance with the laws of mental development.

§ 2. If the teacher knows nothing of psychology

1

as a science, he must copy in detail the methods of others, and rely on his general knowledge of human nature derived from experience. Like all uneducated workmen, he may succeed after a sort by following tradition unaided by science, but he will not develop beyond a narrow degree of perfection in details. He will have no insight into the general relations of his work. He can not safely deviate from routine, nor venture to criticise his own work or the work of others. If he has learned good models, he may pass for a good teacher; if he has learned bad ones, he is unable to perceive their defects. Possessing no scientific knowledge of the mind, he can not lift himself above the details of his art to the principles which govern them, and become himself an original source of directive energy. Some knowledge of the mind every successful teacher must have, although in so many cases it is unsystematic, and consequently unscientific. Ordinary experience differs from science through its lack of completeness and consistency. It is fragmentary and disconnected. Science compensates the inequalities of individual experience by re-enforcing it with the aggregate of all other experiences.

§ 3. Psychology is of two kinds: empirical and rational.

(*a*) Empirical psychology aims to inventory the facts of mind and to arrange them systematically, so that each fact may help to explain all other facts, and in its turn be explained by all. .

(*b*) Rational psychology, on the other hand, deals with the philosophical presuppositions of mental life, with what may be investigated *a priori*, and is found to be necessarily, rather than accidentally, true.

It is confessed that psychology has hitherto borne the reputation of being the driest and least interesting of all the sciences. This is partly due to the circumstance that an inventory of facts of consciousness contains only what is already familiar to us in the fragmentary form of experience. It seems a waste of time to go over and collect with so much painstaking what is already known. Other sciences collect fresh and interesting facts. Psychology by introspection seems to be a sterile occupation, dealing with what is trite and stale. But this is not so. Introspection begins with this dull process of inventorying the already familiar facts of mind, but it forthwith proceeds to the second and higher process of reflecting on the general form of our mental processes. It then enters on a field of generalization entirely unknown to ordinary consciousness and full of astonishing results. By reflecting on the forms of mental activity, we enter the province of rational psychology, and come for the first time to see the real nature of mind. We begin to discern those most important of all fruits of human knowledge— the truths that sit supreme as directive powers on the throne of life—the truths of God, freedom, and immortality.

§ 4. Here we are reminded that there are two hostile schools of psychology. There is one founded

.

upon physiology, which attempts to explain mind as a function of the body. It condemns introspection, and teaches that the soul has no subsistence apart from the body: all individuality is corporeal. The other school, founded on introspection, contends that true individuality is not corporeal by any possibility. The corporeal is moved by external forces, and is divisible, changeable, and perishable, while self-active energy, which is the substance of mind, is incorporeal and the source of all individuality. It denies, moreover, that any really psychical facts may be discovered by external observation—by taste, smell, touch, hearing, or seeing. To understand this stricture on the physiological view, we must take notice of the broad distinction that exists between external and internal observation. There are two distinct and thoroughly marked attitudes of mind. The first is directed outward to the facts in space, and may be called objective perception, or sense-perception. Its characteristic is found in the circumstance that it always sees things as related to environments. To it all things are dependent and relative. The other attitude of mind is directed within, and beholds the self-activities of the mind itself. Self-activity is essentially different from relative and dependent being, because it does not receive its determinations from its environment, but originates them itself, in the form of feelings, volitions, and thoughts. All objects of introspection belong to one of these three classes, and every possible feeling, idea, or volition is a determination of an activity which is, so to speak, polarized into subject and object. Each feeling, idea, or volition is the product of an energy which is both subject and object: it is therefore said to be self-determined. While external observation sees its object as separated into thing and environment, or effect and cause, internal observation sees its object as one unity containing both effect and cause in one. It is what Spinoza called *causa sui.* This is true individuality—called by Aristotle "entelechy," and by Leibnitz the "monad." Be this as it may, all must concede that no form of external experience applies or can apply to internal experience; our apparatus for observing material objects can not perceive feelings or thoughts. This being so, it is evident that physiological psychology can make no progress whatever without introspection. It is limited to noting the relation of concomitance and succession between two orders of observation, the objects of the one being movements and changes of organic matter, and the objects of the other being feelings, ideas, and volitions. The progress of this science will be marked with approximating accuracy in locating and defining physiological functions as connected with mental activities.

There has been recognised from the first an interconnection between the mind and the body. Decapitation has always been recognised as a means of disconnecting the mind from the body. Alcohol, tobacco, coffee, opium, and many other drugs have been used since prehistoric times for their supposed mental effects—effects negative rather than positive, as they dull the action of the nerves of sensation or diminish the mental control over the nerves of motion, and thereby allay the pain of weariness or the worry that arises from a vivid consciousness of the outer world. Physiology is engaged in determining more precisely the location of such effects and their extent, although it will not discover how the corporeal becomes mental or how the external becomes internal, for the reason that objective experience can never perceive thoughts and feelings, yet it will yield rich results in all departments wherein the mind uses the body as an instrument to gain knowledge or to execute its volitions. Insanity, idiocy, the use and abuse of the five organs of sense, all that relates to the proper care of the body, the influence of age, sex, climate, race, the phenomena of sleep, dreams, somnambulism, catalepsy—whatever relates to these and the like important topics will receive elucidation, and, more especially, educational theory will be enriched by investigations of the causes of arrested development.

§ 5. It is believed that arrested development of the higher mental and moral faculties is caused in many cases by the school. The habit of teaching with too much thoroughness and too long-continued drill the semi-mechanical branches of study, such as arithmetic, spelling, the discrimination of colours, the observation of surface and solid forms, and even the distinctions of formal grammar, often leaves the pupil fixed in lower stages of growth and unable to exercise the higher functions of thought.

It is necessary to ascertain the effect of every sort of training or method of instruction upon the further growth of the child. For instance, do methods of teaching arithmetic by the use of blocks, objects, and other illustrative material advance the child or retard him in his ability to master the higher branches of mathematics? What effect upon the pupil's ability to understand motives and actions in history does great thoroughness in arithmetical instruction have? For instance, does it make any difference whether there is only one lesson in arithmetic a day, or one each in written arithmetic and in mental arithmetic? Does a careful training in discriminating fine shades of colour and in naming them, continued for twenty weeks to half a year in the primary school, permanently set the mind of the pupil toward the mischievous habit of observing tints of colour to such an extent as to make the mind oblivious of differences in form or shape, and especially inattentive to relations which arise from the interaction of one object upon another? Questions of this kind are endless in number, and they relate directly to the formation of the course of study and the school programme. They can not be settled by rational or *a priori* psychology, but only by careful experimental study. In the settlement of these questions one is to expect great assistance from the laboratories of physiological psychology.—Notwithstanding the efficiency of the school to help the child enter upon the fruits of civilization, it is to be feared that to the school is due very much arrested development. In our day numerous and concerted efforts are made to study the child with a view to throw light on educational methods. Not very much success in this line of investigation can be expected, however, from those enthusiasts in child-study who do not as yet know the alphabet of rational psychology. Those who can not discriminate the three kinds of thinking are not likely to recognise them in their study of children. Those who have no idea of arrested development will not be likely to undertake the careful and delicate observations which explain why certain children stop growing at various points in different studies, and require patient and persevering effort on the part of the teacher to help them over their mental difficulties. The neglected child who lives the life of a street Arab has become cunning and self-helpful, but at the expense of intellect and morals. Child-study should take up his case and make a thorough inventory of his capacities and limitations, and learn the processes by which these have developed. Child-study in this way will furnish us more valuable information for the conduct of our schools than any other fields of investigation have yet done.

§ 6. In rational psychology we learn that there are three stages of the development of the thinking power. The first stage is that of sense-perception; its form of thinking conceives all objects as having independent being and as existing apart from all relation to other objects. It would set up an atomic theory of the universe if it were questioned closely. The second stage of knowing is that which sees everything as depending upon the environment. Everything is relative, and can not exist apart from its relations to other things. The theory of the universe from this stage of thinking is pantheistic. There is one absolute unity of all things, and this unity alone is independent, and all else is dependent. Things are phenomenal and the unity is the absolute. Pantheism conceives the universe as one vast sea of being, in which the particular waves lose their individuality after a brief manifestation. The third stage of thinking arrives at the insight that true being is self-active or self-determined. True being is therefore self-conscious being, and exists as intellect and will; all else is phenomenal being. On this insight depend the doctrines of God, freedom, and immortality. They may be held, it is true, by a kind of blind faith, when one's thinking is in the first or second stage, but such faith is unstable, because it is contradicted by its mental conviction. The most important end of intellectual education is to take the pupil safely through the world theory of the first and second stages—namely, sense-perception and the relativity doctrine—up to the insight into the personal nature of the absolute. All parts and pieces of school education and all other education should have in view this development of the intellect.

The two attitudes of mind in observation spoken of in § 4 correspond roughly to the second and third stages of thinking here described and more fully discussed in Chapter IV. The negative conditions of mental unfolding will be discovered and defined by empirical psychology. But that which is an original energy can not be explained by its environment because it is independent; nor is it, strictly speaking, correlated to the body, although it uses it in sense-perception and in volition as an instrument of communication with the outer world.

FIRST PART.

PSYCHOLOGIC METHOD.

11

FIRST PART.

PSYCHOLOGIC METHOD.

§ 7. In Part I of this work the chief themes of educational·psychology are treated unsystematically, the main object being to develop the several *aperçus* or insights which furnish the method of such psychology. The use of method to build a strict system is left for Part II, for the insight into a systematic procedure requires more mental grasp than the understanding of a principle or a method. But all insights in this department of inquiry are difficult to reach. Hence the importance of postponing whatever relates to a complete system, if it is possible, until the student gets some familiarity with the simpler aspects of the principle which furnishes the method. That principle will be found to be self-determination. How its development unites the phases of the intellect and the intellect to the will, and how both arise from feeling and return into it, will be discussed in Part II. Certain inquiries into

13

the application of psychology to the settlement of
practical questions in education are reserved for
Part III.

CHAPTER I.

What is meant by Educational Psychology?

§ 8. ALL activities of man have an internal or
mental side, even when they are directed upon the
external world. There is a mental or subjective coefficient as well as an objective one. The mind acts
and reacts in all manner of human deeds. Hence
everything relating to man has a psychological element in it and is in so far educative. There is a psychology to sociology and to individual biography.
There is a psychology of the family, the industrial
community, the state, the Church, and also of the
school. There is a psychology of each branch of
study—grammar, arithmetic, history, poetry, art,
philosophy. The business of psychology is to find
this subjective coefficient wherever it exists. Educational psychology deals with all phases of the
action and reaction of the mind by itself or in the
presence of objects, by which the mind develops or
unfolds, or is arrested, or degenerates.

Psychology in general deals with mind and mental phenomena. In untechnical speech, soul, spirit, reason, intelligence are used as synonyms of mind. Feeling, intellect, and will are said to be the different forms of activity of mind. Psychology investigates the forms of mental activity and their development or evolution. The word "development" suggests the phase of psychology which is of chief interest to education. Psychology as a general science is interested in all phases of mental processes and results. Education is interested especially in methods of mental development, and in the ideals of perfection that can be attained. Education attempts to change what is into what ought to be; it seeks to realize an ideal. As such it is rather an art than a science; but, of course, there is a science of education—that is to say, a science of the subject-matter, the aims and the methods which belong to the art of education. This science of education has to draw from psychology one of its most important elements —the theory of the method of developing the mind. Its ideals are derived from religion, political history, literature, and ethics, proximately· at least. But ethics itself is more or less based on psychology. Psychology, in fact, is so fundamental that it conditions, in large measure, all the sciences based on the spiritual nature of man—ethics, theology, politics, sociology, æsthetics, and all forms of philosophy. Our question involves many considerations; for instance, the question of the relation of psychology to physiology. Physiology is the science of living bodies. Is mind only a function of a living body, or is it an individuality wholly spiritual? Certainly all must admit that there is interaction—that the condition of the body affects the manifestation of feeling, knowing, and willing, being favourable or unfavourable to such manifestation. On the other hand, the operations of feeling, knowing, and willing affect various bodily functions, retarding some and accelerating others. For how many thousand years has mankind known and prized the stimulants and narcotics for their influence on the mind? Alcohol, tobacco, coffee, tea, opium, betel, hasheesh—all have been sought for their psy-

chical effects. Whether their influence is positive or negative, whether stimulants furnish so-called mental force,
or whether they simply paralyze or benumb the body so
as to relieve the mind of the distraction which a consciousness of its physical organs occasions (especially to acutely
nervous persons), this, we see, is a crucial question. In § 4
this topic has already been alluded to and the suggestion
made that the influence of stimulants is negative rather
than positive. "Physiological psychology," as it chooses
to call itself, has a great field for investigation. But even
if the soul is only a bodily function, it is certain that
physiology can not make any progress without borrow-
ing at every step the data derived from psychology by
introspection. For feeling, knowing, and volition are,
as already pointed out, not matters of external observation, but only of internal observation or introspection.
Physiology, like other natural sciences, conducts its investigations by the aid of external observation, mapping
out provinces in the world, inventorying their contents,
and finally classifying and systematizing facts by relating
them to principles. By principles I mean energies acting
according to laws: a cause that explains a phenomenon
is a principle. But to external observation there is no
psychical fact visible. We can behold things occupying
space, and events or actions filling time, but we can not
see a feeling with the eye nor hear it with the ear; nor
can we taste it, or smell it, or touch it. A feeling can be
perceived only by consciousness. So, too, the processes
of knowing and willing can not be perceived except by
consciousness. The most that physiological psychology
can do is to investigate the relations of two orders of observation. It must compare the facts of physiology, the
changes of the body, with the facts of mental action in
the form of feelings, thoughts, and volitions. Introspection is therefore utterly indispensable to physiological
psychology.

CHAPTER II.

What is Introspection?

§ 9. INTROSPECTION is internal observation—our consciousness of the activity of the mind itself. The subject who observes is the object observed. Consciousness is knowing of self. This seems to be the characteristic of mind and mental phenomena—there is always some degree of self-relation; there is self-feeling or self-knowledge. Even in mere life—in the vegetative soul—there is self-relation: this we shall study as our chief object of interest in psychology. We shall note first the contrast between external and internal observation. Outward observation is objective perception or sense-perception. It perceives things and environments. Things are always relative to their environment. Things are therefore dependent beings. They stand in causal relation to other things, and if moved are moved from without by external forces. Introspection, or internal observation, on the other hand, perceives the activity of the mind, and this is self-activity, and not a movement caused by external forces. Feelings, thoughts, volitions, are phases of self-activity. This we shall consider more in detail. Let us note that a feeling, a thought, or a volition implies subject and object. I feel a sensation of pain or a desire for food. There is a self that feels the pain or the desire, and an object that is felt. I think of the relation between the angles of a triangle and its sides—there is a self that thinks and an object thought. So I will an act—the self wills and the act is its object. Each is an activity, and an activity of the self. External perception does not perceive any self. It perceives only what is extended in time and space and what is consequently multiple, what is moved by something else and not self-moved. If it beholds living objects, it does not behold the self that animates the body, but only the body that is organically formed by the self. But introspection beholds the self.

This is a very important distinction between the two orders of observation, external and internal. The former can perceive only phenomena, the latter can perceive noumena. The former can perceive only what is relative, and dependent on something else; the latter can perceive what is independent and self-determined, a primary cause and source of movement. To pass from the first order of observation, which perceives external things, to the second order of observation, which perceives self-activity, is to take a great step. We are dimly conscious of our entire mental activity, but we do not (until we have acquired psychologic skill) distinguish and separately identify its several phases. It is the same in the outer world: we know many things in ordinary consciousness, but only in science do we unite the items of our knowledge systematically so as to make each assist in the explanation of all. Common knowledge lacks unity and system. In the inner world, too, there is common introspection, unsystematized and devoid of unity—the light of our ordinary consciousness. But there is a higher scientific introspection which discovers both unity and system.

§ 10. The scientific view finds the general or universal. First, it discovers classes; next, laws; then causal principles. Science inventories facts, identifying them as falling under classes. Then it goes back of the idea of class and regards the energy that produces a class of facts by continual action according to a fixed form. This fixed form of action is called law. It rises above the idea of law to the idea of purpose or adaptation to end. That is to say, it discovers evolution or progressive development. In the view of evolution there is a goal toward which relatively lower orders are progressing, and the facts, forces, and laws are seen as parts of a great world-process which explains all. At this point science rises into philosophy. Philosophy is science which investigates all facts and phenomena in view of a final or ultimate principle—the first principle of the universe. When science comes to study all objects in view of the principle of evolution, it has transcended the stage of mind whose highest object is to discover classes; likewise the stage that makes law an ultimate. Be-

sides efficient cause, which makes or produces some
new state or condition, there is " final cause " or purpose—design or " end and aim." The theory of evolution takes into consideration this idea of the " end
and aim " of changes in Nature. It ranges or ranks
all phenomena according to their development or realization of an ideal. Now it is evident that purpose,
design, or " final cause " is an ideal that can have
existence (i. e., conscious existence) for a being only
in so far as it is a soul or mind. A living being like
a plant, which can grow but not feel, does not perceive or feel its ideal, and yet its ideal guides and
directs the activity of its efficient cause or active force.
The ideal is only " law " to the plant. But in the
lowest form of animal life there is a feeling of want
—that is to say, the want of an ideal condition different from its real. We can observe even the lowest
animals moving in order to adjust themselves to the
environment, or to appropriate the environment for
food. As an external phenomenon we should never
be able to explain such movements, because we can
not perceive ideals with our external senses. We interpret such movements through our own introspection. We can feel wants and be conscious of motives. We ascribe these wants and motives to animals
and men around us. Clifford calls such attribution

of motives to other beings "ejects." To recognise another being as having a subject or self like ourselves is not merely to perceive an object, but an "eject." We can therefore recognise in a being the existence of introspection in the form of feeling, or in some higher form, only because we exercise the activity of introspection ourselves.

Strange as it may appear, therefore, we conduct even external observation by means of introspection. Natural science in adopting the theory of evolution advances to the stage wherein it makes it its chief object to recognise development from a lower stage toward a higher—the progressive realization of an ideal. The ideal is unconscious in the inorganic world and in the plant world, but acts only as law or as vitality. In the animal world it is conscious of this ideal, and feels it as appetite or represents it in the form of a mental image. To recognise an animal is to perceive an "eject," as W. Kingdon Clifford explains in his essay on The Nature of Things-in-themselves.

§ 11. The evolution theory recognises introspection as existing in the objective world—it sees in Nature a tendency to develop such beings as possess internality and energize to realize their ideals. It is curious to note that this movement in science begins by the utter repudiation of what is called teleology; i. e., it sets aside the old doctrine of design which looked for marks of external adaptation of Nature to ulterior spiritual uses—such external design as one.

finds in a watch, where the various parts are artificially
adapted to produce what they never would have produced naturally.   Such external teleology ignored
the immanent teleology of Nature.   By rejecting the
old mechanical teleology, which makes Nature a machine in the hand of God, evolution has come to see
the teleology which God has breathed into Nature—
to see, in short, that Nature is through and through
teleological.   Nature is, in every particle of it, governed by ideals.   Matter is heavy, and falls, for example, only because it obeys an ideal—an ideal of
which it is entirely unconscious, and yet which is
manifested in it in the form of weight.   Gravity is
the manifestation of the unity of one body with another.   The unity is ideal or potential, but its manifestation is real force, real attraction.

This subject of introspection thus leads out to the
end of the world, and reappears underneath the method
of modern natural science, which studies all objects in
their history—in their evolution.   Strangely enough, the
scientists of the present day decry in psychology what
they call the "introspective method."   And just as in the
case of the repudiation of teleology, they are bound to
return to some other form of what they repudiate.   Renounce teleology, and you find nothing but teleology in
everything.   Renounce introspection, and you are to find
introspection the fundamental moving principle of all
Nature.   All things have their explanation in a blind attempt on the part of Nature to look at itself.   Nature, said
Plotinus (Ennead III, book viii, chapter iii), is philothea-

mon, or greedy of beholding herself. A blind tendency in Nature to develop some ideal implies as its logical condition a completely realized ideal in the absolute first principle through which Nature is given its being. If Nature is evolution—a process moving toward self-consciousness—it is no complete and independent process, but a means used by an absolute personal being—God—for the creation of living souls in his own image.

CHAPTER III.

What is Self-activity?

§ 12. WHAT is the great central fact to be kept in view in the study of the mind? To this question there is only one answer—it is self-activity. But the answer is likely to be a sphinx riddle to the beginner. Who has not heard it often repeated that the end and aim of education is to arouse self-activity in the pupil? And yet who means anything by that word? The moment that one calls attention to its true implication he is met by the objection: It is impossible to conceive the origination of activity; it is impossible to frame a concept of what is both subject and object at the same time; self-activity and self-consciousness are inconceivable. " The words exist, it is true, but the mind is unable to realize in thought what is signified by them." Herbert Spencer (First Principles, page 65 of first edition) says of self-consciousness: "Clearly a true cognition of self implies a state in which the knowing and known are one, in which the subject and object are identified; and this Mr. Mansell rightly holds to be the annihilation of both." Just the difficulty found in the conception of self-consciousness is found in that of self-activity. We can not form a mental picture of self-activity, nor of self-consciousness. We can not picture an activity in which the origin is also the point of return. But this does not surprise us so much when we learn that we can not form a mental picture of any activity of any kind whatever. We can not picture even a movement in space, although we may picture the two places between which the motion occurs. So, too, becoming and change can not be pictured in the mind, although we may picture the states of being before and after the transition. We may picture an object as here or there, but not as moving. The ancient sceptics expressed this fact by denying motion altogether. "A thing," said they, "can not move where it is, because it is there already, and of course it can not move where it is not; hence it can not move at all."

The unwary listener who supposes that he is thinking the elements of the problem when he merely exercises his imagination, finds himself drawn into a logical conclusion that contradicts all his experience. To deny motion, in fact, makes experience impossible. Take all motion out of the world and there could be no experience; for experience involves motion in the subject that perceives, or in the object perceived, or in both. And yet we can not form a mental picture of motion or change. We picture different states or conditions of an object that is undergoing change, and different positions occupied by a moving thing. But the element of change and motion we do not picture.

§ 13. It is not surprising that we can not form for ourselves a mental picture of self-activity, since we are unable to picture in our minds any sort of activity, movement, or change. And yet, as before stated, the thought of motion, change, and activity is necessary to explain the world of experience—nay, even to perceive or observe it. So, too, the thought of self-activity is necessary in order to explain motion, change, and activity.

To make this clear, consider the following: (*a*) That which moves, moves either because it is impelled to move by another, or because it impels itself to move. (*b*) In the latter case, that of self-impulsion, we have self-activity at once. (*c*) In the former case, that of impulsion through another, we have self-activity implied as origin of the motion. Either the one which moves it is directly self-active, or else it receives and transmits, without originating, the energy causing motion. (*d*) Were there no originating source of movement it is obvious that there could be no motion to transmit. Suppose, for once, that all things received and transmitted, and yet none originated energy. Then all phenomena of movement would be de-

rived, but from no source; all would be effects, but effected by no cause. The chain of transmitting links may
be infinite in extent, but it is only an infinite effect without a cause. Here we contradict ourselves. If there is no
self-active cause from which the energy proceeds, and
from which it is received by the infinite transmitting
series, then that series does not derive its energy, but
originates it and is self-active. Hence self-activity must
be either within the series or outside it, and in any case
self-activity is the essential idea presupposed as the logical
condition of any thought of motion whatever.

§ 14. We have been obliged to discuss at length
this notion of self-activity in order to prepare the
road for genuine psychological observation. If the
reader denies the existence of self-activity, he is un-
prepared to see or observe it, and psychology does
not and can not exist for him so long as he holds consistently to his denial. He may make some progress
in the study of physics, perhaps, but he can not learn
even the physiology of plants or animals without the
idea of self-activity. He may study anatomy as the
structure of dead bodies, but he can not study life
and organism without recognising self-activity in
one of its forms—assimilation, sensation, volition,
thought. Of course psychology is impossible to him
when he can not even enter physiology.

§ 15. What phenomena are attributed to self-
activity? In the first place, we recognise it in plants.
All human observation, whether of civilized or of

savage peoples, takes note of self-activity in the phenomena of vegetation. The plant grows, puts out new buds, leaves, branches, blossoms, fruit; adds layers to its thickness, extends its roots. It does this by its own activity, and its growth is not the effect of some outside being, although outside conditions must be favourable or else the energy of the plant is not able to overcome the obstacle. The plant must grow by adding to itself matter that it takes up from its environment—water, salts, carbon, etc. Notice that the plant-energy attacks its surroundings of air, moisture, and earth, and appropriates to itself its environment after transforming it. One may admit that the environment acts on the plant, but he must contend for the essential fact that the plant reacts on its environment, originating motion itself, and meeting and modifying external influences. The plant builds its structure according to an ideal model; not a conscious model, of course. Its shape and size, its roots and branches, its leaves and flowers and fruit, resemble the ideal (model or type) of its kind or species, and not the ideal of some other species. The self-activity of the plant is manifested in action upon its environment, which results in building up its own individuality. It not only acts, but acts for itself; it is self-related. Again, notice that the

5

plant acts destructively on other things, and strips
off their individuality and transforms their substance into its own tissue, making it into vegetable
cells.

The self-activity of the plant is then a formative
power that can conquer other forms and impose its
own form upon them.

§ 16. In the next place, consider the kind of energy that we call the self-activity in animals. The
individual animal is also a formative energy, destroying other forms, eating up plants, for example, con-
suming the oxygen of the air, and making over the
matter into animal cells. But the animal shows
self-activity in other ways. It not only appropriates
and assimilates, but it moves its limbs and feels. In
the plant there is movement of circulation and
growth, and this is also found in the animal. But
locomotion is a new feature of self-activity. It enables the animal to change his environment. The
animal can use some part of itself as an instrument
for providing food, or as a lever by which to move its
whole body. Self-activity is manifested also in locomotion, and especially in its conformity to design or
purpose. The animal moves in order to realize a purpose. With purpose or design, we have reached internality.

Purpose or design implies a distinction between what is and what is not. The lowest and blindest feeling that exists deals with this discrimination. Pleasure and pain, comfort and discomfort, appetite and aversion, all imply discrimination between one's organism and the environment, as well as between the organism as it is and the organism as it should be. There is in all feeling a discrimination of limit and a passing beyond limit. This transcending of the limit to the organism by the self-activity constitutes sensibility. However obscure this may appear at first, it will grow clear and clearer upon further study.

§ 17. Feeling is an activity; it is a self-activity; it is like assimilation or digestion, a reaction against an environment. The environment negates or limits the organism; feeling perceives the limitation, or discriminates itself as organism from its not-self as environment. Feeling, therefore, transcends its organism, and unites two factors—organic self and environment. The self moves in order to relieve itself of the pain or discomfort attending this negative action of the environment. Hunger and cold, all varieties of appetite and desire, have this elemental discrimination between organism and environment, and a further discrimination between the being of the self and the non-being of the self, so that something not yet existent (some ideal state) is presented. This presentation of the ideal is the essential element in desire and sensation, as well as in all higher forms of self-activity, say of thought and will.

It is important to recognise the existence of discrimination in this lowest stage of blind feeling—the most rudimentary animal soul. Feeling, in the act of discriminating between the existing self and its possible self, is constructive ideally, for it repeats to itself its limitation. The limit to its organism exists, and it is in interaction with its environment. But the self-activity in this higher phase of feeling (higher than the vegetative function of digestion) constructs ideally the limit of the organism and changes the limit for other possible limits, comparing it with them. This comparison of one limit with other possible ones is the element of discrimination in feeling. All this is automatic or so nearly unconscious as to require long and careful introspection to discover it. Feeling is not, as it at first seems, a simple activity or passivity, but a very complex process.

§ 18. Sensation is an ideal reproduction of the actual limit to the organism. It involves also the simultaneous production of other possible limitations, and hence contains a reference to itself, a feeling of self in its total capacity. On a background, so to speak, of the general possibility of feeling is marked off this particular limit which reproduces or represents the existent. The contrast between it and the general potentiality of feeling is the birth of purpose or design, and (glancing upward) of all the ideals that arise in the human soul, moral, æsthetic, and religious. Self-activity as assimilation or digestion (vegetative soul), as feeling and locomotion (animal soul), and as thinking (human soul), is to be studied as the fundamental unity of psychology and physiology. It is not in itself an object of external observation, although external observation offers us phenomena that we explain by assuming self-activity as the individuality which causes them. Self-activity itself we perceive in ourselves by introspection. When we look within we become aware of free energy which acts as subject and object under the forms of feeling, thought, and volition. Becoming acquainted with the characteristic of these activities within ourselves, we learn to recognise their manifestations in the external world.

A restatement of this theory in Part II of this work will bring out new points of view and assist the reader in grasping it. Undoubtedly the matter is one of the most obscure in psychology, because, although very complex, nearly all of the process lies below the threshold of consciousness. In the case of assimilation (or digestion), mere vitality, all is unconscious.

CHAPTER IV.

The Three Stages of Thought.

§ 19. THE most important discovery ever made in psychology is this one of the three ascending steps or grades of thought which any one may take with due study and meditation. It is attributed to Plato.

(a) The lowest stage of thinking supposes that its objects are all independent one of another. Each thing is self-existent, and a " solid reality." To be sure, the mind in this stage thinks relations between things, but it places no special value on relations. To it things seem to exist apart from relations, and relations appear for the most part to be the arbitrary product of thought or reflection. Things, it is true, are composite and divisible into smaller things, and smaller things are divisible again. All things are composed of smallest things or atoms. This is the mechanical point of view. This lowest stage of thinking, it appears, explains all by the two categories of " thing " and " composition." All differences seem to arise through combination or composition. But since differences include all that needs explanation, it follows that this stage of thinking de-ceives itself in supposing that *things* are the essential elements in its view of the world, and that *relations* are the unessential. A little development of the power of thought produces for us the consciousness that some relations, at least, are the essential elements of our experience.

§ 20. (*b*) This first stage of thinking, nearest allied to sense-perception, supposes that *things* are the essential elements of all being. The second stage of thought, which we may call the *understanding,* knows better what is essential; it regards *relations* as essential. By relations it does not mean arbitrary comparisons, or the result of idle reflections. It has made the discovery of truly essential relations. It deals with the category of relativity, in short, and goes so far as to affirm that if a grain of sand were to be destroyed, all beings in space would be changed more or less. Each thing is relative to every other, and there is reciprocal or mutual dependence.

Isaac Newton's thought of universal gravitation deserves all the fame it has acquired, because it sets up in modern thinking this category of relativity, and all thinking in our day is being gradually trained into its use by the application constantly made of it. Isaac Newton is thus a perpetual schoolmaster to the race. Herbert Spencer owes his reputation to his faithful adherence to the thought of relativity in his expositions. Our knowledge is all relative, says he (with the exception of that very important

knowledge, the knowledge of the principle of relativity
itself), and things, too, are all relative. Essential relativity means dependence. A is dependent on B, so that
the being of B is also the being of A. Such is the law of
relativity. This stage of thought refuses to think an
ultimate concrete principle as origin of all. It says: A
depends on B; B, again, on C; C on D; and so on, in
infinite progression. Relativity, as a supreme principle,
is pantheistic. It makes all being dependent on something beyond it. Hence it denies ultimate individuality. Everything is phenomenal. All individuality is a
transient result of some underlying abstract principle, a
" persistent force," for example. Individual things are the
transient products (static equilibria) of forces. Forces,
again, are modes of manifestation of some persistent energy into which they all vanish. This second stage of
thinking attains its most perfect form in the doctrine of
the correlation of forces. It is also the ancient scepticism
of Pyrrho and Sextus Empiricus. It underlies, too, the
Buddhist religion and all pantheistic theories of the world.
Nothing is so common among men of science in our day
as theories based on relativity. It is often set up by those
who still hold the non-relational theory of the lower plane
of thought, though if held with logical strictness it is
incompatible with the preceding stage. The first stage
explains by the category of things, or independent non-
relational beings, while the second stage explains by the
category of *force* or essential relation. Take notice that
force does not need a nucleus of things as a basis of effi-
cacy; for things are themselves only systems of forces
held in equilibria by force.

§ 21. (*c*) Relativity presupposes self-relation.
Self-relation is the category of the *reason*, just as relativity is the category of the *understanding*, or non-
relativity (atomism) the category of *sense-perception*.
Dependence implies transference of energy—else how

could energy be borrowed? That which originates energy is independent being. Reflection discovers relativity or dependence, and hence unites beings into systems. Deepest reflection discovers total systems and the self-determining principles which originate systems of dependent being. The reason looks for complete, independent, or total beings. Hence the reason finds the self-active or its results everywhere.

Sense-perception is atheistic; it finds each thing sufficient for itself—that is to say, self-existent and yet without self-activity. The understanding is pantheistic; it finds everything finite and relative, and dependent on an absolute that transcends all qualities and attributes— "an unknown and unknowable persistent force," which is the negative of all particular forces. The reason is theistic because it finds self-activity or self-determination, and identifies this with mind. *Mind* is self-activity in a perfect form, while *life* is the same in a less developed stage. (This will be discussed in Part II.) Every whole is an independent being, and hence self-determined or self-active. Were it not self-determined, it would have no determinations (qualities, marks, or attributes), and be pure nothing; or, having determinations, it must originate them itself or else receive them from outside itself. But in case it receives its determinations from outside, it is a dependent being. Reason sees this disjunctive syllogism. While Buddhism and Brahmanism are religions of the understanding, Christianity is essentially a religion of the reason, and furnishes a sort of universal education for the mind in habits of thinking according to reason. It teaches by authority the view-of-the-world that reason thinks.

§ 22. (*d*) It has appeared that each of the three stages of thinking is a view-of-the-world, and that it is

not a theory of things worn for ornament, so to speak,
or only on holidays, but a silent presupposition that
tinges all one's thinking.

A person may wear his religion on Sabbath days, and
put it off on week days, possibly. But his view-of-the-world
shows itself in all that he does. All things take on a different appearance when viewed by the light of the reason.
For reason is insight; it "sees all things in God," as
Malebranche expressed it. For it looks at each thing to
discover in it the purpose of the whole universe. To see
the whole in the part is justly esteemed characteristic of
divine intelligence.—The oft-asserted ability of great men
of science—that of Cuvier to see the whole animal in a
single bone of its skeleton—that of Lyell to read the history of the Glacial period in a pebble—that of Agassiz
to recognise the whole fish by one of its scales—that of
Asa Gray to see all botany in a single plant—these are in-
dications of the arrival at the third stage of knowing on
the part of scientific men within their departments.
Goethe's Homunculus, in the second part of Faust, symbolizes this power of insight which within a limited sphere
(its bottle!) is able to recognise the whole in each fragment.—The spirit of specialization in our time aims to exhaust one by one the provinces of investigation with a
view to acquire this power to see totalities. This is what
Plato meant by describing this third stage of thinking as
a power of knowing-by-wholes (totalities). Learn to comprehend each thing in its entire history: this is the maxim
of science guided by the reason. Always bear in mind
that self-activity is the ultimate reality—all dependent
being is a fragment, the totality is self-active. The things
of the world all have their explanation in the manifestation of self-activity. All is for the development of individuality and ultimate free union of souls in the kingdom
of God.—To sum up: The lowest thinking activity inventories things but neglects relations; the middle stage of

thinking inventories relations, forces, and processes, and sees things in their essences, but neglects self-relation or totality; the highest stage of thinking knows that all independent being has the form of life or mind, and that the absolute is a person; it studies all things to discern traces of the creative energy which is the form of the totality. The theory of evolution rightly comprehended as the movement of all things in time and space toward the development of individuality—that is to say, toward a more perfect manifestation or reflection of the Creator, who is above time and space—this theory is, properly understood, the theory of the reason. The theory of gravitation, as a world-view, on the other hand, is that of the understanding.

CHAPTER V.

A Concept is not a Mental Picture.

§ 23. Perceptions relate to individual objects; concepts relate to general classes or to abstractions: such is the current doctrine of psychology. As the mental acts of perceiving and conceiving form important topics in psychology, we must make several studies upon them. It is profitable here to discuss the differences between mental images and concepts. The origin of general notions will be considered in Chapter XI on the third figure of the syllogism. Let us now take up the inquiry, What constitutes a general notion or concept? To this we may reply

that it is not a mental image, but a definition. My
general notion *tree* should include all trees of whatever description, and it is expressed by a definition. But no sooner do I attempt to conceive the
notion tree than I form a mental image. The image,
however, is not general enough to suit the notion.
I imagine a particular specimen of a tree—an oak, for
example. If I imagine it vividly, it is an individual
just as much as the oak that I may see before me in
the forest. My concept of tree in general recognises
the inadequacy of the image, and dismisses it or permits it to be replaced by another image which presents a different specimen. Thus the mental act of
conceiving uses images only as illustrations or examples, and dismisses them as promptly as it calls them
up. It breaks images as well as makes them. Perhaps we have never noticed this relation of images to
the concept. We are conscious of only a few phases
of our mental activity until we have cultivated our
powers of introspection. Notice carefully the art of
realizing any general concept. We shall discover that
our definition is a sort of rule for the formation of images, rather than an image.* What concept do we
form of bird? We think of a flying animal—of

---

* Dr. J. H. Stirling has suggested this.

feathers, wings, bills, claws, and various appurtenances which we unite in the idea of bird. We call up images and dismiss them as we go over the elements of our definition, for we recognise the images to be too special or particular to correspond to the concept.

In the rudest and least developed intellects, whether of savages or children, the same process is repeated. Is this a bird? Yes; it has a bill, claws, feathers, wings, etc. But it does not have either of these in general. Its bill is a particular specimen of bill, having one of the many shapes, or colours, or magnitudes possible to a bill. So, too, of its feathers, wings, claws, etc. The image of our bird was not of a bird in general, but of a hawk or duck, a hen or pigeon, or of some other species of birds. Nor was the image that of a hawk or a duck, etc., *in general*, but of a particular variety; and not even of a variety in general, but finally of a possible or remembered individual specimen of a variety. So, too, the features of the bird are only individual specimens or examples that fall under the general conception of claws, feathers, bills, wings, etc. The definition which we have formed for ourselves serves as a rule by which we form an image that will illustrate it, noticing at the same time the defects of each image. This difference between the concept and the specimen is known to the child and the savage, though it is not consciously reflected upon. Take up a different class of concepts. Take the abstractions of colour, taste, smell, sound, or touch; for example, redness, sourness, fragrance, loudness, hardness, etc. Our concept includes infinite degrees of possible intensity, while our image or recalled experience is of some definite degree, and does not correspond to the general notion.

§ 24. We have considered objects and classes of objects that admit of images as illustrations. These images, if vague, seem to approximate concepts; if vivid, to depart from them. But no image can be so vague as to correspond to any concept. Let us take more general notions, such as force, matter, quality, being. For force, make an image, if one can, of some action of gravitation or of heat. If some image or experience can be called up, it is felt to be a special example that covers only a very small part of the province of force in general. But no image, strictly considered, can be made of force at all, or of any special example of force. We can image some object that is acted upon by force—we can image it before it is acted upon and after it is acted upon. That is to say, we can image the results of the force, but not the force itself. We can think of force, but not image it. If we conceive existence, and image some existent thing; if we conceive quantity in general and image a series of things that can be numbered, or an extension or degree that may be measured; if we conceive relation in general, and try to illustrate it by imaging particular objects between which there is a relation —in all these and similar cases we can hardly help being conscious of the vast difference between the image and the concept. In realizing the concept of relation, as in that of force or energy, we do not image even an example or specimen of a relation or force,

but we image only the conditions or termini of a specimen relation; but the relation itself must be seized
by thought, if it is cognized at all, just as any force
must be thought but can not be imaged. We can
think relations, but not image them.

Here we notice that we have a lurking conviction that
these general ideas or concepts are not so valid and true
to reality as our images are, or as our immediate perceptions are. Concepts, we are apt to think, are vague and
faint impressions of sensation. "Ideas are the faint images
of sense-impressions," said Hume.—Nominalism says that
there is nothing in reality corresponding to our general
concepts, and that such concepts are mere devices of ours
for convenience in knowing and reasoning. If so, our
images are truer than our concepts. Herbert Spencer says
(in his First Principles, chapter i) that our concepts are
mere symbols of objects too great or too multitudinous to
be mentally represented.—If the views of Hume and Herbert Spencer were true in regard to our general notions,
psychology would have a very different lesson in it—very
different from that which we have found. To us the images
are far less true than our concepts. The images stand
for fleeting or evanescent forms, while the concepts state
the eternal and abiding laws, the causal energies that
constitute the essence of all phenomena.—When we are
contemplating the world as a congeries of things (recall
the " lowest stage of thinking " described in Chapter IV)
we seem to be convinced that all true reality has the
form of things. But when we begin to reflect on what
our experience teaches, we see that all things are the
results of forces, and that they (the things) are in a process of change into other things. The underlying reality,
then, is force, and even Herbert Spencer assures us that
the ultimate reality is a persistent force—persistent under
all the special forces. These forces form and transform

things. Now force or energy is more real than the fleeting things in which it manifests itself, and the persistent force is more substantial still.—Here we find ourselves arrived at another conviction than nominalism. We see that general concepts correspond more nearly to the deeper realities (the formative and destructive forces) which manifest themselves in the process of the world. In fact, psychology ought to recognise that the mental act of forming general concepts is the attempt to go over in the mind the real process in which things are explained by our experience. We find the history of things—we trace them from one shape to another, and we name the process and define it. Hence arise our general notions. The oak and the acorn are two things to perception. But experience discovers that there is an individual energy which manifests itself as acorn, and then as sapling, and again as oak bearing a crop of acorns. From acorn to acorn again there is a process. Our word oak signifies this general concept, which corresponds to the deeper reality of energy which reveals itself in the whole process. This leads us from the question of mental images to the question of the reality which we learn to know through experience. We learn to estimate at their proper value things and dead results, and to look beyond them to the energies that cause them to be and to change. In the changes we see revealed the generic causes and the laws or forms of manifestation. We learn in the order of the growth of an oak or of a human being what is the energy that is there incarnated and what is the law of the inner essential form.

CHAPTER VI.

Time, Space, and Causality—Three Ideas that make Experience possible.

§ 25. AFTER the doctrine of the three stages of thinking expounded in Chapter IV, the next in importance is the doctrine of *a priori* ideas or forms of the mind that make experience possible. Kant has proved that they are *a priori* by showing that they are necessary in order to make experience possible, and hence can not ever have been derived from experience. They belong to the very structure, so to speak, of our *ego.* Our discussion has made it clear that a conception is not a mental picture, but a sort of rule or definition for the formation of mental pictures. The mental pictures thus formed are only illustrations. The mental picture called up by the word *oak* is an illustration, but does not exhaust the idea of oak. The idea of oak includes an infinite number of possible examples, illustrations, or specimens, all differing one from another, while the picture that we form in the mind is only a particular individual of one species. Inasmuch as all particular specimens of the oak have grown to be what they are (or what they were) by the action of an oak-producing energy, the idea or conscious conception that we form of oak corresponds not to the individual, but to the energy which produces the individual. Moreover, the energy that brings the individual example of an oak into being—causing it to sprout and become a sapling, grow to maturity and bear its crop of acorns, continually appropriating from its environment air, moisture, salts, and other material that it needs, and converting them into vegetable cells—this energy is a more potent reality than its effect, the individual oak. It is the generic process, in fact, and does not stop with one oak, nor a forest of oaks. Our general idea of oaks corresponds to this generic energy, and hence has a deeper reality corresponding to it than the mere individual oak or oaks that we see by the aid of our senses. Sense-perception does not, in fact, amount to much until it is aided by the formation of concepts or general ideas.

§ 26. Previous to the formation of general ideas, sense-perception is merely the ceaseless flow of individual impressions without observed connection with one another. In fact, we do not perceive at all, strictly speaking, until we bring general ideas to the aid of our sense-impressions. For we do not perceive *things* except by combining our different sense-impressions—that is to say, uniting them by means of the ideas of Time, Space, and Causality. These three ideas are the chief among the conditions necessary *for* and are not derived *from* experience—in other words, they are not externally perceived as objects, or learned by contact with them as individual examples. We know that this is so by considering their nature, and especially by noting that they are necessary as conditions for each and every act of experience. We do not mean, of course, that we must be conscious of these ideas of time, space, and causality before any act of experience; nor would we deny that we became conscious of those ideas by analyzing experience (separating it into matter and form, time, space, and causality being the form, and the particular results the matter). What we deny is that they were furnished by sense-impressions; what we affirm is that they were furnished by the mind in its unconscious act of appropriating the sense-impressions and converting them into perception. The mind's self-activity is the source of such ideas. This doctrine is, as above noted, the immortal service of Kant to philosophy, and it inaugurates the era of modern philosophy, furnishing for it an adequate psychological basis. We find these ideas *in* experience, but as furnished by the self-activity of the mind itself, and not as derived from sense-impressions. We may each and all convince ourselves of the impossibility of deriving these ideas from sense-impressions by giving attention to their peculiar nature. We shall see, in fact, that no act of experience can be completed without these ideas. Immanuel Kant called them "forms of the mind"—they may be said to belong to the constitution of the mind itself, because it uses these ideas in the first act of experience, and in all acts of experience. Why could not these ideas be furnished by experience, like ideas of trees and animals, of earth and sky? The answer is: Because the ideas of time and space involve infinitude, and the idea of causality involves absoluteness; and neither of these ideas could by any possibility be received through the senses. For we can see, hear, and feel only that which is here and now, and not that which is everywhere and always. And it is not correct to say that we derive even ideas of trees and animals, earth and sky, from sense-impressions, because sense-impressions can not become ideas until they are brought under the forms of time, space, and causality. Before this they are merely sensations; after this they are ideas of possible or real objects existing in the world.

Let the psychologist who believes that all ideas are derived from sense-impressions explain how we could receive by such means the idea of what is infinite and absolute. Is not any sense-perception limited to what is here and now? How can we perceive by the senses what is omnipresent and eternal? The follower of Hamilton will answer, perhaps: " We can not, it is true, perceive what is infinite and eternal by means of the senses, nor can we conceive or think such ideas by any means whatever. In fact, we do not have such ideas. Time and space and causality do not, as you assert, imply conceptions of infinitude or absoluteness. All supposed conceptions of the infinite and absolute are merely negative ideas, which express our incapacity to conceive the infinite rather than our positive comprehension of it." The issue being fairly presented, we may test the matter for ourselves.

§ 27. Do we think space to be infinite, or simply as indefinite? Do we not think space as having such a nature that it can only be limited by itself? In other words, would not any limited space or spaces imply space beyond them, and thus be *continued* rather than limited? Let any one try this thought and see if he does not find it necessary to think space as infinite, for the very reason that all spatial limitation implies space beyond the limit. Space as such therefore can not be limited; the limitation must belong always to that which is *within* space. An attempt to conceive space itself as limited results in thinking the limited space as within a larger space. Space is of such a nature that it can only be thought as self-continuous, for its very limitations continue it. A limited portion of space is bounded only by another space. The limited portion of space is continuous with its environment of space.

§ 28. This is a positive idea and not a negative one. It is most important to consider carefully this point. The idea would be a negative idea if our thinking of it could not transcend the limit—that is to say, if we could not think space beyond the limit. But as our thought of space is not thus conditioned (we are, in fact, obliged to think a continuous space under all spatial limitations) space is a positive or affirmative idea. We see that the mind thinks a positive infinite space under any idea of a thing extended in space.— Let us state this in another way: We perceive or think things as having environments—each thing as being related to something else or to other things surrounding it. This is the thought of relativity. But we think both things and environments as contained in pure space—and pure space is not limited or finite, because all limitation implies space beyond.

The difficulty in this psychological question arises through a confusion of imagination with conception or thinking. While we conceive infinite space positively, and are unable to think space otherwise than as infinite or self-continued, yet, on the other hand, we can not image, or envisage, or form a mental picture of, infinite space. This inability to imagine infinite space has been supposed by Sir William Hamilton (see his Lectures on Metaphysics, page 527 of the American edition) to contradict our thought of infinite space. His doctrine was adopted by Mansell and from him borrowed by Herbert Spencer, who made it the foundation thought of his "Unknowable" (First Principles, Part I, chapter i). Now, a little reflection (and introspection) will convince us that this incapacity of imagination to picture infinite space is not a proof that we can not conceive or think that idea, but the contrary: Our incapacity to image infinite space is another proof of the infinitude of space!

§ 29. When we form a mental picture of space, why do we know that that picture does not represent all space? Simply because we are conscious that our thought of the mental picture finds boundaries to that picture, and that these boundaries imply space beyond them; hence the limited picture (and all images and pictures must be limited) includes a portion of space, but not all space. Thus it is our thought of space as infinite, or self-continued, that makes us conscious of the inadequacy of the mental picture. If we *could* form a mental picture of all space, then it would follow of necessity that the whole of space is finite. In that case imagination would contradict thinking or conceiving. As it is, however, imagination confirms conception. Thinking says that space is infinite because it is of such a nature that all limitations posit space beyond them, and thus only continue space instead of bound it. Imagination tries to picture space as a limited whole, but finds it impossible because all its limitations fall *within* space, and do not include space as a bounded whole. Thus both mental operations agree. The one is a negative confirmation of the other. Thinking reason sees positively that space is infinite, while imagination sees that it can not be imagined as finite.

§ 30. Time is also infinite. Any beginning presupposes a time previous to it. Posit a beginning to time itself, and we merely posit a time previous to time itself. Time can be limited by time only. The now is limited by time past and by time future; no, it is not correct to say that it is *limited*, for it is *continued* by them. Time did not begin; nor will it end. But one can not perceive an event without thinking it under the idea of time. No sensation that man may have had could be construed as a change, or event happening in the world, except by the idea of time. But it is impossible to derive the idea of time, such as we have it, from sense-impressions, for any one or any series of such impressions could not furnish an infinite time nor the idea of a necessary condition. Nor could the experience of any limited extension give us the idea of infinite space, or of the necessity of space as a condition of that experience.

If it seems as if this discussion belongs to metaphysics rather than psychology, this suggestion is made: Psychology treats of the nature of the mind. It treats of the forms which the mind gives to its contents. Hence it relates above all to our world-views, in so far as these are *a priori* and reveal the structure of cognition. It relates to the theory of knowledge in its most general form, and concerns, too, all concrete theories of the world, as well as the abstract questions of knowledge. In fact, the attitude of modern science against philosophy—the attitude of positivism against metaphysics—the attitude of mysticism and " theosophy " against Christianity—in short, all agnosticism and pantheism branch out at the point treated in this chapter. Most of it starts professedly from Sir William Hamilton's supposed proof that the idea of the infinite is merely a negative idea—an incapacity instead of a real insight. From the psychological doctrine of the negativity of our ideas of the infinite and absolute (first applied by Hamilton in his famous critique of Cousin) it is easy to establish the world-view of pantheism and to deny the doctrine of the personality of God. Surely that part of psychology which treats of the capacity of the mind to know ultimate reality is the foundation of the rest! To him who asserts that psychology is not important for the teacher it may be replied: Upon it depends the spirit of his instruction whether he gives a pantheistical or a theistical implication to the science and literature that he teaches. Psychology, as a mere classification of so-called faculties, or as a mechanical theory of sense-perception, conception, imagination, will, and emotions, is undoubtedly of little worth; but as revealing to us the foundations of ultimate principles in our view of the world it is of decidedly great importance! It is true that the psychology offered to teachers is often only a mere classification of the activities of the mind. But in order that psychology shall be more than a classification—namely, an investigation of the essential forms of mind itself—it is indispensable that its operations shall be studied before they are classified. Without such study it is easy to pass off a spurious theory of ideas—a theory, for example, that all ideas are derived from sense-impressions. On such a theory agnosticism may sit securely and deny God, freedom, and immortality.

CHAPTER VII.

Causality and the Absolute.

§ 31. In the preceding chapter we have discussed space and time as ideas that involve the conception of infinity. We trust that every one who has carefully considered the exposition has become convinced that we actually think space and time as infinite— that, in short, we think the infinite positively, or affirmatively, and not negatively. In this chapter we must discuss another idea that is equally essential to experience. Without the idea of Causality there could be no experience; experience can not begin until the idea of causality awakens in the mind. Space and time are not derived from external perception, but they are perceived by insight, or the mind's own self-activity; they are perceived as necessary conditions for the existence of things and events. Space and time are not mere subjective ideas which have no objective validity. They are the primary logical conditions which make an objective world possible. So, too, causality is equally fundamental for the existence of experience and the world which it reveals. Without using the idea of causality the mind can not recognise itself as the producer of its deeds, nor can it recognise anything objectively existing as the producer of its sense-impressions. All sense-impressions are mere feelings and are subjective. How do we ever come to recognise objects as the causes of our sense-impressions? We can see that it is impossible for us to derive the idea of cause from experience, because we have to use that idea in order to begin experience. The perception of the objective is possible only by the act of passing beyond our subjective sensations and referring them to external objects as causes of them. Whether I refer the cause of my sensations to objects and thereby perceive, or whether I trace the impressions to my own organism and detect an illusion of my senses in place of a real perception—in both cases I use the idea of causality. The object is a cause, or else I am the sole cause.

" When we are aware of something that begins to be, we are, by the necessity of our intelligence, constrained to believe that it has a cause," says Sir William Hamilton. The idea of causality contains the idea of energy or self-activity (or self-determination), and it is not a mere impotence of the mind, but a positive idea that reveals to us, more than any other, the transcendence of mind.

But Hamilton (Metaphysics, pages 533, 555) refers causality to "a negative impotence" of the mind: "We can not conceive any new existence to commence, therefore all that now is seen to arise under a new appearance had previously an existence under a prior form." This is his explanation of causality: What exists now must have existed somehow before; "There is conceived an absolute tautology between the effect and its cause. . . . We necessarily deny in thought that the object which appears to begin to be really so begins, and we necessarily identify its present with its past existence." Here we see the, defect of Hamilton's analysis. He eliminates the idea of cause or energy, and has left only one of its factors—that of continuity or continuous existence. The element of difference or distinction is omitted and ignored. (Hume reduced the idea of cause to that of invariable sequence—i. e., to invariable variety.)

§ 32. In our idea of causality we conceive something as producing something different from itself, or as originating a distinction, a difference. Change involves the origination of something new, something that did not exist before. This is one of its elements. On the other hand, causality involves the identification of this new determination with what existed before. But this is not all. The difference and identity are united in a deeper idea; the idea of cause contains the unity of difference and identity in a deeper idea—the idea of energy. Energy is deeper than existence because it is the originator of its form. We think the cause as an energy that gives rise to changes. It gives rise to new distinctions and differences—something, through the action of a cause, becomes different from what it was before. The action of the energy is the essential element in the idea of cause, and Hamilton's analysis omits just this, and reduces the idea of an activity to a sequence of existence, and thus adopts Hume's analysis.

Experience would be utterly impossible with such an idea as Hamilton's or Hume's in place of the causal idea. We should say, as Hamilton does say, in fact, *ex nihilo nihil*—that is to say, there can be no origination, but only a persistence, of being.

§ 33. The idea of causality involves this: A reality which is an energy shall by its activity originate a distinction within itself, and by the same activity transfer this distinction to something else, thus producing a change. A cause sends a stream of influence to an effect. It must, therefore, separate this stream from itself. Self-separation is therefore the fundamental idea in causality. Unless the cause is a self-separating energy, it can not be conceived as acting on something else. The action of causality is based on self-activity.

The attempt to form a mental image of causality is futile. We can imagine existences, but not the origination of them. We can not image time and space as we conceive them. We can not image causality as we conceive and think it.—It is, in fact, the most repugnant idea to a mind that clings to mental pictures as the only form of thinking. Such a mind fails to discriminate clearly between efficient cause and transmitting links or agents. By doing this it produces an infinite regress of causes which are at the same time effects. In this way it succeeds in losing the idea of efficient cause altogether. (This is done in the third antinomy of Kant's Critique of Pure Reason.) For example: a change, A, is caused by B, another change; B is caused by C, a third change; C by D, and D by E, and so on, *ad infinitum*. Here we have a change A, which, being an effect, must have a cause. We look first for the cause in B, but, upon examination, we see that B is only a transmitter of the cause: it is an instrument or agent through which the causal energy passes on its way from beyond. We successively trace it through C, D, E, etc. The imagination says, " so on forever." This, of course, means that a true originating cause is not to be found at all in the series. But if this is so, it follows likewise that there are no effects in the series unless there is a cause beyond the series, for there is no effect without a cause. Here we see that there is a fallacy in the idea of infinite progress (or regress) in causes. The infinite regress can not be in the cause, but only in the effect. For A, B, C, D, E, etc., are all effects. But just as sure as we see that these are effects, so sure are we that there is an efficient cause to produce them. The infinite series of links or transmitting members of the series change or transmit by reason of the activity of a true cause. If any one denies this, he denies that the changes are effects. To deny that a change is an effect does not escape the law of causality, but it asserts that the change is self-caused or spontaneous. But this is only to come to the same result that one finds if he asserts that the change is caused by something else, for it asserts causality. A real cause is an originator of changes, or new forms of existence. It is not something that demands another cause behind it, for it is self-active. The chain of relativity ends in a true cause, and can not be conceived without it.—The true cause is an absolute, inasmuch as it is independent. That which receives its form from another is dependent and relative. That which is self-active or a

true cause gives form to itself or to others, and is itself
independent of others. That which can supply itself
does not need others to supply it.—Our idea of cause,
therefore, is the nucleus of our idea of an absolute. It is
the basis of our idea of freedom, of moral responsibility,
of selfhood, of immortality, and, finally, of God.

§ 34. All realities owe their qualities, marks,
and attributes either to causes outside themselves
or to their own causality. If the former—that
is, if they are what they are through others—they
are dependent beings, and can not be free, or responsible, or immortal. If the latter—if they are
what they are through their own causality—they are
free and morally responsible, immortal selves, and
they are in the image of God, the Creator of all
things, who has endowed them with causal energy—
that is to say, with the power to build themselves,
and he has not built them or furnished them ready-
made. The causal reality may be perfect as God,
or it may be partially actualized and partially potential, as in the case of man. (" Partially potential "
—that is to say, man has not fully realized himself,
although he has the power thus to realize himself.)

The idea of a whole or complete being is realized in
our minds solely through the idea of cause. Any dependent being is relative to another and involved with it,
so that it can not be detached from it and exist by itself.
It is no centre of formation and transformation. Our
idea of life or living being also has this causal idea as

its basis. When one does not confound the idea of causality with the application of it to this or that case, but sees the absolute certainty which he possesses that there can be no change without an efficient cause—and the like certainty that the true cause is an originator of movement and of new forms—then he sees that experience can not furnish the idea because it can not begin without it, and because the external senses can never perceive a true cause at all.

CHAPTER VIII.

The Psychological Meaning of the Infinite and Absolute.

§ 35. WE have seen the grounds for our conclusion that time and space are not externally perceived as objects or learned by contact with them as individual examples—in short, we have seen that the ideas of time and space are not derived from sense-perception. From the nature of the case, sense-perception is limited to what is present (here and now), and can not furnish us objects that are infinite, like time and space. We have considered the idea of the infinite, and noted the fact that it is a positive idea and not a negative idea. Time and space are the logical conditions of existence of all things and events in the world. The ideas of time and space make experience possible. This is very important, and must be borne in mind constantly in the psychology of education, or else we can not rightly adjudge the value or worthlessness of ideas that lie at the bottom of so much that is offered us in literature, science, history, and philosophy in our day.

In thinking these ideas we think the infinite in an affirmative manner. Through the mistake of Hamilton and Mansel, Herbert Spencer and nearly all of his disciples have been led into agnosticism, and many of the men of science and literature have followed them. If their doctrine of the inconceivability of the infinite is based on false psychology, we may see at once how much literature needs correction. Herbert Spencer, in his First Principles, denies the conceivability of all " ultimate religious ideas "—such, for example, as self-existence, self-creation, and creation by an external agency. Nor can we conceive (according to him) of First Cause as infinite and absolute. He quotes Mansel: " The absolute can not be conceived as conscious, neither can it be conceived as unconscious; it can not be conceived as complex, neither can it be conceived as simple; it can not be conceived by difference, neither can it be conceived by the absence of difference; it can not be identified with the universe, neither can it be distinguished from it." " The fundamental conceptions of rational theology," according to Mansel and Spencer, " are thus self-destructive." All these negative conclusions are based on the false psychology here exposed. Spencer says (page 31, first edition of First Principles): " Self-existence therefore necessarily means existence without a beginning; and to form a conception of self-existence is to form a conception of existence without a beginning. Now by no mental effort can we do this. To conceive existence through infinite past time, implies the conception of infinite past time, which is an impossi-

7

bility." To us this all rests on the confusion of mental images with logical thought. We can not image infinite time simply because it is infinite. That it is infinite we can know, however, by thinking on its nature. We can see that any limited time is limited by time previous and subsequent, and that these three times—present, past, and future—all are parts of the same time. In fact, had Spencer been acquainted with Kant's Critique he would have noticed his own contradiction. For while he denies the possibility of conceiving self-existence in the first chapters of his book, he does not hesitate to set up " persistent force " as the highest scientific truth in the latter part of his book. His " persistent force," for the reason that it " implies the conception of infinite past time, which is an impossibility," is a phrase that could have no idea corresponding to it according to his philosophy. Now, if we really can know the infinity of space and time and the absoluteness implied in causality, it is a matter of great concern; for science is coming to be written and taught with these agnostic assumptions explicitly stated at every turn. There is nothing about natural science that warrants such agnosticism. It is due only to the teachers and expounders of it who have adopted a false psychology and who give science their own point of view.

§ 36. The true doctrine of causality leads to valid conceptions of self-activity. In Chapter IV of these discussions we have described the three stages of thought. The second stage sets up relativity as a supreme principle, and is pantheistic. The lowest stage of thought is atheistic, because it makes all things alike independent realities. The second stage makes all things dependent and subordinate to an ultimate blind force, which swallows up all special forms of existence. The third stage of thinking reaches the ideas of the infinite and the absolute, and comprehends and recognises the attributes of life, moral freedom, immortality, and the divine, as belonging to whatever has the form of true or independent being. All totalities or independent wholes must be self-active, for they would be dependent on others, and hence not totalities if they were not self-active.— The writings of the Scholastics or "Schoolmen" abound in expressions for this distinction. A totality is called a "perfect being." Descartes uses "perfect" in this sense in his celebrated proof of the being of God (in his Third Meditation).

With a belief that the words "infinite" and "absolute" do not express anything to which we may think any meaning, all religious, all moral, and all æsthetic ideas must be set aside as unthinkable or else explained physiologically, or, perhaps, shown up as "survivals" of crude early epochs of development. Religious ideas have been explained as a "disease of language." The sun myths that have furnished the symbols and metaphors for religious ideas are looked upon rather as the substantial meaning, and the spiritual ideas which have found expression in those symbols are regarded by such agnostics as spurious and unwarranted outgrowths.—So freedom and moral responsibility, the sheet-anchor of man's higher life in institutions, has been denied, and is still denied, by all who deny the true import of causality and who set up in its place an "invariable sequence." Herbert Spencer, in the first American edition of his Data of Psychology (page 220), says: "Psychical changes either conform to law or they do not. If they do not conform to law, this work;

in common with all works on the subject, is sheer nonsense; no science of psychology is possible. If they do conform to law, there can not be any such thing as free will." Here "conformity to law" means dependence on other beings belonging to the series. Mr. Spencer supposes that freedom is not as rational and fundamental as fate. (This will be considered in detail in Chapters XVII, XVIII, and XIX.)—The physiological psychologists, instead of explaining the nerves and brain as servants of mind, are prone to make them the originating source and masters of mind. But we are forced to see the soul as a substantial self-activity and original cause, which acts on its environment *really* in assimilation and digestion, taking up matter and converting it into living tissue—vegetable or animal cells; and it reacts *ideally* against its environment in sense-perception, representation, and thought. It constructs the ideas of objects, projects them in space and time, and thereby perceives those objects—not destroying them by the operation, as the process of digestion does.

CHAPTER IX.

The Logic of Sense-Perception.* What Figure of the Syllogism Apperception uses.

§ 37. THE exposition of the structure of the mind —of its forms used in sense-perception, or reasoning, belongs to psychology. Hence formal logic is

---

* I was incited to inquire into the significance or function of the three logical figures by a study of the modes *Baroko* and *Bocardo*, undertaken twenty years ago.— W. T. H.

a part of psychology, and a very important one. A consideration of its significance will throw light on the structure of sense-perception. Sense-perception is not a simple act that can be no further analyzed. In its most elementary forms one may readily find the entire structure of reason. The difference between the higher and lower forms of intelligence consists not in the presence or absence of phases of thought, but in the degree of completeness of the consciousness of them—the whole is present, but is not consciously perceived to be present, in the lower forms. The whole structure of reason functions not only in every act of mind, no matter how low in the scale—say even in the animal intelligence—nay, more, in the life of the plant which has not yet reached the plane of intellect—yes, even in the movement of inorganic matter: in the laws of celestial gravitation there is manifested the structural framework of reason. "The hand that made us is divine." The advance of human intellect, therefore, consists not in realizing more of the logical structure of reason, but in attaining a more adequate consciousness of its entire scope. Let us imagine, for illustration, an entire circle, and liken the self-activity to it. (Self-determination is a movement of return to itself, like the circle.) The lowest form of life (the plant) is not conscious of the smallest arc of this circle; but the animal with the smallest amount of sensation is conscious of points or small arcs of it. The lowest human intelligence knows at least half a circle. The discovery of ethical laws, of philosophic principles, of religious truths, gradually brings the remaining arc of the entire circle under the focus of consciousness. What is more wonderful is this: There are degrees of higher consciousness. The lower consciousness may be a mere feeling or emotion—much smoke and little flame of intellect. There are, in fact, degrees of emotional consciousness, covering the entire scale: First, the small arcs or points; next, the half circle; finally, the whole. Think of emotions that concern only selfish wants; next, of emotions that are æsthetic, relating to art; next, of emotions that are ethical and altruistic; then, of religious emotions relating to the vision of the whole and perfect. Next above the purely emotional (all smoke and no flame of abstract intellect), think of the long course of human history in which man becomes conscious of his nature in more abstract forms, and finally reaches science. The progress is from object to subject, and finally to the method that unites both. We act, and then become conscious of our action, and finally see its method.

§ 38. The structure of reason is revealed in logic. Logic is thus a portion of psychology—it is " rational psychology." Let us examine sense-perception and see what logical forms make themselves manifest. Take the most ordinary act of seeing; what is the operation involved there? Is it not the recognition of something? We make out the object first as something in space before us; then as something limited in space; then as something coloured; then as something of a definite shape; and thus on until we recognise in it a definite object of a kind familiar to us. The perception of an object is thus a series of recognitions—a series of acts of predication or judgment: " This is an object before me in space; it is coloured gray; it looms through the fog like a tree; no, it is pointed like a steeple; I see what looks like a belfry; I make out the cross on the top of the spire; I recognise it to be a church spire." Or, again: " Something appears in the distance; it is moving; it moves its limbs; it is not a quadruped; it is a biped; it is a boy walking this way; he has a basket on his arm; it is James." First we recognise a sense-impression, and through that impression an object; then the nature of the object; its identities with well-known kinds of objects; its individual differences from those well-known kinds of objects. But the differences are recognised as identical with well-known kinds of difference. It is the combination of different classes or kinds of attributes that enables us to recognise the individuality of this object. It is like all others and different from all others. Let us notice what logical forms we have used. First, the act of recognition uses the second figure of the syllogism. The second figure says S is M; P is M; hence S is P; or, in the case of sense-perception, (a) this object (the logical subject) has a cross on the summit of its spire, or is a cross-crowned spire; (b) church spires are cross-crowned; (c) hence this object is a church spire. We notice that the syllogism is not necessarily true. It may be true, but it is not logically certain to be true. This uncertainty attaches to sense-perception. Its first act is to recognise, and this takes place in the second figure of the syllogism, which has "valid modes" (or necessary conclusions) only in the negative. But sense-perception uses *in-valid* modes— i. e., syllogisms which do not furnish correct inferences. Sense-perception, using a *valid* mode of the second figure (the mode called "Cesare"), might have said:

No natural tree is cross-crowned.

This object is cross-crowned.

Hence this object can not be a natural tree.

(No P is M; S is M; hence S is not P.)

The structure of reason, as revealed in logic, shows us always universal, particular, and individual ideas united in the form of inference or a syllogism.

Grammar shows us the logical structure of language. Language is the instrument of, and reveals the structure of, reason. Grammar finds that all speech has the form of a judgment. A is B—something is something. All sense-perception is a recognition of this sort: Something (an object before me) is something (an attribute or class which I have known before). This is an act of apperception or an identification of the new with what is already familiar. But this recognition or apperception takes place through some common mark or property that belongs to the object and to the well-known class—this mark or property being the middle term. Hence the judgment is grounded on other judgments, and the whole act of sense-perception is a syllogism. The mind acts in the form of a syllogism, but is dimly conscious or quite unconscious of the form in which it acts when it is engaged in sense-perception. I perceive that this is a church steeple. But I do not reflect on the form of mental activity by which I have recognised it. If asked, "How do you know that it is a church steeple?" then I elevate into consciousness some of the steps of the process, and say, "Because I saw its cross-crowned summit." This implies the syllogism in the second figure: (a) Church spires have cross-crowned summits; (b) this object has a cross-crowned summit; (c) hence it is a church spire. But this is not a necessary conclusion—it is not a "valid mode" of the second figure. The mind knows this, but is not conscious of it at the time. An objection may be raised which will at once draw into consciousness a valid mode. Let it be objected: "The object that you see is a monument in the cemetery." The reply is, "Monuments do not have belfries, but this object has a belfry." Here sense-perception has noted a

further attribute—the belfry. Its conclusion is simply
negative: "It is not a monument, because it has a belfry,"
and it concludes this in a "valid mode" of the second
figure (Cesare). (*a*) No monuments have belfries; (*b*) this
object has a belfry; (*c*) hence it is not a monument. If
the premises (*a* and *b*) are correct, the conclusion necessarily follows.

§ 39. In the first act of recognition the second
figure is used. The characteristic of the second figure
is this: Its middle term is the predicate in both
propositions (the major proposition or premise, and
the minor proposition or premise). There are four
"modes" in this figure which are valid—that is to
say, four modes in which necessary truth may be
inferred. The conclusions of these are all negative,
and run as follows:

1. This is the "mode" called "Cesare": (*a*)
No P is M; (*b*) all S is M; (*c*) hence no S is P.

2. ("Camestres"): (*a*) All P is M; (*b*) no S is
M; (*c*) hence no S is P.

3. ("Festino"): (*a*) No P is M; (*b*) some S is
M; (*c*) hence some S is not P.

4. ("Baroco"): (*a*) All P is M; (*b*) some S is
not M; (*c*) hence some S is not P.*

---

* Let the reader not familiar with logic, who desires to
learn more of it than is explained here, read the first eight
chapters of Aristotle's Prior Analytics, and he will see
the subject as presented by its first discoverer. Or any

In the *first figure* the middle term is subject of the major premise and predicate of the minor premise, thus: (*a*) M is P; (*b*) S is M; (*c*) hence S is P.*

In the *second figure* (as shown above) the middle term is the predicate of both premises, thus: (*a*) P is M; (*b*) S is M; (*c*) hence S is P.

In the *third figure* the middle term is. the subject of both premises, thus: (*a*) M is P; (*b*) M is S; (*c*) hence S is P.

In the *first figure* we unite the subject (S) to the predicate (P) because of a middle term (M) that contains the subject, but which is itself contained in the predicate: All men are mortal; Socrates is a man; hence Socrates is mortal. Here man is the middle term (M) which contains Socrates, the subject (S), and is contained in the more general class of mortal beings, the predicate (P).

In the *second figure* we unite the subject to the predicate because of a middle term that *includes* both—that is to say, is *predicate* of both (because the predicate includes its subject). All men are language-using beings; no monkeys are language-using beings; hence no monkeys are men. Here monkeys are discriminated from men by the middle term, " language-using," which includes all men and excludes all monkeys.

---

ordinary compend of logic will give the essential details. For this psychological purpose note in particular the nature of the three figures which are distinguished by the way in which they employ the middle term (the term which unites or divides the subject and predicate of the conclusion).

* S is used to denote the word Subject; M to denote the word Middle (term); P is used to denote the word Predicate. S and P are respectively subject and predicate of the proposition that expresses the conclusion or inference. M is the middle term that brings together S and P, as it is subject or predicate to the other terms. S, P, and M are called " terms," and the first two propositions are called, respectively, ", major " and " minor " premise.

In the *third figure* we unite the subject to the predicate because of a middle term which is included in both—i. e., is subject of both (because the subject is included in the predicate). All men are animals; all men are rational; hence some animals are rational. Here animals (the subject) is united with rational (the predicate) through the middle term, man.

CHAPTER X.

How Sense-perception uses the First Figure of the Syllogism to re-enforce its First Act which takes place in the Second Figure.

§ 40. WE have seen that sense-perception uses the second figure of the syllogism in its first act. The proof of this may be found in the fact that the object can not be perceived except in so far as it is recognised or identified. Identification takes place in the second figure of the syllogism. Before one can notice the differences of a thing one must identify it as an object. And he must identify it as a sensation before he can identify the sensation as a sensation of an object. One may not be able to take account of differences except in so far as he has a basis of identity to go upon. The primary form of seizing the object—the form of " presentation," as certain psy-

chologists call it—is that of the second figure. But
immediately after its presentation in the second
figure begins the activity of the first figure. No
sooner have I recognised and classified the object by
one of its marks than I begin to look after the other
marks which I have learned in my previous experience to belong to objects of its class. I recognise the
object to be a church steeple by its cross-crowned
summit, and begin at once to look for other characteristics of a church steeple, such as a belfry, for example. I also look for the well-known outlines of a
spire, for the roof of the church to which it is united,
and so on. If the first step of the process of sense-
perception is in the form of the second figure, the
second step is in the form of the first figure. By the
second figure I have identified the object as a church
spire. To classify is to refer the new object to what is
well known. It is possible now to re-enforce the
present perception by bringing to it all the stored-up
treasures of experience. I begin at once to draw out
of the treasure-house of the general class a series of
inferences: If it is a church spire, it is likely to have
a belfry—possibly a clock, a steep slope above, shin-
gled with slate or wood, joined below to the body
of the church at the ridge of the roof or else at the
corner of the edifice, etc. Hence I look again and

again; being now helped by my previous experience
I collect much information in a very short interval
of time. The form of this second activity in the first
figure is (*a*) M is P; (*b*) S is M; (*c*) S is P. " This
object is a church steeple " is the conclusion of the
second figure or first act of perception. Then by the
first figure (though not with one of the four valid
modes) I conclude: (some) church steeples have belfries; this is a church steeple; hence it has (or may
have) a belfry. And I continue to look for characteristics which the first figure infers to be present in
a steeple. I see a dark opening at the bottom of the
steeple, and I infer the existence of a belfry by the
second figure, thus: (*a*) A belfry has the appearance
of a dark opening at the base of the steeple; (*b*) this
object has that appearance; (*c*) hence it is a belfry.
This again is a not-valid mode, and infers only possibility or probability.

Thus to and fro moves the syllogizing without coming to full and clear consciousness. The mind acts without reflecting on the form of its acts. The classification of
the object (belfry) being effected by the second figure, I go
on to infer by the first figure what I may expect to find there
—namely, a bell—and I look for it and see a portion of a
wheel in the dark opening. I infer a bell from this. The
steps are very complex: I recognised the wheel by some
characteristic appearance that belongs to a wheel. The
wheel is attached to the axis that turns the bell. Thus
we have a series of middle terms, each one of which has

been used first as predicate in a syllogism of the second figure and then as middle term in one of the first figure.

§ 41. The modes of the syllogism ordinarily used by sense-perception are not the so-called valid modes; that is, they deduce only possible or probable knowledge at best, while the valid modes infer necessary conclusions. The cross-crowned object may be something else than a steeple; the dark space below may be something else than a belfry; the wheel may be there with no bell attached to the axle; the axle may not be there; the appearance of the wheel may be deceptive. Sense-perception abounds in deception. The second figure, of identification, is corrected by the use of the first figure, of deduction, which offers a number of additional marks for verification. By verification we decrease the possibility of error according to the law of probabilities. Every additional mark verified increases the probability.

The first figure acts in very subtle ways in the early stages of a given observation. I look out through the fog in a given direction and see some object so dimly that I should not be able to say what it is. But I know where I am, and that in the direction where I am looking there is a village. In a village church steeples are wont to be seen, and hence I am led to expect that the most prominent object will be such a steeple. Here the first figure acts to suggest what I may expect to see. It acts in a not-valid mood, thus: (a) Some villages have churches with steeples; (b) this is a village; (c) it has (or may have) a steeple. And again (second figure): (*a*) Steeples are prominent objects; (*b*) you behold a prominent object; (*c*) it is (or may be) a steeple.—The identification of the present place (the " here ") and the present time (the " now ") leads to a number of anticipations of perception by the aid of the first figure. And these lead to verification by means of the second figure.—Besides these very general anticipations there are more abstract ones, and even *a priori* anticipations which guide our sense-perception. The general idea of space as a major premise suggests externality and the anticipation that the object is limited on all sides; and sense-perception is directed to look for boundaries.—Next, the idea of time suggests movement, and the object is examined for changes.—Then the idea of causality suggests functions, and these, too, are anticipated, and the object is observed to find its relations to other things. These " anticipations of perception " are not conscious ordinarily, although they may become so in case doubt suggests investigation and verification.

§ 42. The educational significance of these facts of sense-perception is worth noting. The school labours to give the pupil the results of human experience. This stored-up material furnishes anticipations of experience to each, so that he may know what to look for when the object is presented to him. In a brief time he verifies all that experience has recorded of an object. By the first figure of the syllogism the individual re-enforces his present vision by all his past experience. More than this, he re-enforces it by the experience of the race. This makes human progress possible, and by accumulation develops civilization.

To teach powers of quick perception it is not necessary simply to use one's senses (although a false psychology often tells us so). It is necessary to store up, in the
form of scientific generalizations, the observations of the
race, and then (for this is not all) learn to verify these
observations and critically test them so as not to mimic
the former observers and repeat their errors. To master
the results of the past sharpens one's observation by setting up in the mind a myriad anticipations of experience
which test and cross-question observation at every turn,
and make the alert and critical observer. One learns how
to eliminate the personal co-efficient from his observations.
This personal co-efficient is due to the individual peculiarity of the observer—to his defects and weaknesses. As
no two persons are likely to have the same defects of sense-
perception, it is possible for each one to correct the errors
due to his own personal coefficient by the aid of the observation of others. Formal logic has fallen into great
contempt in modern times. This contempt is not deserved.
The study of logic as an industry by which we are to learn
the art of reasoning—this, perhaps, deserves all the contempt it has received; but as a science of the spiritual
structure of cognition—a science of the forms of perception—it is not contemptible.

§ 43. Formal logic, as the exposition of the structure of mind—the forms of its functions—is a very
important part of psychology, and a key to all the unconscious activities of the mind. Treatises on logic
usually hold the doctrine that logic is the form of
reflection, and of conscious reflection alone. Hence
they suppose that sense-perception and feeling are
not syllogistic in their structure. Hegel was the first
to show explicitly that every form of life has a syllo-

8

gistic structure, and that even the inorganic world is dominated by the same form. He was led to this by seeing that the universal or general term, while it means only a class taken superficially, when taken profoundly and in its entire compass stands for the idea of an energy—a producing cause—just as Plato's Ideas are such (see Chapters V and VI). The universal concept (*der allgemeine Begriff*) of Hegel corresponds to the creating cause of the species—oak means the oak-producing energy. He did not, it is true, make the analysis of sense-perception here given, but he pointed out the dependence of the first figure on the third, and likewise that of the second on the first, for the proof of its major premise. Hegel alone of students of logic has looked to the distinction of figures as having a profound significance. The major premise of each figure needs proof; that of the first figure is proved by the third; that of the third by the second figure; and finally the major premise of the second figure requires the first figure for its proof. Hence Hegel changed the order that Aristotle gave for the second and third figures. In the psychology of sense-perception, as expounded here, we change the order of the use of the figures to the following: second, first, third.

There are four valid modes in the first figure—four modes in which a conclusion may be deduced with absolute certainty from the premises given—that is to say, if the premises are true in these four modes the conclusion must be true. These are as follows:

1. (*Barbara*): (*a*) All M are P; (*b*) all S are M; (*c*) hence all S are P. Illustrating this symbolism: (*a*) All men are mortal (all M are P, or all of the middle term, men, are mortal, mortal being the predicate of the conclusion); (*b*) all Indians are men (all S are M, or all of the subject of the conclusion, Indians, are men, the middle term); (*c*) hence all Indians are mortal (all S are P, all of the subject, Indians, are mortal, the predicate).

2. (*Celarent*): (*a*) No M are P; (*b*) all S are M; (*c*) hence no S are P.

3. (*Darii*): (*a*) All M are P; (*b*) some S are M; (*c*) hence some S are P.

4. (*Ferio*): (*a*) No M are P; (*b*) some S are M; (*c*) hence some S are not P.

There are sixteen modes (or moods) possible in each figure, as one may see by calculating the permutations possible in two terms, each one of which has four possible forms. Each term, S, M, P, may be universal affirmative—all are (indicated in logic by the letter *a*); universal negative—none are (indicated by the letter *e*); particular affirmative—some are (indicated by the letter *i*); particular negative—some are not (indicated by the letter *o*). But of the sixteen possible modes in each figure only a few are valid, or draw necessary conclusions. There are only four valid modes in the first figure; the same in the second figure; and six valid modes in the third figure.

CHAPTER XI.

*How General Concepts arise.   How Sense-Perception
uses the Third Figure of the Syllogism to store
up its Experience in General Terms.*

§ 44. THE activity of the second figure gives occasion to that of the first figure.   Then the stored-up
experience leads through the application of the first
figure to a number of anticipations of perception,
which are verified or tested.   But by what process do
classes, species, genera, and all the universals which
furnish the major premise of the first figure arise?
The answer to this brings us to the consideration of
the third figure.   Its schema is: M is P; M is S;
hence S is P.   Man is a biped; man is rational; hence
(some) rational being is a biped.   Here man is the
middle term, and it is the subject in both premises.
In the third figure, as used in sense-perception, the
middle term is the object perceived, and the two
extremes are connected with each other by the
fact that they both belong to the same object.   Now,
since the middle term is subsumed under both extremes, it follows that only particular affirmative
conclusions can be made in it—we can only say

some S is P and not all S is P. *Some* rational beings are bipeds. This may be seen by considering that the middle term (which is the object) participates in the predicate (major premise: horse is an animal), and participates also in the subject (the minor: horse is a quadruped). Hence the subject is connected with the predicate through the object (horse), which is in all cases only a part of the logical sphere of the predicate, and likewise only a part of the sphere of the subject. It follows that this conclusion connects a part of the subject with the predicate.

There are six valid modes in this figure—three particular affirmative and three particular negative conclusions. These are named, respectively:

Darapti—all M is P; all M is S; hence some S is P.

Disamis—some M is P; all M is S; hence some S is P.

Datisi—all M is P; some M is S; hence some S is P.

Felapton—no M is P; all M is S; hence some S is not P.

Bocardo—some M is not P; all M is S; hence some S is not P.

Ferison—no M is P; some M is S; hence some S is not P.

These valid modes, useful as they are in deducing necessary conclusions, like the valid modes of the second and first figures, are nevertheless not of much use in sense-perception. Certainty in experience comes from repetition and verification, rather than from single necessary conclusions.

Explanation of the Artificial Words used to Name the Modes.—Aristotle, and after him nearly all other writers on logic, hold that the first figure gives the purest and simplest form of the syllogism. The other figures are conceived to rest on it in such a way that the mind in using

them unconsciously travels through the first in reaching
a conclusion. The road travelled is explained by Aristotle
and his followers. The mnemonic words indicate not only
the quality (positive or negative) and the quantity (universal or particular) of the major, minor, and conclusion, but also the changes necessary to turn the mode
into a corresponding one of the first figure. Thus, in *Barbara* the three *a*'s show three universal affirmative propositions, each expressed by *all are; e* in *Celarent* means *none
are; i* in *Darii, some are; o* in *Ferio, some are not.* In the
first figure the consonants are not significant, except that
the first letters, B, C, D, F, are the first four consonants of
the alphabet, and are taken only as the distinguishing
characteristics of the modes of that figure. When used in
the modes of the other figures they indicate that the mode
beginning with one of these letters is to be explained or
resolved by transforming it into the mode of the first
figure to which the letter belongs. *Camestres* is to be
changed into *Celarent; Festino* into *Ferio; Baroco* into *Barbara*, etc. The consonants, *s, m, p,* used in one of the
modes of the second and third figures, indicate the changes
necessary to transform it into a mode of first figure. S
denotes simple conversion—i. e., the proposition indicated
by the previous vowel must be converted or changed, so that
its predicate becomes the subject. *Cesare*, for example,
beginning with *C*, must be changed to *Celarent* in first
figure. The *s* indicates that the universal negative proposition, symbolized by the vowel *e* before it, must be converted simply, its subject and predicate changing places.
No man is a bird, converted simply would read *no bird is
a man.* Simple conversion can happen in universal nega-
tives and in particular affirmatives; *some birds are waders*,
converted, reads *some waders are birds.* Universal affirmatives convert into particular affirmatives, as, the conversion
of *all men are mortal* is not *all mortals are men*, but *some
mortals are men*, because the subject is only a part of the
extent of the predicate. Conversion of a universal affirmative into a particular is conversion *per accidens*, and is indicated by the letter *p* after the vowel representing the

proposition. Thus, in *Darapti* the *p* indicates that the minor premise, a universal affirmative, represented by the second *a*, should be converted into a particular affirmative. *Per accidens*—by accident—means that the form of necessity indicated by allness has been lost and the accidental assumed. If some are and some are not, accident determines which. Finally, *m* in the mnemonic word indicates that the major and minor premises must be exchanged one for the other. Thus, in *Disamis* not only must the major premise indicated by the first letter *i* be converted simply, but it must also exchange places with the minor premise (metathesis or transposition). The *c* in *Baroco* and *Bocardo* indicates that the proposition symbolized by the preceding vowel must be changed into its contradictory (*all are* into *some are not; all are not* into *some are*), when an absurd result will show itself, and prove that any other than the first conclusion is absurd. *Baroco* and *Bocardo* are the modes not satisfactorily explained by the logicians.* The circuitous method of reduction by the *ad absurdum*, although Aristotle's method, is perplexing and unsatisfactory. Take as examples the following: BAROCO—*Every animal is endowed with feeling;* some living beings are not endowed with feeling; hence some living beings are not animals (the plants, for instance). Here it seems perfectly easy for the mind to come to a direct conclusion from the premises without any process of *reductio ad absurdum;* for there is a middle term, *endowed with feeling*, which contains or comprehends all animals, but excludes some living beings. It is a simple logical step to conclude that the *some living beings* not in the middle term are not in the major term, animals, which is in the middle term. This

---

* See Hamilton's Lectures on Logic, pages 312 and 316, where he says that they " have been at once the *cruces* and the *opprobria* of logicians. . . . So intricate was *Bocardo* considered that it was looked upon as a trap, into which, if you once got, it was no easy matter to find an exit." See also, on page 317, his astonishing attempt to analyze *Bocardo*.

is as clear as *Ferio:* No non-sentient beings are animals; some living beings are non-sentient; hence some living beings are not animals. Take *Bocardo:* Some animals are not bipeds; all animals are self-moving; some self-moving beings are not bipeds. Here, as in *Baroco*, the inference is direct, because all the middle is in the subject and yet is partly outside the predicate; hence the subject is partly outside the predicate, and this insight can not be stated in a form any clearer than it is in *Bocardo*.

§ 45. The third figure follows the second figure, and can not precede its activity because each of its premises presupposes the action of identifying. The object M is S (horses are quadrupeds—S [quadruped] is recognised in the object). The object M is P (horses are shod with hoofs—P [shod] is now recognised). Thus there are two identifications, one for each premise (both using the second figure of the syllogism), before the third figure can begin to function. Now it acts and connects the two phases of the object (S P), making a new predication, which may serve for a new major premise of the first figure (collecting in the definition of horse the ideas of quadruped and hoofs). Hereafter we may say: Such objects as those (M) are S P, and when we see one of this kind we may recognise it in the second figure at once. Let us suppose that our object before had been a black eagle, a well-known object. Now we recognise eagle and white-head by two acts of the second figure;

white-headed (bald-headed) eagle makes a new class,
derived by the third figure. Hereafter, an object may
be recognised as white-headed (or bald-headed) eagle
by the second figure, and all its other peculiarities
stored up in observation deduced by the first figure.

§ 46. The second figure identifies in sense-perception; the first figure anticipates further identification; but it is the third figure that distinguishes, divides, and determines, and by making a new synthesis
of already familiar marks defines new classes. The
new class arises by adding a special new attribute
to an old class. Every new combination of marks discovered in an object is potentially a new class. All
other specimens discovered like it are recognised, and
their peculiarities, stored up by experience, may be
deduced by the first figure in such a way as to abridge
the act of perception and make it swift and com-
pendious.

§ 47. The third figure notices the striking characteristics of an object, and unites them through this
middle term, which is the object itself; these are
characteristics of one and the same object, and distinguish it from other objects, making it belong to the
S-P class. Inasmuch as the characteristics S and P
exist together in the same object, there is some deeper
unity to be sought for them. This leads to the appli-

cation of the principle of causality. S and P are
related in some way causally. They are means, or
ends, or agents, or results, in the same process. The
a priori principle of causality here acts as an " anticipation of perception," and sets mental activity in the
third figure to looking for a synthesis of causality
between the attributes discovered in the same object.

§ 48. The causal relation has many phases; these
fall under two classes—(*a*) subjective and (*b*) objective. (*a*) As relating to manifestations to sense—
colour, noise (especially), taste, touch, smell—the
object may be obtrusive on our attention; conspicu-
ous, attractive, monopolizing attention. Here the
causative energy is subjective in the sense that its
effect is chiefly upon our senses, and not an essential
element in the process of the object itself.

(*b*) The causal relation, secondly, is that of self-
activity for the object's own sake. The activity of
limbs in locomotion—legs, fins, wings; or in prehen-
sion, as arms, hands, claws, jaws; or in growth, implying assimilation, as of trees, etc.—The object is a producer of effects on its environment.

The activity of the syllogism thus far treated is supposed to be unconscious in various degrees; but the activity in the third figure comes nearest to being a conscious
one, because it notes what is new and announces the results of synthesis in a new definition.

§ 49. It would seem from this study of the third figure in sense-perception that the formation of general terms is not conducted after the manner supposed in ordinary treatises on psychology. We do not proceed by abstraction, comparison, generalization, etc., to classification. We make a synthesis of traits, and, although we have only one case before us, this synthesis is a definition of a possible class. If we observe a second, like the first, we use this synthetic concept (S P) and subsume the object under it. We recognise by the second figure any other specimen of the same. Thus each synthesis performed by the third figure becomes a class definition under which an indefinite amount of experience may be stored up by the second and first figures. Should no new examples occur, the synthetic characteristic S P drops into the background and remains an individual mark, or it may get lost altogether and forgotten.

§ 50. Here is the natural system of mnemonics: The mind classifies, and each class definition is a mental pigeonhole in which it places facts of experience that belong there. The act of noticing the particular distinction that forms the subclass assists powerfully in retaining the observation in the memory. The operation of this third figure may be compared not only to a case with pigeonholes, but more aptly to a series of hands that clutch and hold tightly the particular experience. Think how vividly we remember an object that possessed a peculiarity—a white crow, a tailless squirrel, a sheep with hair, or a horse with wool, etc. Whatever is peculiar gets clutched by this third figure, and it may become familiar if experience furnishes a number of examples to be subsumed under it; otherwise it remains an exceptional fact or a " curiosity."

§ 51. The lower use of the third figure notes the obtrusive characteristics—those which strike the senses first—and usually not the characteristics important to the object itself. Its means of self-preservation are most important to the object; its means of procuring subsistence, and defending itself—what it uses as a means of survival in its struggle for existence.

Herein is objective causality manifest, and our general terms get something objective to correspond to them. In the case of subjective characteristics which are prolific in giving names to the lower varieties, we do not have an objective universal named, but only a subjective—a constant for the form of obtrusion on the sense; for example, shade-tail for squirrel ($\sigma\kappa\iota o\nu\rho o s$—$\sigma\kappa\iota d$ = shadow, and $o\dot{\nu}\rho d$ = tail). The striking characteristic of the squirrel is his bushy, upturned tail. The animal seated on his haunches struck the Greek imagination as an animal sitting in the shadow of his tail, or his tail appeared as a materialized shadow of him. The name falcon is from its curved beak—

here the name indicates the objective causal process—its instrument of attack. So rodent is a gnawer—another example of an objective causal process. The act of gnawing is the means by which this class of animals makes itself valid. Cow, and the many words for kine, come from *gu*, to low, to bellow (old Indo-European root; see Fick, Vergleich. Wörterbuch Indo-German. Sprachen, i, 577), just as bos, *bous*, in the Greek and Latin come from the root *bu*, to low, to bellow (see Fick, iv, 178). The most important thing about the use of the third figure is this apprehension of causality—this formation of concepts based on the causal connection between two attributes belonging to the object. This is an explaining process—the reaching of a universal that is universal because it is a process that begets many examples (see Chapter V, on Concepts). It is a self-producing power like life.

§ 52. The action of the third figure, as we have seen, produces a definition because it unites two characteristics in one object. It is the figure of definition or determination. The definition may or may not be valid for many subsequent specimens. The test is the further experience which stamps the definition with currency or leaves it an exceptional case.

Says Aristotle: "When one thing without difference invariably prevails, there is then first a universal in the soul; for the singular is indeed perceived by the sense, but sense is of the universal—as of man, but not the man Callias." It perceives individually, but it is the universal or potentially universal that sense perceives in the individual. It recognises, or identifies the new percept with other percepts as one with them "without difference"—this by the second figure; then it notes new properties or characteristics by the third figure, and thereby gets definitions of subclasses. Each definition is used by the first figure in such a manner as to facilitate the observation of the marks of the object. For further illustration here are a few examples of the action of sense-perception in the third figure, by which two attributes are united by a causal idea: Tree, evergreen, resinous sap (resisting the action of cold). Bird, hooked beak, for tearing its prey. Bird, sharp talons, clutches living prey. Beast, chews cud, extra stomach. Beast, chews cud, divided hoofs (this contrast to the former is a mere subjective class, no causality being obvious). Beast, large pupil to eye, prowls at night. Desert plant, dew-absorbing, no rain. *Summary.*—The second figure classifies, using a property as its middle term. The first figure adds to the present observation the results of past observation, using the class as a middle term. The third figure, using the object as a middle term, perceives a new property and adds it to the class, making a new definition of a possible subclass, of which the object before it is an example.—There are three terms in sense-perception— the object, its class, its properties. The appropriate middle term is the object in the third figure, the class in the first figure, and a property in the second.—In Chapter V we have seen that a conception is not a mental picture, but a definition. Here we have found the process by which the definition arises.

§ 53. The ultimate consequences of this principle in psychology are important as touching the doctrine of ·categories of the mind. Sense-perception uses these categories unconsciously. Reflection subsequently discovers their existence, and finally their genesis. The fundamental act of mind, as self-determining, discriminates self from the special modification in which the self finds itself. The self is the general capacity for feeling, willing, knowing; but it is at a given moment determined as one of these, if not exclusively, at least predominantly. Every act of perception begins with identification (second figure). This is an act of removal of the special limitation from the object—a dissolving of it in the general self as a capacity for any and all sensation, volition, or thought. Because to see an individual as a class is to neglect an infinite number of characteristics, and contemplate only the few belonging to the definition of this class. It is this first act that gives rise to the category of being, and the category of negation born with it is next perceived. All other categories arise from division of this most general of categories (*summum genus*). The third figure shows how these arise by progressive definition. The categories, in so far as they do not imply in their definition any properties derived from sense-perception, are called categories of pure thought or logic. Hegel undertakes to show the process of progressive definition by which these arise, in his logic (Wissenschaft der Logik). ·

CHAPTER XII.

The Body and the Mind.

§ 54. In the last three chapters we have discussed the structure of the mind as revealed in its logical forms. The intellect has a logical constitution; it uses the syllogism in all its activity. It is a process of determining or of descent from the general to the particular, as in the third figure, or it is a process in the opposite direction, from the particular to the general, as in the second figure, which identifies particulars with general terms. In these investigations there can be no doubt that we have the real nature of the mind revealed to us. It is a self-activity whose forms of action are these three logical figures. In the present chapter we are to look at another method of studying the mind, that of the so-called physiological psychology. This method begins with the living organism and studies the correlation of mental phenomena with bodily changes. It seeks to find what phenomena of the soul correspond to various bodily stimuli. It is evident at the outset that there is some connection between the soul and the body; all human experience presupposes this. We use the body in two ways: we perceive the external world by means of it, and we use the body as an instrument in order to produce changes on the world that we see. Here we have inward movement and outward movement through nerves—centripetal nerve-currents and centrifugal nerve-currents. Sensation is the sequence of the centripetal, and motor-impulse the antecedent of the centrifugal. The motor-impulse may proceed from the brain, or it may proceed from some ganglion of the spinal marrow. In both these currents we have what may be explained as mechanical action. It may be so explained, but it is not as yet so explained. Mechanical action borrows all its energy from another—it merely transmits it, and does not originate it. Vital action is self-activity in combination with mechanical action; it originates activity and guides it. The process of digestion, common to animals and plants, is a vital activity. It takes possession of matter in its environment, and acts first destructively on its existing form, preparing it for food by fire, extinguishing its inherent vitality if it has any, and then subjecting it to processes of mastication and digestion, which deprive it of its other independent properties, and converting it into its own kind of animal cells. Here it acts constructively, giv-

9

ing to the matter its own form and converting it into
cellular tissue. In this process there is a struggle
between the vital activity and the matter which it
uses for food. The plant or animal, as vital, originates
energy. Even if one claims that there is here a con-
servation of energy, and that the plant or animal derives or appropriates energy from its food, still it
must be admitted that the plant or animal guides or
directs this energy, and thus gives to it its psychical
form. To guide or direct energy requires energy; it
requires force to confine a force. Moreover, it is
necessary that the guiding force be as strong as the
force it guides. According to one view, the sequence
of centripetal nerve-action, or the act of sensation, is
self-active, and also the antecedent of the motor-
action is a self-activity, while the two nerve-currents
themselves are mechanical. But according to another
view, both nerve-currents are vital and not mechanical. But the self-activity ends somewhere and the
mechanical begins, it may be in one place or in another. The action produced by the muscles and the
bones is certainly mechanical. The origination of
motion before the nerves receive it is certainly self-
activity. The spiritual individuality of the soul
builds its body and uses it in interaction with the
world, in perception and in volition.

Physiological psychology investigates the two kinds of action—centripetal and centrifugal—and traces their paths and termini. It finds that the sensor current may come to the cerebrum before a corresponding motor-current originates, or it may only proceed so far as some nervous ganglion. In the former case there is conscious volition; in the latter case there is only reflex action of some kind. Great efforts have been made to discover the several turning points, or centres, in which centripetal and centrifugal currents are connected. It is certainly one of the most worthy objects in natural science to trace out these relations of the mechanical, vital, and spiritual. No field of Nature has demanded more patience and skill on the part of scientific men than the nervous system. We may be sure that no field of Nature will yield more valuable results. As the science of physiological psychology is in its infancy, it is too early to expect much from it yet. I shall endeavour to sum up the more significant of its discoveries in the next two chapters.

CHAPTER XIII.

Brain Centres of Sensation and Motion.

§ 55. The distinction between sensor and motor nerves is made by Rufus Ephesius in his work on the names of different parts of the body. He lived in the time of Trajan (97–117 A. D.), but he refers this discovery to the famous physician and anatomist Erasistratus, who lived 300 B. C., and discovered the cause of the illness of the king's son. Antiochus, the son

of Seleucus Nicator, King of Syria, was pining away,
and no physician could detect the cause until Erasistratus noticed the quickening of his pulse on the
approach of the beautiful Stratonice (etc., see the
classical dictionary). Although this important discrimination between efferent and afferent nerves is
two thousand years old, yet the connection between
these two orders of nerves was only vaguely known
until recently. Erasistratus, according to Galen, had
discovered by dissection that the motor nerves arise
in the substance of the brain, while the sensor nerves
connect only with the cerebral membranes. Modern
researches show that both sets of nerves arise in the
great ganglia at the base of the brain.

§ 56. The spinal cord, after passing from the
spine into the skull, thickens and forms the medulla
oblongata. Above this it expands laterally, sending
out bundles of nerve-fibres to connect and unite the
spinal cord with the two hemispheres of the brain,
thus forming a sort of bridge, called the pons Varo-
lii. Above this, one on each side of the middle line,
are the optic thalami, " continuous with the gray
matter of the spinal cord, which thus ascends into
the interior of the brain." * Above and before the

---

* J. Luys, in Appletons' International Scientific Series,
The Brain and its Functions.

optic thalami, and also farther outward from the middle line on each side, are two ganglia of gray matter, called the corpora striata, or "streaked bodies." The important concern for us is the func- tion of these great ganglia. It is supposed that the optic thalami furnish the co-ordinating centre for all the nerves of sensation, while the corpora striata fur- nish a like centre for all nerves of motion; co-ordinat- ing in the sense that they adjust, harmonize, and reduce to unity contrary and conflicting nerve im- pulses. The sense-impressions from the surface of the body are collected, by aid of the spinal cord, in the optic thalami, and thence transmitted to the gray matter (cortex) of the large brain (cerebrum). Here some elaborative process goes on. When the mind is " made up " to act, there proceeds a motor-impulse to the corpora striata, and thence to the muscles of the body that are to be moved.

A French specialist, who has made discoveries in this field, describes it: " Through the tissues of the optic thala- mi pass vibrations of all kinds, those which radiate from the external world, as well as those which emanate from vegetative life (i. e., from the digestive organs). There in the midst of their cells, in the secret chambers of their peculiar activity, these vibrations are diffused, and make a preparatory halt; and thence they are darted out in all directions, in a new and already more animalized and more assimilable form to afford food for the activity of the tis- sues of the cortical substance which only live and work

under the impulse of their stimulating excitement." The
same author, with his somewhat lively imagination, describes the functions of both ganglia (sensor and motor)
thus: "The elements of the optic thalami purify and
transform by their peculiar metabolic action impressions
radiating from without, which they launch in an intel-
lectualized form toward the different regions of the cortical substance. The elements of the corpus striatum, on
the contrary, have an inverse influence upon the stimula
starting from these same regions of the cortical substance.
They absorb, condense, and materialize them by their
intervention; and, having amplified and incorporated them
more and more with the organism, they project them in
a new form in the direction of the different motor gan-
glions of the spinal axis, where they thus become one of
the multiple stimulations destined to bring the muscular
fibres into play." *

§ 57. These two ganglia are, moreover, intercon-
nected by nerve-fibres, and there is possible a direct
communication between the optic thalami and the
corpora striata, as well as the indirect communication
through the gray matter of the cerebrum.   Here is a
physiological basis for the distinction between reflex
movements and deliberative movements.   The spinal
cord and medulla oblongata are especially the seat
of a large number of reflex actions, such, for example,
as the closing of the eye to keep out a cinder, or the
involuntary gesture of the hand to protect the head
from a blow aimed at it.   The sensory impulse is con-

---

* Luys, pp. 45 and 58.

verted into a motor impulse through a central organ, a ganglion of the spinal cord. It is a column or pile of centres in which such conversion takes place. Automatic actions do not need external stimulus, and are not reflex, although they seem to be impelled from the same centres as reflex actions; breathing, digestion, movement of the heart are automatic. More complicated reflex action and automatic centres in the medulla oblongata, and still more complex reflexes, involve both the optic thalami or corpora quadrigemina (for the sensory side) and the corpora striata (for the motor side). The medulla oblongata is claimed to be the centre of a large number of automatic centres, such as breathing, swallowing, sneezing, coughing, vomiting, laughing, weeping, etc. If there is a direct communication between the optic thalami and the corpora striata without the mediation of the cerebrum, we have a reflex action of a higher order than those which go out from centres in the spinal cord. If, finally, there are two higher centres in the gray matter of the cerebrum—a sensory centre and a volitional centre—the action becomes deliberative, conscious, and responsible.

It must be understood that the optic thalami form a sort of crown to the back portion of the spinal cord, while the corpora striata crown in like manner the front portion. In the cord the sensory regions occupy the back part, while the motor regions occupy the front. It is necessary to add here, however, that the researches of the German physiologists seem to prove that there are other bodies—e. g., the corpora quadrigemina—that share in the functions above attributed (on French authority) solely to the optic thalami. These facts point to localization of functions in the cerebrum. Some portion of it would seem to be used for initiating volitions, and some portion of it for elaborating the data of sense-perception.

CHAPTER XIV.

The Localization of Functions in the Brain.

§ 58. IN the previous chapters we have glanced at the distinction between sensor and motor nerves, and the corresponding distinction between the great ganglia at the base of the brain which perform the function of co-ordinating centres of these two orders of nervous impressions. The optic thalami (together with the corpora quadrigemina?) are supposed to collect and co-ordinate the sense-impressions and transmit them to the cerebrum, while the corpora striata receive motor-impressions from the cerebrum and transmit them to the muscles of the various limbs. The localization of functions in the cerebrum has naturally occupied much attention. In fact, this is a very old investigation, although it has not begun to yield trustworthy results until quite recently.

Herophilus of Bithynia (300 B. C.) is reported by Galen as the first who held the doctrine that the brain is the seat of the mind. Galen himself (130-200 A. D.) adopts this view. Indeed, the father of medicine, Hippocrates (460-370 B. C.), is mentioned as having the same opinion.—The influence of Aristotle was against the localization of mental functions in the brain. The heart was thought to be fittest for such functions. In later times different phases of the mind came to be assigned to different parts of the body. The spleen was supposed to be the seat of hilarity and good spirits (splene rident); wisdom dwelt in the heart (corde sapiunt); anger in the gall (felle irascuntur); love in the liver (jecore amant); vanity in the lungs (pulmone jactantur). Albertus Magnus, the great Schoolman (A. D. 1200-1280), not only located the mind in the brain, but distributed the faculties, assigning judgment and reason to the frontal portion, imagination to the middle portion, and memory to the posterior regions. His ideas had been influenced by the Arabian commentator Averrhoes, who supported Galen's views against Aristotle. It was thought that the empty cavities (ventricles) formed between the great ganglia at the base of the brain were the seat of the vital spirits or forces of the soul. Malpighi and Willis (about 1680) first called attention to the gray matter of the surface of the cerebrum as the true seat of the spiritual forces, but the basal ganglia were favoured by many anatomists of the sixteenth and seventeenth centuries as the location of the soul and its faculties. Prochaska, of Vienna, published a work in 1784 looking toward a system of phrenology.

§ 59. Gall, in 1798, gave the first impulse to the widespread movement under the name of phrenology. He was joined by Spurzheim, in 1804, who carried

.

the system to England and the United States, gaining many disciples in both countries, while Gall
made many influential converts in Paris. Gall
mapped out on the skull the locations of mental
peculiarities, which he named, from their excessive
manifestation, organs of murder, theft, cunning,
pride, vanity, on the other hand, Spurzheim attempted
to systematize the organs into groups, and to name
them from their normal manifestation. The feelings
were located in the middle and back parts of the head,
and include (1) propensities or blind impulses like
love and hate, appetite and avarice; (2) sentiments
like self-esteem and caution, benevolence and con-
scientiousness, firmness, hope, the sense of the beautiful and of the ludicrous. In the front of the head
were located the intellectual faculties, those of perception being behind the frontal sinus, with the reflective faculties above them.

§ 60. The observations of Gall are original and
of some value, but those of Spurzheim and the other
phrenologists are hampered by theory and can not
be relied upon. A psychologic theory settles the
definitions of the separate faculties, and determines
in advance what is to be found. But the definitions
are very imperfect, and some of the phrenological
faculties are only modifications of others, as, for in-

stance, "comparison" includes "causality," and "form" includes "individuality," according to the definitions given. Also, many of the higher intellectual powers are omitted altogether, because Spurzheim possessed them feebly and had no power to observe them. For instance, the power to perceive in thought what is complete and independent in itself is a different faculty from that which perceives causal relations in the external world. Yet it is the most important of all intellectual powers. Theologians and poets of the highest order, as well as original philosophers—St. Paul and Athanasius, Dante and Shakespeare, Plato and Kant—possess this "faculty." "Comparison" should relate to the discernment of analogies, and be the poetic faculty of discovering correspondences between the material and spiritual, but this is a different mental activity from the essentially prosaic faculty of discrimination which notices differences rather than analogies. Besides this, the faculty of "ideality" (called "poesie" by Gall) encroaches on the province of this mental activity.

§ 61. But, aside from this *a priori* system of psychology based on crude introspection, a serious objection to phrenology is to be found in the fact that the so-called "organs" are protuberances of the skull, and do not correspond to natural divisions of the brain. The "organs" of perception, twelve in all, crowded together behind the eyes are formed by the protrusion of the outer wall of the skull, while the inner table, keeping close to the brain, leaves a "sinus," or chasm, between it and the outer. Moreover, the convolutions, which are distinctly marked by well-established fissures or furrows (sulci), in no case agree with the "organs" as mapped out. Some organs are located over fissures; some unite portions of different convolutions. The organ of amativeness belongs to the cerebellum, while that of alimentiveness (another "propensity") belongs to the cerebrum. Bony processes on the skull for the insertion of muscles are (as in the case of "combativeness") mistaken for brain protuberances. No account is made of the convolutions in the "island of Reil," or of those which are found in the median longitudinal fissure which separates the two hemispheres of the brain.

§ 62. Phrenology, however, led to the more systematic study of the brain. Magendie and Desmoulins attempted a description of the brain in 1825, but Rolando, in 1830, was the first to start on the right track by a study of the great fissure which separates the frontal lobe from the rest of the brain. The fissure of Sylvius (named from the Leyden anatomist Sylvius, 1672) is the largest and most important, and is formed, as it were, by folding the entire brain in the form of an arch, the concave surface closing together over the fissure. The spinal marrow folds back upon itself and thus forms the cerebrum, leaving the Sylvian fissure to show the fold. This fissure is parallel to a line drawn from the end of the nose to the external opening of the ear, and about two inches above it, its middle point being over the ear. Below this fissure, and parallel to it, extend the three convolutions of the temporo-sphenoidal lobe, separated by two minor fissures (the larger one named the " parallel temporal fissure ").

§ 63. The second great fissure is likewise named from the anatomist who first described it (Rolando, of Turin, in 1830). It arises near the middle and a half inch above the Sylvian fissure, and extends upward and backward about four inches to the median line separating the two hemispheres. It divides the frontal lobe from the parietal. It runs for its entire length between two convolutions, the ascending frontal and ascending parietal, very important because in them have been made the recent discoveries of localized functions. Three parallel convolutions (upper, middle, and lower) spring from the ascending frontal and extend to the median line of the forehead. Behind the ascending parietal convolution, and separated from it by a long and deep fissure (the intra-parietal, third in size and importance), is the supra-marginal convolution, and below this the angular con-volution, also important because it is the centre for the movements of the eyes. There is a fissure (the parieto-occipital) that separates the parietal from the occipital lobe, which also has three convolutions (upper, middle, and lower).

§ 64. This is an outline map of the convolu-tions.* Now look at the results of recent investiga-tions. The anatomists who examined the claims of phrenologists fifty years ago found only negative re-sults. Longet, Magendie, Flourens, Matteucci, Schiff, and others declared that their experiments showed no evidence of such localization. . Longet tried me-chanical irritation, cauterization, and even galvanic currents on the brains of dogs, rabbits, and kids, with-out obtaining any sign of muscular contraction. But, in 1861, Broca, of Paris, gave a report of two cases of aphasia, and announced that loss of speech is caused by the disease of the back portion of the lower frontal convolution on the left side of the head (a point three inches above and forward of the orifice of the ear).

---

* The subjoined is a roughly constructed cut of the brain, showing the main features.

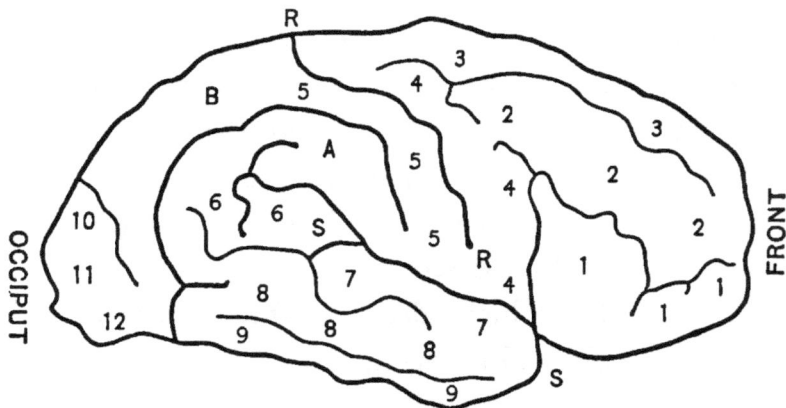

FISSURES.

S–S, Fissure of Sylvius.
R–R, Fissure of Rolando.

CONVOLUTIONS.

1, 1, 1, Inferior frontal (below the inferior frontal fissure).
2, 2, 2, Middle frontal (between inferior and superior frontal fissures).
3, 3, Superior frontal (above superior frontal fissure).
4, 4, 4, Ascending frontal (front of the fissure of Rolando).
5, 5, 5, Ascending parietal (between the Rolando and intraparietal fissures).
6, 6, Angular (above the parallel fissure.)
7, 7, Superior temporo-sphenoidal (between the Sylvian and parallel fissures).
8, 8, 8, Middle temporo-sphenoidal (below parallel fissure).
9, 9, Inferior temporo-sphenoidal.
10, Superior occipital (behind the parieto-occipital fissure).
11, Middle occipital.
12, Inferior occipital.
A, Supra-marginal (under the parietal eminence).
B, Postero-parietal.

Eckhard, six years later, discovered that convulsive movements in the extremities may be caused by removing portions of the cortical substance, or gray matter of the brain. (The cortical substance, or gray matter of the brain, is about one tenth of an inch in thickness, and covers the whole brain like a cortex or bark.) Meynert before this had arrived at the conclusion that the front part of the brain is used for functions of movement, while the back part is used for sensation.

§ 65. During the Franco-Prussian War, in 1870, Dr. Hitzig applied a galvanic current to a portion of the exposed brain of a wounded soldier, and noticed that it caused a contraction of the eyelids. After the war he and Dr. Fritsch made systematic experiments on lower animals with a continuous current, and were able to locate five centres of movement in the convolutions near the fissure of Rolando. Besides the centre for the movement of the tongue, already mentioned as discovered by Broca, they located the centre for the movements of the eyelids and upper part of the face just above the former; the centre for the muscles of the neck is situated in the back part of the upper frontal convolution; the centre for the movement of the arms (or fore legs) in the upper end of the ascending frontal; the centre for the movement of the hind legs just opposite of the former, across the fissure of Rolando, in the upper part of the ascending parietal convolution; the centre for the movement of the eyeballs in the angular convolution, just below and back of the marginal protuberances at the side of the head. The publication of these discoveries made an epoch in the study of the brain. Dr. David Ferrier, of London, used a faradic current instead of the continuous current, and succeeded eventually in locating fifteen centres of movement in the brain of the monkey.

These centres, if stimulated, produce the following movements (the numbers and letters referring to Ferrier's map): (1) Advance the legs, as in walking; (2) complex movements of leg, foot, and trunk; (3) movements of tail; (4) movements forward and backward of fore limbs; (5) extension of arm and hand to reach something; a, b, c, d—movements of fingers and wrists and clinching of fist; (6) forearm raised to the mouth; (7) angle of mouth drawn back and elevated; (8) nose and upper lip elevated and lower lip depressed so as to expose the canine teeth; (9) mouth opened and tongue protruded; (10) mouth opened and tongue drawn back; (11) angle of mouth drawn back; (12) eyes opened widely, head and eyes turned to one side; (13 and 13*) rolling of eyeballs to one side; (14) drawing back of ears; (15) twisting of lip and nostril on one side. It will be readily seen that these are chiefly further specifications of the areas discovered by Hitzig and Fritsch: for movements of the hind legs (marked on maps of the brain E, in the upper portion of the ascending parietal convolution) we have No. 1 of Ferrier located in the same region.—Hitzig's fore-limb movements (marked D on maps of the brain, located in the upper portion of the ascending frontal) correspond to Nos. 4, 5, 6, a, b, c, d, of Ferrier, of which 5 and 6 occupy an area a little below D, and the others cover the middle and lower portions of the ascending parietal. The tail movement (No. 3) is between Nos. 4 and 5. Hitzig's neck and head movement (marked C, in back part of upper frontal) corresponds to No. 12 of Ferrier in locality. His face movements (marked B, in back part of middle frontal) correspond to Ferrier's Nos. 7, 8, 9, 10, and 11, all relating to the mouth in some way. Nos. 6 (which carries

10

hand to mouth), 7, 8, 9, 10 occupy the middle and lower portions of the ascending frontal, and are separated by a fissure from B. No. 11 is in the lowest part of the ascending parietal. Hitzig's centre for movement of the eyeball (marked F, in the supramarginal and angular convolutions) corresponds to Ferrier's 13 and 13*, which extend from the locality of F down some distance on both sides of the parallel temporo-sphenoidal fissure. Ferrier's No. 14 covers the whole of the upper temporo-sphenoidal convolution, and corresponds to G, the old location of the centre for movements of the ear, which was placed only in the forward end of that convolution. His No. 15 is in the convolution at the base of the brain (subiculum cornu ammonis).

§ 66. The results of Ferrier's experiments in the main confirm and carry out those of Hitzig and Fritsch. More recently Horsley and Schäfer have discovered areas associated with movements of the thorax, abdomen, and pelvis. The experiments of Munk, who removed portions of the brain of animals and noted carefully the disturbances of motion that occurred, confirm in general the location of the motor area. It was his opinion that there is a sensor area back of the motor region. It will be noted that these views and results contradict the phrenological hypothesis which placed the organs of sense-perception in the extreme frontal portion of the brain, while the motor organs (propensities) are in the occipital and temporo-sphenoidal portions. Munk's theory of the action of these areas is more interesting than the details of location. He rejects the view that makes these to be direct motor centres, and supposes that they are really centres of mental images of those parts of the body which are moved. Lose the mental image of the hand, and one can not will it to move.

§ 67. Goltz, of Strasburg, who also made experiments in extirpation of brain tracts by a method invented by himself, using a jet of water to avoid hæmorrhage, thinks that it is possible to explain all these facts of location by inhibitory action on lower centres, and that there are no experiments that show beyond question the existence of detached centres of movement. But he agrees with Munk that the cerebrum has to do with sensory activities. Destruction of the cortical substance, says the latter, produces physical blindness, inability to form an intelligent comprehension of the visual impressions received. The gray matter over the occipital lobes would have to do with the elaboration of simple visual impressions into clear perceptions. Destroy it, and the animal still sees, but can not convert his seeing into acting, because he can not connect it with his previous experience; not unite it into a consistent perception; not interpret it by his wants and desires. The cortex (gray matter) of the brain would have to do with attention.

Dr. Ferrier has adopted a somewhat similar view:
"After the animals, which were selected on account of
their intelligent character, were operated upon and a part
of the brain removed, they remained apathetic or dull,
or dozed off to sleep, responding only to sensations or impressions of the moment, or varying their listlessness
with restless and purposeless wanderings to and fro. Instead of, as before, being actively interested in their surroundings, and curiously prying into all that came within
the field of their observation, they had lost, to all appearance, the faculty of attentive and intelligent observation."
The movements in the eyes, occasioned by stimulating the
angular convolution, he regards as "merely reflex movements on the excitation of subjective visual sensation."
It was not motor paralysis, but the loss of intellectual
images. (To use the logical explanation for it, it was
the inability to employ the second figure of the syllogism
and recognise the impressions made on their senses. Not
recognising the object, they could not re-enforce their perception by the first figure, the deductive syllogism, and
hence could not find motives for action.) Ferrier thinks
that the auditory centre is in the upper temporo-sphenoidal
convolution, and that this explains the movement of the
animal's ears under the electrical excitement of that convolution. Taste and smell he referred to the lower temporo-sphenoidal convolution, and touch to a convolution
called the hippocampus major at the base of the brain.

§ 68. Another line of investigation has been undertaken with great industry by Prof. Exner. He
read all the cases of cerebral disease that had been
followed by post-mortem examination—several thousand in all. Comparatively few of these were sufficiently circumstantial and trustworthy to be received
as evidence; only one hundred and sixty-nine cases,

in fact, were available as test cases. He constructed charts showing what areas of the brain showed lesion in the case of each mental disturbance recorded. His careful induction has confirmed the other methods of localization. He found that lesions of the brain in which some disturbance of function followed were mostly located in that part of the brain lying near the fissure of Rolando, and that lesions in the left hemisphere of the brain are most likely to be followed by disturbance of function. From his data it has been inferred that the left side of the brain has to do with motion, while the right side has more to do with sensibility. But this is a mere conjecture. Although this field of investigation has been opened within twenty years, there are now many scientific men at work in it, and there is constant and rapid addition made to the stock of knowledge. The mutual criticisms, the different working hypotheses, and, above all, the different methods of investigation invented, help to sift out erroneous conjectures and confirm the sound theories. Munk and Ferrier, Goltz and Luciana, Exner and Lepine, Luys, Pitres, Tamburini, and their co-workers have assisted one another by sharp criticism as much as by newly discovered data. It is important to arrive at a theory which will unite and harmonize the observations and suggest new experiments for verification.

§ 69. In concluding this meagre summary of that part of physiological psychology which relates to the localization of mental functions in the brain a word must be added as to its results.* When interpreted by introspective psychology and compared with its results, we do not discover any new grounds for distrusting the spiritual theory of the soul, nor do we see in these researches much that throws any light on the real nature of the mind itself. Self-activity, which is the object of introspection, is necessarily presupposed to explain life in plants and animals—not to speak of man. The plant acts on its surroundings, and, laying hold of foreign matter, strips off from it its form, and then assimilates it or stamps upon it its own peculiar form of vegetative cell. Graft the cells of one plant upon another

---

* The reader who wishes the most serviceable book on this subject in the English language should get Prof. George T. Ladd's Elements of Physiological Psychology (New York: Charles Scribner's Sons). The articles in the Encyclopædia Britannica may be consulted to advantage; see the titles "Anatomy," "Physiology," "Aphasia," "Psychology." But no one else has ever written so entertainingly on the subject as Prof. William James in The Principles of Psychology, two volumes (New York: Henry Holt & Co., 1890).

plant, and they retain their own individuality and produce their own kind. In the act of digestion the animal organism manifests the self-activity of the individual just as the plant does. Life is the manifestation of originating energy in an individual form.

§ 70. Self-activity is plainly manifest in the process of digestion common to plants and animals. But feeling, which is a higher manifestation of self-activity, does not seem to be higher, for the reason that we are prone to look upon it as a passivity affected by external influences. Feeling is higher, however, than assimilation, because in it the soul makes or repeats for itself the form of the environment. In digestion the soul gives its form to matter; in sensation it gives form to itself without matter. We do not do any violence to external objects in perceiving them or hearing them; we form representations of them for ourselves. In the rational intellect the soul contemplates universals, forming them by self-definition. It sees causal energies as the essence of phenomena, and to these causal energies correspond the general terms of language. As will, the soul shows its individuality and independence in the most direct way.

§ 71. The matter of the brain and nerves is constantly changing. The living individual energy of the soul aggregates matter and organizes it into an instrument adapted for its purposes: First, it learns the world through the sensory nerves; secondly, it acts on the world through its motor nerves and realizes its ideals by its will. It is incorrect to call a living organism a " mechanism," for a mechanism is wholly a means, and not an end; it is moved by causation from without, while in an organism its parts are alike means and ends to the whole. But while the body is organic, the soul is not organic, but a higher form of being—namely, a pure self-activity which makes its product (that is to say, its organism) for the sake of self-relevation.

CHAPTER XV.

The Will.

§ 72. In our last three chapters we have attempted to give an outline of what has been discovered up to date in what is called physiological psychology as far as it relates to the general theory of the two sorts of nerves, the two ganglionic centres at the base of the brain, and the localization of functions in the cerebrum. We have omitted any notice of the fields of labour now diligently worked in the psycho-

physiological laboratories of America and Europe—
namely, the ascertainment by exact quantitative experiments of the velocity and intensity of nerve-currents to the brain from various organs, or outwardly
from the former to the latter. All quantitative measurement is useful in the process of inventorying
Nature, and there is no doubt that the devotees of
" psycho-physics " will discover much that is valuable on their road. De Soto and others went in search
of the " Fountain of Youth," and discovered vast
rivers and the details of the continent, though the
object of their expeditions was a figment of the imagination. " Saul, the son of Kish, went out to find
his father's asses, but found a kingdom." Many people have done the reverse of this, and men of average
capacity are usually well satisfied if in their search
for kingdoms they are rewarded by finding useful
beasts of burden. In the laboratories of the students
of psychology no metaphysical results, nor results in
pure psychology of a positive character, will be arrived
at, it is safe enough to say. But it is equally safe to
expect very useful discoveries relating to the proper
care and nurture of our nervous system—in short,
a stock of pathological and educational knowledge,
and scientific insight into the relation of man to
other animals, and to his own historic evolution.

§ 73. We take up now the topic of the will. In our three chapters on the logical structure of sense-perception we have called attention to the inner or spiritual structure of mind as contradistinguished from the physiological structure of its instruments of manifestation, which is the subject investigated by the laboratory students whose chief discoveries have been noticed in the three chapters preceding this. The will, inasmuch as it is the most direct and immediate form of self-activity, lies within the field of observation open to introspection. It is a fact of consciousness. Nevertheless, its existence is denied freely on metaphysical grounds urged against self-activity by minds that have reached the second stage of thought. If there is no such thing as self-activity or self-determination, there is certainly no such thing as will-power. We have already discussed the so-called inconceivability of self-activity in Chapters III and V, and will ask the reader who denies spontaneity or freedom or will-power, on account of the dogma of inconceivability, to go over once more, and yet again, the arguments already submitted to remove his objection.

The centre of pure psychology is this principle of self-activity which we have so many times considered. It has been found to be the presupposition of all causal action;

of all influence of one body upon another; of all dependence, all change, and all motion. Finally, in the will as we are aware of it in our actions, it is not a presupposition inferred as the logical condition of the existence of some perceived thing or event, but the direct and immediate object of our inner consciousness, although we do not picture this object. We see ourselves as self-active in volition—originating motion in our bodies, acting on the external world, and setting things in motion to realize thoughts or ideals which we conceive in our minds. We are conscious of ourselves, therefore, as feeling, thinking, and willing, and, strange to say, we have many grades of consciousness of these activities. The child or the savage has some dim consciousness of these activities; the cultured man has a reflective consciousness of them, and grasps them much more firmly and clearly. The scientific state of mind has a still more thorough grasp of them by means of a third degree of consciousness, a new reflection, so to speak, upon them. For the philosopher or scientific student of psychology not only has these activities and the dim consciousness of them, and, secondly, the reflective consciousness of them, which the cultured man adds to the first or dim inward perception, but he also has a higher order of reflection on them which seizes them as special objects of observation, neglects the particular subject-matter with which they deal, and confines itself to their form.—To illustrate: I touch the surface of this paper and feel its texture with my hand, just as a child or savage might do, and am conscious of the sensuous impression it makes, and at the same time I am dimly conscious of myself as subject of the feeling—I know that it is *my* hand that feels, and my self that perceives the sense-impression. The child or savage makes this reference to himself spontaneously as I now do to myself; but he does not reflect on this reference as I am doing, for his mind is directed to the object and not to the act of perception— his perception is a so-called " objective " perception, and the inward perception of consciousness is not by itself the object of special attention, but occurs without anything more than momentary notice. The cultured man differs from the child or savage in paying more attention to the subjective phases of perception. He reflects on the relation of the object to his sense-organs and is aware of a series of doubts as to the accuracy of his perceptions, and therefore is apt to make experiments to eliminate the deceptive phases that arise through the defects of his sense-organs. Finally, the philosophic or scientific consciousness notes the form of perceiving as its chief object, and neglects the object perceived, upon which the child had concentrated *his* attention. The philosophic consciousness discovers that the mind is active even in the lowest sense-impression, and that feeling is itself an ideal reconstruction of the environment (as pointed out in Chapter III). It is conscious that it feels and knows much of the subjective defects of its perception, and also it knows its selfhood as an independent and original cause, a responsible will-power in the universe.

§ 74. Self-activity is freedom. The so-called " freedom of the will " belongs to the highest degree of self-activity. But freedom of the will seems impossible to all persons who have reached the first degree of reflection, which is the second stage of thought mentioned in Chapter IV. It is the stage of thinking that makes the doctrine of the relativity of all things its supreme principle—it is Herbert Spencer's first principle. Those who hold this set up what was called by the ancients the category of quality—" all things have environments and are what they are because necessitated through their environments to be such as they are." Ordinary " common sense " is in this habit of contemplating all beings as having environments—it supposes, in short, that the form of external perception is truly universal and valid for every being that exists. It denies, therefore, the existence of self-activity as mind or will. It pays no attention to the form of internal perception or consciousness which considers solely what is self-active, as feeling, thinking, or willing.

There are two difficulties which students encounter in this part of psychology. The first one is to get over from this external mode of thinking which reaches the category of necessity as the supreme thought beyond which there is no further progress—to get over from this thought to the insight into freedom as the logical presupposition of necessity itself. The second difficulty is that form of fatalism which urges the impossibility of resisting the strongest motive. "The strongest motive determines the will, and hence there can be no free will," is their statement of the case.

CHAPTER XVI.

The Fallacy of the Doctrine that the Strongest Motive governs the Will, and therefore the Will is not Free.

§ 75. I SHALL discuss in this chapter the question of motives. The will is not free, because the strongest motive always constrains it—this is the conclusion that many thinkers have drawn. Is it true, and, if not, why does it happen to seem true? These are the questions that a true psychology must solve. First let us notice that the argument quietly assumes that motives are beings independent of the will, a sort of controlling environment, in fact. The argument practically assumes that all reality takes the form of external perception, the form of " thing and environment," and not the form of internal perception, which is that of self-activity. Hence it fails to notice how utterly inept its conclusion is. It assumes that motives are things really existing which have an actual power to condition the energy of the will. Look now for a moment at the true psychological facts involved.

1. A motive is not a reality, not an existing thing, not a force or energy. It is an ideal, a mere possibil-

ity, a mere thought, or a mere feeling. When it is realized it will become a fact, and will lose its character of motive. It is a purpose or design, an ideal of something different and more desirable than what exists. For a motive involves the change of what is into something else that is not as yet. It involves the realization of a possibility.

2. Let me see a fine ripe fruit and desire to eat it. The motive presents itself to me to do something that is not done, and to change the condition of something from what it is to a condition that is merely possible. I think of the apple as already in the process of being devoured. I think of its juices on my tongue and of its flavour. But the juices are not on my tongue nor am I tasting its flavour. The motive contains the idea of what is not existent.

3. I must, by my mental activity, go out beyond the circle of existence before me in order to conceive a motive, or indeed to feel a motive. I must imagine something as happening to the reality, that has not happened, in order to have a motive. The mind, in fact, has to make an abstraction as the first condition for the existence of a motive. The motive is not a real independent thing, but an idea existing in some intelligence as a product of the activity of that intelligence which has put an ideal in the place of the real.

4. To say that a motive constrains the will is therefore to say that something acts before it exists; for the motive has only ideal and not actual existence, until it is realized.

5. The motive becomes a real thing or fact through the act of the will. This realizing of the motive is at the same time an annulment of the motive as motive. After I have eaten the apple there is no motive any longer to eat it.

§ 76. 6. Thus the will is creative or self-determining in two ways or forms in this process of volition. The will first creates the motive by thinking away the form of something that really exists and thinking an ideal or possible form in its place. The being of the motive is caused by the will, and the motive is wholly dependent on the self-activity of the mind for its existence. Secondly, if the motive gets realized, it is the will that realizes it. Thus the will is creator of the motive as ideal, and of its realization, and to say that the motive constrains the will is to say that a possible something constrains the actual that creates it, or, in other words, that something acts before it exists.

7. The motive, in fact, is a condition and means of freedom or spontaneity (self-activity); for there can be no free act, nor any sort of act, where there is

no possibility of change or of an ideal different from the real. The possibility which may be substituted for the reality breaks the tyrannical necessity of existing environment.

§ 77. 8. I have supposed a motive of appetite—a motive to eat a fruit. Even this sort of motive makes for freedom. But there are much higher motives. Let us suppose that when I am about to eat the apple I think of the idea of property—" Whose apple is this? " I recall the fact that this apple belongs to my neighbour. I at once think that to eat his apple violates my neighbour's right to his own. A moral motive now comes in and I annul the motive to eat the apple, and repress my appetite. What seemed desirable no longer seems desirable. Instead of this trivial matter of the apple, let it be something more than the good things of life; let it be life itself, and weigh this against moral integrity. The moral motive outweighs all motives of earthly reward. The patriot chooses the post that is sure to bring death for the sake of his country. The suicide proves his transcendental freedom by cutting even the thread of life with his own hand.

9. In the case of moral motive the will sets up its own ideal self as motive. In the case of appetite it sets up an ideal condition of some thing or fact as a

11

motive. In the moral ideal the mind conceives the true form of its own highest being—the form of social co-operation with a universe of intelligent beings.

10. The will can so act in its freedom as to contradict itself. For example, it may act so as to create a fate outside itself. It can act so as to prevent the realization of possibilities in the external world favourable to the development of mind in knowledge of truth and right. It can thus work against the freedom of others—not against their spontaneity, but against their realization of highest motives.

§ 78. 11. Here we come to a great distinction—that between spontaneity, or formal freedom, and moral freedom or true freedom. The worm has spontaneity, but only a minimum of moral freedom. The will is essentially a social being. It may create and realize motives of a purely individualistic order—motives that when realized result in appropriating for one's selfish interest things and facts which it at the same time prevents from being useful to others. Secondly, it may create and realize motives of an altruistic order. It may change things and events so that they benefit others. In other words, a will may co-operate with other wills or it may come into antagonism with other wills. The ideal of action that re-enforces all wills and does not thwart any is the ideal called morality: "So act that thy deed will not contradict itself if it is made the universal act of all intelligent beings."

12. If one person steals the property of another, he acts immorally, because, if all persons steal, no one is left in the safe possession of what he steals—all property is annulled. But property is a means of rational freedom. It is a means of conquest over time and space; a means by which all wills may re-enforce each will; a means of elevating the individual into the species. Add to each will the aggregate will of all intelligent beings in the universe and you make each will infinite.

13. There is, therefore, a spontaneous or formal will and a moral or rational will. Both are free so far as the ordinary sense of the word "free" is concerned, because both are self-active and both create and use motives. But in a higher sense only the moral will is free, because it alone progressively conquers its environment. It effects this conquest in two ways: First, as regards the environment of things and events, the world of material and non-spiritual existence, it makes combinations which result in the production of food, clothing, shelter, and means of intercommunication. Secondly, as regards the human environment, it makes social combination by adopting ethical forms

—forms in which all may act without contradiction and with mutual help and co-operation.

§ 79. 14. The moral motive is now seen to be the highest motive, because it is the form that consolidates all intelligent will-power into one power, so that the action of each assists the action of all. This one power is the will of the social whole. Hence it is properly called by Hegel the form of *pure will*, because it places as supreme motive the harmony of all wills—the mutual re-enforcement of all wills. Outside of the moral form of action each will contradicts others and also itself; for its acts of one day contradict those of a previous day and reduce them to zero. The immoral man is perpetually annulling his own action; the moral man continually re-enforces the days by the years and the moments by eternity.

Thus our psychology of the will has brought us into the presence of the psychology of morals.

Let us consider in the next chapter the psychology that underlies the metaphysical thought of Necessity or Fate, an idea or thought which causes so much confusion in the moral world that it has long been regarded as one of the most important objects of higher education to bring the pupil out of its enthralment. It has also had baneful effects in religion.

CHAPTER XVII.

Freedom versus Fate.

§ 80. I HAVE already pointed out that psychology furnishes a solution of the problem of free will. It shows how the category of quality (or " thing and environment ") seems to exhaust the entire range of possibilities and to shut out that of freedom completely. But the category of self-activity is as much a fact of internal observation as quality is a fact of external observation, and, as we shall see, even things and their environments presuppose self-activity in the beings on which they depend. Our thinking, feeling, and willing are forms of self-activity, and inconceivable without admitting it. Moreover, self-activity must be assumed in order to explain any form of living being. We have discussed this in Chapter III, in the case of the plant and the animal.

§ 81. We now come to the very important question how to reconcile these two categories—self-activity and quality; for quality is the category of fate, while self-activity is the category of freedom. In other words, we are here to study the fundamental nature of these two forms of thinking and see which is the most substantial. Does freedom presuppose fate as its ground, or, on the other hand, does fate presuppose freedom? If they are co-ordinate and equally valid, there is a contradiction in the very nature of our thought. Kant and Fichte apparently come to this result in their psychologies. They assert that the mind arrives at insoluble contradictions, but they affirm that all practical life, all moral life, presupposes that the category of freedom is the ultimate and absolute one. Fate would, according to them, apply only to appearances or phenomena, while freedom would apply to being-in-itself or to all true reality.

§ 82. The following argument is offered as a specimen of the dialectic method of investigating the psychological value of such categories of the mind. We first assume the universal and absolute validity of the category in question, defining it in its widest scope, and then look at the result as regards its own validity. In other words, we apply it to itself and see whether it contradicts itself. If a category contradicts itself when made universal, it is manifestly not a category of the absolute, but only one side of some more comprehensive category. Thus we shall see that fate or necessity is only one side of the more comprehensive category of self-activity or freedom. (Compare this argument with Chapters III and VII.)

First, state the law or point of view of fate thus:

1. All things are necessitated; each thing is necessitated by the totality of conditions; hence whatever is must be as it is, and under the conditions can not be otherwise.

It will be noted that this makes each thing dependent on its environment and derivative from that environment. If it has anything original and underived, it is to that extent not necessitated by external conditions, but is self-existent. But derivation implies change—something to be derived must have passed over from an original state of being, in the cause or condition, to a derivative state of being, in the effect or condition. Hence we have to consider next the phase of change necessarily involved in the assumption of beings determined by fate.

2. Change exists and must have existed if there is such a thing as derivation. In change, something new begins and something old ceases to be. But according to the above definition of fate, the thing before the change was necessitated to be what it was by the totality of conditions, and the thing after the change, likewise, is necessitated to be what it is by the totality of conditions. Under the same conditions a thing must always remain as it is and can not change. Here it becomes evident, therefore, that any change of thing or event presupposes a change in the totality of conditions, and this is the rock on which our law of fate suffers shipwreck, as we shall see.

§ 83. 3. Any change whatever presupposes an anterior change in the totality of conditions. For as the two states of the thing, the one before and the other after the change, are different, they require two different totalities of conditions to make them possible according to the law of fate. Otherwise the totality of conditions would admit two different things, and could not be said to necessitate either. A mould that could cast a cube or a globe equally well could not be said to mould or give form to either. Hence unless we admit change into the totality of conditions, we are constrained to deny the necessity of proceeding from that totality and to affirm chance or contingency in its place. If things change, their change is a proof that there was no constraining necessity in the shape of a totality of existing conditions. There must have been a contingency—this thing had other possibilities of existence, and it was not necessitated to remain in one state of reality rather than some other state which was possible to it. But the category of chance does not explain anything, but, on the contrary, needs explanation itself; for that which can change a possible state of a thing into a real state of it must be a causal energy. Hence with the idea of chance, as well as with the idea of two different totalities of conditions, we are thrown back upon the idea of causal energy, which lifts us above the idea of fate, as we shall see in the next consideration.

§ 84. 4. How can we construe the change in the totality of conditions? If change exists, it either disproves necessity altogether, or else presupposes change in the totality of conditions. The totality changes, but there is nothing outside of the totality to necessitate it; if it is necessitated, it necessitates itself. If it moves, it moves itself, for there is no environment from which it can derive its motion or change. The totality includes all the conditions. If the totality of conditions changes, it changes itself, and we have found self-activity, therefore, as the ultimate ground of all change, and of all conditioning necessity as well. Self-activity, self-determination, *causa sui* (self-cause), spontaneity, freedom, will-power, life, cognition, instinct—these all involve phases of this necessity that necessitates itself, and is therefore self-active.

§ 85. 5. The thought of necessity or fate—which is the thought of thing and environment elevated to a universal category, the category of quality—therefore shows itself, when dialectically considered, to be grounded in the idea of freedom (self-activity or self-determination), and we have now before us the explanation of the psychological difficulty which makes the thought of the freedom of the will seem impossible to agnostics and to all people just beginning to think logically. It has never occurred to their minds that such a category as quality can possibly be limited and subordinate. It is the category of all external observation, and it seems to be absolute. It contradicts the internal category of self-activity, and the novitiate thinker sets the latter aside, supposing that if one of the two categories is illusory it must be that of self-activity, for he can perceive by his senses the actual existence of things with environments, while he can not even fancy or represent self-activity as having being. But careful reflection will show him, as it shows us, that the two categories do not contradict, but that the category of fate or necessity belongs to a lower order than the category of self-activity —fate is partial; self-activity, total. The category of necessity belongs to the realm of effects, of phenomena, or manifestations, while the category of self-activity or self-determination belongs to the realm of noumena, or self-existences and causal energies. Necessity belongs to dependent being; self-activity and freedom to independent being.

This is one of the most important of all subjects in psychology, because it is the foundation of the doctrine of moral responsibility, and of jurisprudence as well as of religion. Quality is the category of *otherness* (θάτερον) of Plato (see The Sophist, 255-259); the *somewhat and other*

(*Etwas und Anderes*) of Hegel (Logik, second edition, vol. i, p. 116); the finite opposed to the infinite of theology.

§ 86. One should be careful not to confound logical necessity with fatalistic necessity. Logical necessity is the necessity of consistency between form and content—a formal necessity and not an external necessity, although it is often confounded with it, as the following will show: Logical necessity is a necessity of self-identity. Creation is a necessary attribute of God, because freedom implies creative power or origination of energy and determination. Hence God, if free, is creative because it is a necessity of his being, since it belongs to his perfection. If it did not belong to him he would be imperfect. " God must be perfect " is therefore an equivalent statement to " God must be free " or " God must be creative." Creation is a free act; though necessary, it is not compelled by any external necessity. It is only a logical necessity, and not an external necessity. It is a logical necessity that the first principle should be self-active or self-determining, and hence free intelligence. But such logical necessity does not imply or involve fate or external constraint. This is a dialectic circle: (1) The first is necessarily free, (2) but is therefore necessitated and is not free; (3) hence not being free, it is not *necessitated* to be free, (4) and hence *is* free in spite of (2). *Logical* necessity is spoken of in (1); fatalistic necessity in (2) and (3); (2) and (3) cancel each other and leave (1) or (4).

In this chapter we have considered the general psychological conditions of the entire thought of freedom of the will, and we have seen that the difficulty arises further back than the question of the will. Most persons deny the freedom of the will because they do not see the possibility of any freedom whatever in the universe —not even the possibility of God's freedom.

CHAPTER XVIII.

Old and New Psychologies compared as to their Provinces and their Results for Education. A Review.

§ 87. As a review of Part I, I will in this concluding chapter offer some general considerations of a popular character in the nature of a summary of the educational bearings of the old and new psychologies. Under the term "new psychology" I include only two classes of investigation—namely, what is known as "physiological psychology," dating from the discovery of Broca in 1861 (see above, § 64), and what is known as "child study." * All other studies

---

* Including the researches of Prof. Preyer and of Dr. Stanley Hall, their co-workers and disciples.

of mind, from ancient times to the present time, whether based on induction or deduction, whether *a priori,* as rational psychology, or *a posteriori,* as empirical psychology, are called the " old psychology." Both of those psychologies are of importance, and neither one is a substitute for the other, or to be neglected by the teacher who wishes to know scientifically the mind that he is supposed to educate.

§ 88. In the first place, from the old psychology we learn that there is a constitution of the mind common to all rational beings—a rational nature which may be discovered by introspection and distinguished from the transient and variable characteristics which are determined in large manner by environment and conditions of development. By far the most important knowledge from this source is the distinction of the soul into several stages, as that manifested in plant life, called by Aristotle the nutritive, or vegetative, soul; the soul as active in sensation and locomotion, or the animal soul; the rational soul manifested in imagination, memory, reflection, and in pure thought.* The distinctions of active and passive reason made by Aristotle in his famous treatise on the soul, and so often rediscovered or verified by pro-

---

* Treated summarily in Chapter IV.

found thinkers, in the history of philosophy, is the principle of this classification of soul-activities. On it is founded the philosophical doctrine of the immortality of the soul. In fact, not only the doctrine of immortality, but also the doctrines of theism and the freedom of the will, are based on this rock of the old psychology, developed by Aristotle out of the hints of Plato or Socrates. God, freedom, and immortality are the three good gifts of philosophy, according to Novalis; * they are all derived from the insight that finds in pure thought the independent self-activity of the soul and sees in it the only possible type of independent being, the only form that a first principle of the world—a Creator—can have. The idea of self-activity is, moreover, the basal idea of free will.

> The very concept of will is impossible, on the basis of empirical thinking; for the understanding, as Coleridge defined it, deals with relations between objects, and finds causal relation everywhere, but not self-activity or will. It tries to explain each thing through its environment—and it never rests until it has traced the phenomena of an object to a ground in something else outside.

§ 89. That the fundamental condition of introspection is the admission of this idea of self-activity is evident if we consider that the world of self-consciousness

---

* See Carlyle's essay on Novalis in his Miscellanies.

contains only feelings, volitions, and ideas. Each one of these is twofold, implying subject and object. There are two poles to each; feeling is nothing unless it has a subject that feels, and unless the self that feels is the object of the feeling. So volition implies a self that acts, and, moreover, a determination or limitation of the subject issuing in an objective deed —a volition has the twofold aspect of subject and object. So, too, an idea is always thought as a determination of the self which thinks it—or defines it; it is conceived by the mind; it, too, involves subject and object. Now by no possibility can external observation discover any such twofold object in space and time. All objects of the senses are dead results or in a process of becoming through some external cause. If we discriminate dead objects from living objects, and recognise plants, animals, and men before us, we do it because we interpret the forms, shapes, and movements before us as indicative of a self-determining soul within the object. We transfer to the object by an act of inference an internality of life, feeling, volition, or thought such as we know directly only by introspection, and can only know thus.

To expand this theme, one would show the importance of these distinctions of Aristotle, St. Thomas, and

Leibnitz in making an account of the spiritual life of
man, in inventorying the principles of his civilization and
making clear and consistent his views of the world.—To
live is one thing, but to give a rational and consistent
account of one's life is a different and difficult matter.
The old psychology succeeded in doing this by these fundamental distinctions, and all new attempts at psychology
either prove abortive, or else soon fall into line with the
old psychology, so far as these essentials are concerned—
they end in affirming self-activity as more substantial
than material things, and in the admission of various
grades of realization of this self-activity, or soul.

§ 90. Another very important step in this investigation of the contents of self-consciousness, which the
German thinkers have added to the old psychology, is
the recognition of the characteristic of universality
and necessity as the criterion of what is in the constitution of mind itself as contradistinguished from
experience or empirical content. Time and space,
the categories of quality and quantity, the laws of
causality, identity, and contradiction, the ideas of
self-activity, moral responsibility, and religion, all
transcend experience, and are found by introspection. It is their application which constitutes experience, and experience would be impossible unless
the mind had in itself these powers *a priori*, for
these powers make experience possible. If we could
not furnish the intuitions of infinite space and time,
we could not perceive objects of experience; nor un-

less we could furnish the category of causality could we refer our sensations to objects as causes.

Universal and necessary ideas are furnished by the mind itself, and not derived from experience, although our consciousness of them may date from our application of them to the content of experience. Formal logic, with its judgments and syllogisms, its figures and modes, should be regarded also as a part of rational psychology in so far as it reveals to us the forms of action of thinking reason. All these contributions of the old psychology are of priceless value, as giving us the means to understand the place we occupy in the universe with our ideals of civilization. They furnish us directive power, they give us the regulative ideals of education, religion, jurisprudence, politics, and the general conduct of life.

§ 91. Although the old psychology has furnished these substantial things, it has not furnished all that is desirable. There is a realm of conditions which must be understood before man can be made to realize his ideals. The product of Nature is an animal, and not a civilized man. How can man react upon Nature; how can he ascend out of his own natural conditions; how can he rise from the stage of sense-perception to that of reflection; how from mere reflection to mere thought; how can he put off his state of slavery to the category of thing and environment, and rise to the category of self-activity? This is to ask how we can ascend from a mechanical view of the world to an ethical view of it. Certainly we must

12

know the bodily conditions that limit or enthrall the soul. We must be able to recognise what activity tends to fix the soul in a lower order of thought and action, and what exercise will tend to lift it to a higher order.

To enumerate some of these enthralling conditions through which the soul passes necessarily, if it ever comes to the highest, we must name the influences and attractions of one's habitat, its climate and soil, its outlook, its means of connection with the rest of the world. Then next there is the race and stock of which one comes, black, red, yellow, or white—northern or southern European—inheriting all the evil tendencies and all the good aspirations. Then the temperament and idiosyncrasy of the individual, as his natural talents or his genius—these all lie deep as predetermining causes in his career.—Then come other natural elements to be regarded—those of sex —the seven ages from infancy to senility—the physical conditions that belong to sleep and dreams and the waking state, the health and disease of the body, the insane tendencies, the results of habits in hardening and fixing the life of the individual in some lower round of activity. If he is alone the efficient cause or the free will, at least these conditions of habitat, race, and stock furnish the material that he is to quarry and build into the temple of his life—a Parthenon, a Pantheon, or only a mud hut or a snow house.

§ 92. Of all these, the laws of growth from infancy to mature age especially concern the educator. There is for man, as contrasted with lower animals, a long period of helpless infancy. Prof. John Fiske has shown the importance of this fact to the theory of evolution as applied to man.* Basing his theory on some hints of Wallace and Spencer, he has explained how the differentiation of the primitive savage man from the animal groups must have been acomplished. Where psychical life is complex there is not time for all capacities to become organized before birth. The prolongation of helpless infancy is required for the development of man's adaptations to the spiritual environment implied in the habits and arts and modes of behaviour of the social community into which man is born. He is born first as an infant body, he must be born second as an ethical soul, or else he can not become human. The conditions are of extreme complexity. This is the most important contribution of the doctrine of evolution to education.

§ 93. In the light of this discovery we may see what an important bearing the results of child study and physiological psychology will have on education.

---

* Dr. Nicholas Murray Butler has pointed out that the Greek philosopher Anaximander, more than two thousand years ago, spoke of the prolonged period of infancy as a reason for believing that in the beginning man had an origin from animals of a different species from himself. The Greek did not perceive the relation of this prolonged infancy to the adjustment of the complex physical and spiritual activities of the child to his environment.

For it is evident that if the child is at any epoch of his long period of helplessness inured into any habit or fixed form of activity belonging to a lower stage of development that the tendency will be to arrest growth at that standpoint and make it difficult or next to impossible to continue the growth of the child into higher and more civilized forms of soul activity.

A severe drill in mechanical habits of memorizing or calculating, any overcultivation of sense-perception in tender years, may so arrest the development of the soul in a mechanical method of thinking as to prevent further growth into spiritual insight. Especially on the second plane of thought which follows that of sense-perception and the mechanical stage of thinking—namely, the stage of noticing mere relations and of classifying by mere likeness or difference, or even the search for causal relations—there is most danger of this arrested development. The absorption of the gaze upon adjustments within the machine prevents us from seeing the machine as a whole. The attention to details of colouring and drawing may prevent one from seeing the significance of the great work of art. The habit of parsing every sentence that one sees may prevent one from enjoying a sonnet of Wordsworth. Too much counting and calculating may at a tender age set the mind in the mechanical habit of looking for mere numerical relations in whatever it sees. Certainly the young savage who is taught to see in Nature only the traces that mark the passage of a wild animal, or perhaps of a warrior foe, has stopped his growth of observation at a point not very much above that of the hound that hunts by scent.— And yet all these mechanical studies are necessary at some period in the school; they can not be replaced except by others equally objectionable in the same aspect. The question is, then, where to stop and change to other and higher branches in time to preserve the full momentum of progress that the child has made. Prof. C. M. Woodward has pointed out that the educational effect of manual training is destroyed by having the pupils work for the market. It turns the attention toward the training in skill, and the educational effect which comes of first insight is afterward neglected. The first machine made is an education to its maker; the second and subsequent machines made are only a matter of habit. To keep the intellect out of the abyss of habit, and to make the ethical behaviour more and more a matter of unquestioning habit, seems to be the desideratum.

§ 94. Child study will perhaps find its most profitable field of investigation in this matter of arrested development. If it can tell the teacher how far to push thoroughness toward the borders of mechanical perfection, and where to stop just before induration and arrest set in, it will reform all our methods of teaching.* And it can and will do this. The new

---

* Child study in the United States, under the distinguished leadership of Dr. Stanley Hall, has not, it is true, done much in the study of arrested development. But there is a good reason for it. The province, being almost a new field for science, had to be mapped out first and its objects inventoried. In this work of inventorying an immense task has been accomplished by his disciples, but more especially by Dr. Hall himself. The beginnings must necessarily be quantitative. Take Dr. Hall's excellent study of dolls for an example of the quantitative survey of the field (see Pedagogical Seminary, vol. iv, p. 129), or his study of a sand pile (Princeton Review) for a qualitative inventory of the contents of an interesting specimen of the social education of boys through play. Fix

psychology, in its two phases of direct physiological study of brain and nerves, and its observation of child development, will show us how to realize by education the ideals of the highest civilization. The prolonged infancy of man will be in less danger of curtailment through vicious school methods.

The orphaned and outcast child becomes precociously world-wise. But the school can scarcely reclaim the *gamin* from the streets of Paris or New York. He has become as cunning and self-helpful as the water-rat, but not in ethical or spiritual methods. He should have been held back from the bitter lessons of life by the shielding hand of the family. He would then have become a positive influence for civilization in its height and depth. As a *gamin*,* he can live a life only a little above that of the water-rat, and is fitted only to feed the fires of revolution.

---

the order of succession, the date, duration, the locality, the environment, the extent of the sphere of influence, the number of manifestations and the number of cases of intermittence, and we have an exact inventory of a phenomenon. When stated in quantitative terms, any one's experience is useful to other observers. It is easy to verify it or add an increment to it. By quantification, science grows continually without retrograde movements.

* Victor Hugo has given a picture of the *gamin's* life and shown his genesis through the neglect of family care in infancy, in Parts III, IV, and V of his Les Misérables— little Gavroche and his two brothers, a solemn and pathetic history!

SECOND PART.

PSYCHOLOGIC SYSTEM.

145

SECOND PART.

PSYCHOLOGIC SYSTEM.

CHAPTER XIX.

Method and System in Psychology.

§ 95. A SYSTEM arises through the application of a method to all the details. A method is derived from a principle. Thus principle, method, and system are the three phases of a science. Principle, taken in this sense, includes the generating forces that produce and organize a province of facts. The principle of geology includes the formative forces that produce the earth crust and give it its shape. The principle of psychology includes the self-activity as it realizes itself, on the basis of assimilation, in the activities above plant life. Aristotle, it is true, makes it include the plant life, taking it to be the science of the soul in general—of the plant as well as of the animal and man. But ordinarily we limit the use of the word psychology to the functions above plant

147

life, including feeling, sense-perception, recollection,
memory, imagination, reflection, understanding, reason, will, etc.

§ 96. It is necessary to take the word principle in
the sense of productive cause, when we use it, as here,
in connection with method and system. The formative process that makes the earth crust shows the nature of its action to the geologist, and he comes to
know by degrees its method of working. Method is
the mode of acting of the productive principle. Self-
activity or self-definition manifests its form of acting
or its method, and psychology observes and records
this in various ways. One phase of it is described in
the account of the three figures of the syllogism;
another phase in the deduction of the moral virtues
which show the method by which the will preserves
its freedom. There is a productive principle in art
and literature which reveals its method; another in
sense-perception; still another in sociology; others in
other activities of the soul.

§ 97. In Part I each chapter has given at least
a glimpse of the method of the soul in some one or
other of its phases of action. But no method has been
followed out so far as to form an organic whole. If
method is followed, the parts unite and a systematic
whole arises. It has been said already that science

is a collection of facts systematically united in such a manner that each throws light on all and all on each. This is explained by saying that each fact seen in the light of its producing principle reveals the method of that principle. A series of facts arranged in the order of their production may thus make clear the sequence of the whole action of the cause, and give the entire method.

§ 98. A productive principle will result in a progressive development. At first it will be realized only partially, but later on it will be realized with greater and greater degrees of perfection. It is, in other words, a growth; only a growth can make an organic system. Time reveals the several steps of realization, and each step is the basis for the next. A logical system, it is true, does not take the form of growth in time, but it must be a growth from what is incomplete toward that which is complete— a successive addition of what was implied but not stated.

Aristotle has, in his De Anima, given a sketch of the views regarding the soul held by his predecessors and his contemporaries; then he follows with an account of the vegetative, animal, and rational stages of the development of the soul arranged in as systematic a manner as the knowledge of his time and his philosophic insight admitted. Now, as then, a systematic exposition of psychology will have to connect these phases and show how each is a step in the realization of mind. There will remain facts of observation which we are not able to explain as yet by the productive principle, because we can not yet fix them in their proper places and connect them with the steps that immediately precede or follow. All the sciences have unexplained data which have not yet been thus connected with antecedent and consequent steps, and for this reason are not yet organic parts of the same. But all sciences have succeeded in properly arranging the great provinces of their data in such a way as to explain each by the others and make each in turn help in the explanation of the rest. Some sciences (e. g., geology and botany) have progressed in this work of interpreting their data far into the minute details; others, like psychology and anthropology, have reached the order of genesis of only a few of the typical facts. So long as the place of a fact is not understood, its function can not be comprehended. Suppose that the tadpole were thought to be a higher development of the frog, coming after the full-grown amphibian, evolution would then be reversed. Suppose that sense-perception were taken for the perfection of the intellect, and memory, reflection, and insight taken to be stages of degeneration, the kind of psychology would be as bad as the philosophy of religion which took sun-myths as the normal form of religious thought, and explained all religious ideas as a disease of language. In fact, such a psychology has actually undertaken to explain philosophic thought as a disease of language, differing from religion only by reifying instead of personifying general terms, attributing to abstractions a higher order of existence than the objects of the senses, while religion personifies general terms and makes a mythology.

CHAPTER XX.

The Individuality of Inorganic and Organic Beings.

§ 99. HUMAN experience has distinguished from time immemorial four classes of individualities: (*a*) men, (*b*) animals, (*c*) plants, (*d*) inorganic things. Three classes can be made by including men with animals, or two can be made by uniting men, animals, and plants as the organic or living class of beings, and opposing to it the class of inorganic beings or conditions. Science inherits this distinction into four great classes from the unscientific experience of the race, but it progresses toward a clearer definition of the boundary lines and the laws of transition and development. It reclassifies what had been wrongfully classified. While the savage or ancient man includes many inorganic beings in the class of organic, and peoples Nature with good and evil spirits, science is disposed to find much in organic (or life) processes to be purely inorganic and mechanical.

§ 100. Inorganic being does not possess individuality for itself. A mountain is not an individual in the sense that a tree is. It is an aggregate of substances, but not an organic unity. The unity of place gives certain peculiarities and idiosyncrasies, but the mountain is an aggregate of materials, and its conditions are an aggregate of widely differing temperatures, degrees of illumination, moisture, etc.

§ 101. Atoms, if atoms exist as they are conceived in the atomic theory, can not be true individuals, for they possess attraction and repulsion, and by either of these forces express their dependence on others, and thus submerge their individuality in the mass with which they are connected by attraction or sundered by repulsion. Distance in space changes the properties of the atom—its attraction and repulsion are conceived as depending on distance from other atoms, and its union with other atoms develops new qualities and conceals or changes the old qualities. Hence the environment is essential to the atomic individuality—and this means the denial of its independence. If the environment is a factor, then the individuality is joint product, and the atom is not a true individual, but only a constituent.

§ 102. In an organism each part is reciprocally means and end to all the other parts—all parts are mediated through each. Mere aggregates are not individuals, but aggregates wherein the parts are at all times in mutual reaction with the other parts through and by means of the whole, are individuals. The individual stands in relation to other individuals and to the inorganic world. It is a manifestation of energy acting as conservative of its own individuality, and destructive of other individualities or of inorganic aggregates that form its environment. It assimilates other beings to itself and digests them, or imposes its own form on them and makes them organic parts of itself; or, on the other hand, it eliminates portions from itself, returning to the inorganic what has been a part of itself.

§ 103. Individuality, therefore, is not a mere thing, but an energy manifesting itself in things. In the case of the plant there is this unity of energy, but the unity does not exist for itself in the form of feeling. The animal feels, and, in feeling, the organic energy exists for itself, all parts coming to a unity in this feeling, and realizing an individuality vastly superior to the individuality manifested in the plant.

That which is dependent upon external circumstances, and is only a circumstance itself, is not capable of education. Only a "self" can be educated; and a "self" is a conscious unity—a "self-activity," a being which is through itself, and not one that is made by surrounding conditions. Again, in order that a being possess a capacity for education, it must have the ability to realize within itself what belongs to its species or race. If an acorn could develop itself so that it could realize not only its own possibility as an oak, but its entire species, and all the varieties of oaks within itself, and without losing its particular individuality, it would possess the capacity for education. But an acorn in reality can not develop its possibility without the destruction of its own individuality. The acorn vanishes in the oak tree, and the crop of acorns which succeeds is not again the same acorn, except in *kind* or species. " The species lives, but the individual dies," in the vegetable world. So it is in the animal world. The brute lives his particular life, unable to develop within himself the form of his entire species, and still less the form of all animal life. And yet the animal possesses self-activity in the powers of locomotion, sense-perception, feeling, emotion, and other elementary shapes. Both animal and plant react against surroundings, and possess more or less power to assimilate what is foreign to them. The plant takes moisture and elementary inorganic substances, and converts them into nutriment wherewith to build its cellular growth. The animal has not only this power of nutrition, which assimilates its surroundings, but also the power of *feeling*, which is a wonderful faculty. *Feeling* reproduces within the organism of the animal the external condition; it is an ideal reproduction of the surroundings. The environment of the plant is seized upon and appropriated, being changed into the form of sap for the nourishment of that plant; but there is no ideal reproduction of the environment in the form of *feeling*, as in the animal.

CHAPTER XXI.

Psychologic Functions of Plants and Animals compared.

§ 104. THE plant grows and realizes by its form or shape some phase or phases of the organic energy that constitutes the individuality of the plant. Roots, twigs, buds, blossoms, fruits, and seeds, all together manifest or express that organic energy, but they lack thorough mutual dependence, as compared with the parts of the animal who feels his unity in each part or limb. The individuality of the plant is comparatively an aggregate of individualities, while the animal is a real unity in each part through feeling, and hence there is no such independence in the parts of the animal as in the plant.

§ 105. Feeling, sense-perception, and locomotion characterize the individuality of the animal, although he retains the special powers which made the plant an organic being. The plant could assimilate or digest— that is to say, it could react on its environment and impress it with its own form, making the inorganic into vegetable cells and adding them to its own struc-

13

ture. Feeling, especially in the form of sense-perception, is the process of reproducing the environment
within the organism in an ideal form.

§ 106. Sense-perception thus stands in contrast
to the vegetative power of assimilation or nutrition,
which is the highest form of energy in the plant.
Nutrition is a subordinate energy in the animal, while
it is the supreme energy of the plant. Nutrition relates to its environment only negatively and destructively in the act of assimilating it, or else it adds
mechanically to the environment by separating and
excreting from itself what has become inorganic. But
feeling, even as it exists in the most elementary forms
of sense-perception, can reproduce the environment
ideally; it can form for itself, within, a modification
corresponding to the energy of the objects that make
up its environment. This is the essential thing to
keep constantly before the mind in psychology—that
feeling is not a mere passivity of the soul, but an
activity which makes an internal state responsive to
the external. Compared with the higher faculties,
it is passive because it lacks the repeated self-activities
added by reflection.

§ 107. Sentient being stands in reciprocal action
with its environment, but it seizes the impression received from without and adds to it by its own activity,

so as to reconstruct for itself the external object. It receives an impression, and is in so far passive to the action of its environment; but it reacts on this by forming within itself a counterpart to the impression out of its own energy. The animal individuality is an energy that can form limits within itself. On receiving an impression from the environment, it forms limits to its own energy commensurate with the impression it receives, and thus frames for itself a perception, or an internal copy of the object. It is not a copy so much as an estimate or measure effected by producing a limitation within itself similar to the impression it has received. Its own state, as thus limited to reproduce the impression, is its idea or perception of the external environment as acting upon it.

§ 108. The plant receives impressions from without, but its power of reaction is extremely limited, and does not rise to feeling. The beginnings of such reaction in plants as develops into feeling in animals are studied by intelligent biologists with the liveliest interest, for in this reaction are seen the ascent of individuality through a discrete degree—the ascent from nutrition to feeling.

§ 109. Nutrition is a process of destruction of the individuality of the foreign substance taken up from the environment, and likewise a process of impressing

on it a new individuality, that of the vegetative form,
or the nutritive soul, as Aristotle calls it. Feeling is
a process of reproducing within the individuality, by
self-limitation or self-determination, a form that is
like the external energy that has produced an impression upon it. The sentient being shapes itself
into the form of impression, or reproduces the impression, and thus perceives the character of the external energy by the nature of its own effort required to reproduce the impression.

§ 110. The difference between a nutritive process
and a perceptive or sentient process is one of degree,
but a discrete degree. Both processes are reactions on
what is foreign; but the nutritive is a real process,
destructive of the foreign object, while the sentient
is an ideal or reproductive process that does not affect
the foreign object. The nutritive is thus the opposite of the sentient—it destroys and assimilates; the
latter reproduces. Perception is objective, a self-determination in the form of the object—it transforms
the subject into the object; nutrition is subjective
in that it transmutes the object into the subject and
leaves no object. Perception preserves its own individuality and the individuality of its object while
reproducing it, for it limits itself by its own energy
in reproducing the form of the external.

The growth of the plant is through assimilation of external substances. It reacts against its surroundings and digests them, and grows through the nutrition thus formed. All beings that can not react against surroundings and modify them lack individuality. Individuality begins with this power of reaction and modification of external surroundings. Even the power of cohesion is a rudimentary form of reaction and of special individuality. In the case of the plant, the reaction is *real*, but not also *ideal*. The plant acts upon its food, and digests it, or assimilates it, and imposes its *form* on that which it draws within its organism. It does not, however, reproduce within itself the externality as that external exists for itself. This would be a complete victory over the external —to be able to posit it as well as to negate it. It does not form within itself an idea, or even a feeling of that which is external to it. Its participation in the external world is only that of *real* modification *of* it or through it; either the plant digests the external, or the external limits *it*, and prevents its growth, so that where one begins the other ceases. Hence it is that the elements—the matter of which the plant is composed, that which it has assimilated even—still retain a large degree of foreign power or force—a large degree of externality which the plant has not been able to annul or to digest. The plant-activity subdues its food, changes its shape and its place, subordinates it to its use; but what the matter brings with it and still retains of the world beyond the plant, does not exist for the plant; the plant can not read or interpret the rest of the universe from that small portion of it which it has taken up within its own organism. And yet the history of the universe is impressed on each particle of matter, as well within the plant as outside of it, and it could be understood were there capacities for recognising it. The reaction of the life of the plant upon the external world is not sufficient to constitute a fixed, abiding individuality. With each accretion there is some change of particular individuality. Every addition by growth to a plant is by the sprouting out of new indi-

viduals—new plants—a ceaseless multiplication of individuals, and not the preservation of the same individual.
The species is preserved, but not the particular individual.
Each limb, each twig, even each leaf is a new individual,
which grows out from the previous growth as the first
sprout grew from the seed. Each part furnishes, as it
were, a soil for the next. When a plant no longer sends
out new individuals, we say it is dead. The life of the
plant is only a life of nutrition. Aristotle called vegetable
life "the nutritive soul," and the life of the animal the
"feeling," or *sensitive* soul.—Since nutrition is only an
activity of preservation of the general form in new individuals—only the life of the species, and not the life of
the permanent individual—we see that in the vegetable
world we do not possess a being that can be educated,
for no individual of it can realize *within* itself the species;
its realization of the species is a continual process of
going out of itself into new individuals, but no activity of
return to itself, so as to preserve *the identity* of an individual.

CHAPTER XXII.

Feelings and Emotions.

§ 111. With feeling or sensibility we come to a
being that reacts on the external world in a far higher
manner than nutrition, and realizes a more wonderful
form of individuality. The animal possesses, in common with the plant, a process of assimilation and nutrition. Moreover, he possesses a capacity to *feel*.
Through *feeling*, or sensation, all the parts of his

extended organism are united in one centre. He is one individual, and not a bundle of separate individuals, as a plant is. With feeling, likewise, are joined *locomotion* and *desire*. For these are counterparts of feeling. He feels—i. e., lives as one indivisible unity throughout his organism and controls it, and moves the parts of his body. Desire is more than mere feeling. Mere feeling alone is the perception of the external within the being, hence an ideal reproduction of the external world. In feeling, the animal exists not only within himself, but also passes over his limit, and has for object the reality of the external world that limits him. Hence feeling is the perception of his finiteness—his limits are his defects, his needs, wants, inadequateness—his separation from the world as a whole. In feeling, the animal perceives his separation from the rest of the world, and also his union with it. Feeling expands into appetite and desire when the external world, or some portion of it, is seen as ideally belonging to the limited unity of the animal being. It is beyond the limit, but ought to be assimilated within the limited individuality of the animal: I look on this piece of bread as potentially assimilated and added to my body.

Mere feeling, when attentively considered, is found to contain these wonderful features of self-activity: it reproduces for itself the external world that limits it; it makes for itself an ideal object, which includes its own self and its not-self at the same time. It is a higher form than mere nutrition, for nutrition destroys the nature of such externality as it receives into itself, while feeling preserves the external in its foreign individuality. But through *feeling* the animal ascends to *appetite* and *desire*, and sees the independent externality as an object for its acquisition, and through locomotion it is enabled to seize and appropriate it in a degree which the plant did not possess.

§ 112. Feeling may be said to be intellect and will in an unconscious form. On the side of unconscious intellect we have all the feelings that are passive or contemplative—sensations, emotions, and affections. On the side of unconscious will we have instincts, appetites, and desires. On one side the feelings look toward the intellect, and tend to become conscious and pass over into cognitions, motives, and reflections. On the other side, the feelings tend to rise into conscious volition, and become deliberate and responsible.

A. On the intellectual side we have (*a*) sensation, which is partly physical, using the five sense-organs and the general or common sense—sometimes called the feelings of vitality (as in such sensations as rest and weariness, sickness and health). (*b*) Emotions— (1) hope, terror, despair, fear, contempt, etc.; (2) æsthetic pleasure in the presence of the beautiful and sublime; (3) the religious emotions. (*c*) Affections, benevolence (or kindness, sympathy, pity, mercy, etc.), gratitude, friendship, family love, philanthropy, etc., and the opposite affections of malice, wrath, jealousy, envy, etc.

B. On the will side we have (*a*) instincts which move us unconsciously to acts performed by us as animals—laughing, crying, winking, dodging a missile thrown at one, etc. (*b*) Appetites for food and drink, sleep and exercise, etc. (*c*) Desires for happiness, or pleasure, or knowledge, and such other desires as ambition, avarice, vanity, pride, etc.

It will be noted that division (*b*) of the intellectual feelings presupposes as their basis the third stage of knowing in the æsthetic and religious feelings, and that division (*c*) includes social feelings.

§ 113. How to educate the feelings? They can not be educated directly and as such, precisely because they are feelings and immediate. But they can be educated indirectly through the intellect and will. The good feelings may be strengthened and the evil repressed by correct intellectual views and the adoption of proper motives. The instinctive action, according to bad motives, can be inhibited by the will, and correct habitual action substituted for it.

(A.) Feeling is immediate, a consciousness of a direct impulse of Nature, of that which has become a part of one's nature, and of something alien struggling against absorption by one's nature. Feelings are of two kinds: (a) Primary feelings in order of time, those that are inherited appear in the child at first; (b) secondary feelings in order of time, those that result from intellect and will which adopt a course of action for some conscious purpose, and then by repeated volitions fix that course of action as a habit, in which form the conscious element of purpose and volition fades out and the act becomes unconscious and sinks into the form of feeling again. This secondary kind of feeling is entirely under the control of education.

(B.) A proper view may be taught the intellect and made to become the conviction of the pupil. He may be trained to act habitually according to that conviction; it will soon become a matter of feeling with him. The result of all school education is heart culture, whether intended or not. But if partial, whether of intellect only or will only, the result is not abiding. If the school enforces a correct habit by authority, requiring it strictly of each pupil, say, a courteous bearing toward one's fellows, this will go a long way, but it may be uprooted by a mental conviction which has not been overcome that discourtesy is the proper thing (i. e., for example, that courtesy is insincerity and deceit). So, too, a correct view may be of little avail if the opposite habit is allowed to stand and is not uprooted by the necessary will training in habit. Feeling is not co-ordinate with intelligence and will. Intellect and will are co-ordinate, but feeling is the implicit unity out of which they rise. Education acts on intellect and will, and through habit and fixed conviction supplants the wrong feeling by a new feeling.

§ 114. For the reason that feeling as sensation measures off, as it were, on its own organic energy—which exists for it in the feeling of self—the amount and kind of energy required to produce the impression made on it from without, it follows that sense-perception is not only a reception of impressions, but also an act of introspection. By introspection it interprets the cause or occasion of the impression that is felt. Feeling arises only when the impression made on the organism is reproduced again within the self —only when it recognises the external cause by seeing in and through its own energy the energy that has limited it. The degree of objectivity (or the ability to perceive the reality of the external power) is measured by the degree of introspection or the degree of clearness in which it perceives the amount and limit of the internal energy required to reproduce the impression.

Having noted these important characteristics of feeling and assimilation, and found that *reaction* from the part against the whole—from the internal against the external—belongs to plant life and animal life, we may now briefly consider the ways in which sensation is particularized. In the lower animals it is only the feeling of touch; in higher organisms it becomes also localized as seeing, hearing, taste, and smell. These forms of sense-perception constitute a scale (as it were) of feeling. With touch, there is reproduction of externality, but the ideality of the reproduction is not so complete as in the other forms. With taste, the feeling cognizes the external object as undergoing dissolution, and assimilation within its own organism. We taste only what we are beginning to destroy by the first process of assimilation—that of eating. In smell, we perceive chemical dissolution of bodies —it is more ideal than taste, because it does not proceed from a direct attack of the ego on the individuality of the object, but only from the attack of the entire objective environment on it. In seeing and hearing, we have the forms of *ideal* sensibility. Hearing perceives the attack made on the individuality of an external thing, and its reaction in vibrations, which reveal to us its internal nature—its cohesion, etc. In seeing, we have the highest form of sense-perception as the perception of things in their external independence—not as being destroyed chemically, like the objects of taste and smell; not as being attacked and resisting, like the objects which are known through the ear; not as mere limits to our organism, as in the sense of touch. The action of these forms of sensation must be considered more in detail.

CHAPTER XXIII.

The Five Senses.

§ 115. THE energy presupposed in the act of feeling and sense-perception is a self-activity, but one that manifests itself in reproducing its environment ideally. It presupposes an organic energy of nutrition in which it has assimilated portions of the environment and constructed for itself a body. In the body it has organized stages of feeling, constituting the ascending scale of sense-perception. In the plant the self-activity is limited to the time when it is acting on its food to assimilate it; it is intermittent and dependent on the existence of the food in the environment. But in feeling the self-activity continues as a reaction without attacking the object by a real process, as in the case of digestion. It is as if feeling is in some sort the digestive activity continued without any food from without, the activity being reflected or turned inward and acting upon itself in feeling. Further on, in recollection and memory, the self-activity does not require even the presence of the object for its action. In imagination it does not require even a past object, but creates its object without being tethered to its environment, present or past.

a. First there is the sense of touch, containing all higher senses in potentiality. When the higher senses have not developed, or after they have been destroyed by accident, the sense of touch may become sufficiently delicate to perceive not only contact with bodies, but also the slighter modifications involved in the effects of taste and smell, and even in the vibrations of sound and light.

b. The lowest form of special sense is taste, which is closely allied to nutrition. Taste perceives the phase of assimilation of the object, which is commencing within the mouth. The individuality of the object is attacked and it gives way, its organic product or inorganic aggregate suffering dissolution—taste perceives the dissolution. Substances that do not yield to the attack of the juices of the mouth have no taste. Glass and gold have little taste compared with salt and sugar. The sense of taste differs from the process of nutrition in the fact that it does not assimilate the body tasted, but reproduces ideally the energy that makes the impression on the sense-organ of taste. Even taste, therefore, is an ideal activity, although it is present only when the nutritive energy is assimilating—it perceives the object in a process of dissolution.

c. Smell is another specialization which perceives dissolution of objects in a more general form than taste. Both smell and taste perceive chemical changes that involve dissolution of the object.

d. Hearing is a far more ideal sense, and notes a manifestation of resistance to dissolution. The cohesion of a body is attacked and it resists, the attack and resistance take the form of vibration, and this vibration is perceived by the special sense of hearing. Taste and smell perceive the dissolution of the object, while hearing perceives the defence or successful reaction of an object in presence of an attack. Without elasticity—i. e., reaction on the part of cohesion—there would be no vibration and no sound.

e. The sense of sight perceives the individuality of the object not in a state of dissolution before an attack, as in the case of taste and smell, nor engaged in active resistance to attack, as in case of hearing, but in its independence. Sight is therefore the most ideal sense, inasmuch as it is farthest removed from the real process of assimilation, in which one energy destroys the product of another energy and extends its sway over it. It is the altruistic sense, because it perceives the existence-for-itself of the object, and not merely its existence-for-others or its existence-for-me.

Sense-perception, as the developed realization of the activity of feeling on its intellectual side, belongs to the animal creation, including man as an animal. Locomotion also belongs to animals as the developed realization of feeling on its will side. Plant life does not possess that self-activity which returns into itself in the 'same individual, if we may so express it; it goes out of one individual into another perpetually. Its identity is that of the *species*, but not of the *individual.*—In feeling there is a reaction, just as in the plant. This reaction is, however, in an ideal form—the reproduction of the external without assimilation of it—and especially is this the case in the sense of *sight*, though it is true of all forms of sensation to a less degree.—But all forms of sensibility are limited and special; they refer only to the *present*, in its forms of *here* and *now*. The animal can not feel what is not here and now. Even seeing is limited to what is present before it. When we reflect upon the significance of this limitation of sense-perception, we shall find that we need some higher form of self-activity still before we can realize the species in the individual—i. e., before we can obtain the true individual, the permanent individuality. The defect in plant life was that there was neither identity of individuality in space nor identity in time. The growth of the plant destroyed the individuality of the seed with which we began, so that it was evanescent in time; it served only as the starting point for new individualities, which likewise in turn served again the same purpose, and so its growth in space was a departure from itself as individual. But the animal is a preservation of individuality as regards space. He returns into himself (i. e., makes his self-activity the object of his self-activity, or becomes self-object) in the form of *feeling* or *sensibility;* but as regards time, it is not so, feeling being limited to the present. Without a higher activity than feeling, there is no continuity of individuality in the animal any more than in the plant. Each new moment is a new beginning to a being that has feeling, but not memory. Thus the individuality of mere feeling, although a far more perfect realization of individuality than that found in plant life, is yet, after all, not a continuous individuality for itself, but only for the species. In spite of the ideal self-activity which appertains to feeling in sense-perception, only the species lives in the animal, and the individual dies, unless there be higher forms of activity.

CHAPTER XXIV.

Recollection and Memory.

§ 116. WHILE mere sensation, as such, acts only in the presence of the object, reproducing (ideally, it is true) the external object, the faculty of recollection is a higher form of self-activity (or of reaction against surrounding conditions), because it can recall, at its own pleasure, the ideal object. Here is the beginning of emancipation from the limitations of time. The self-activity of representation can summon before it the object that is no longer present to it. In this the soul's activity is a double one, for it can seize not only what is now and here immediately before it, but it can compare the present with the past object, and identify or distinguish between the two. Thus recollection or representation may become *memory*. We may distinguish memory from mere recollection by letting it denote systematized recollection —recollection organized into wholes of experience— relative wholes, which are called *events*. Memory may thus be regarded as the grouping faculty by whose aid sense-perception becomes a perceiver of species as well as individuals. Memory contains the stores of experience by which the present object is explained and interpreted by the first figure of the syllogism (Chapter X). It therefore uses general ideas or class ideas. It has already become conscious in its act of recollection that it can call up at will the past perceptions. It can summon before it the absent object and represent it. To represent is to create the object subjectively or mentally. The memory which

14

collects and arranges the recollections thus deals with an activity which reproduces individual sense-impressions; it unites the object to the activity that produces it. This activity (memory), accordingly, generates the faculty of perceiving things and events as individuals of species, or members of classes. Human sense-perception is nearly always not simple sense-perception, but complex, being united to memory in such a way that the objects perceived are identified (second figure of syllogism, Chapter IX) or apperceived as specimens of classes. This makes possible language; for language can not be used unless the special object of the senses can be expressed in general terms already become familiar in remembered experience.

As memory, taken in this sense of the organizer of experience into groups by subsuming all particulars under universal or general classes, the mind achieves a form of activity above that of sense-perception or mere recollection. It must be noted carefully that mere recollection or representation, although it holds fast the perception in time (making it permanent), does not necessarily constitute an activity completely emancipated from time, nor, indeed, very far advanced toward it. It is only the beginning of such emancipation. For mere recollection stands in the presence of the imaged object of sense-perception; although the object is no longer present to the senses (or to mere feeling), yet the image is present to the representative perception, and is just as much a particular here and now as the object of sense-perception. There inter-

venes a new activity on the part of the soul before it
arrives at memory. Recollection is not memory, but it
is the activity which grows into it by the aid of the activity of introspection and attention to it (i. e., to the activity of recollection).

§ 117. The activity by which the mind ascends
from sense-perception to memory is the activity of introspection, in this case an unconscious act of attention to the process of recollection.   Here we have the
appearance of the will in intellectual activity, for this
synthesis of the formative power (manifest in representation) with its results, recollected impressions, is
the addition (to the products made) of the will that
makes them.   The act of systematizing the first
stage of representation, which is recollection, therefore introduces attention to subjective processes, which
we call introspection.   But introspection here is far
below the threshold of consciousness, for it is the unnoticed activity which adds the representing process
to its products.   Attention is the control of perception by means of the will, but it is unconscious
will, if we may use the terms attention and will,
at this point of progress.   It directs, however, spontaneously the attention to the process, and causes it to
let go the particular images formed by representation.
The senses shall no longer passively receive and report
what is before them, but they shall choose some defi-

nite point of observation, and neglect all the rest. Here, in the act of attention, we find the elementary form of *abstraction,* and the greater attainment of freedom by the mind. The mind abstracts its view from the many things before it, and concentrates on one point. Educators have for many ages noted that the habit of attention is the first step in intellectual education. With it we have found the point of separation between the animal intellect and the human. Not attention simply—like that with which the cat watches by the hole of a mouse—but attention which arrives at results of abstraction, is the distinguishing characteristic of educative beings (see Chapter XXX).

§ 118. Attention abstracts from some things before it and concentrates on others. In the case here considered it abstracts from the sense-impressions and considers the mental activity of reproducing them by recollection. This is not a conscious act of abstraction, but it is, all the same, an act of the will. When we reflect on it, we discover all the steps that are involved in it and make them conscious. We see that there was discrimination or analysis, and also synthesis. Through attention grows the capacity to discriminate between the special, particular object and its general type. This it does, as already described, by thinking together the reproductive imagination and its products, reaching the concept of particulars produced and held together in a generating cause (see Chapter V—a concept not a mental picture, but a definition of the thing-producing energy). Generalization thus arises, but not what is usually called generalization—only a more elementary form of it— i. e., not generalization as it takes place on the stage of reflective thought, but as it takes place in the swift and unnoticed process of sense-perception and memory. Memory, as the highest form of representation— distinguishing it from mere recollection, which reproduces only what has been perceived—such memory deals with the general forms of objects, their continuity in time. Such activity of memory, therefore, does not reproduce mere images, but only the concepts or general ideas of things, and therefore it belongs to the stage of mind that uses language.

§ 119. *Mnemonics.*—Whatever cultivation of memory tends to the arrest of the power of rational thinking is to be by all means avoided. It seems, therefore, that most of the schemes of mnemonics which are advocated are to be condemned without reservation. Those which proceed upon the principle that memory is to be cultivated by association, and that all kinds of association are equally good, should fall under the ban. For in order to find interesting associations they suggest the search for absurd and ridiculous relations. The philosopher Locke has well said that "the connection in our minds of ideas, in themselves loose and independent of one another, has such an influence and is of so great force to set us wrong in our actions, as well moral and natural, passions, reasonings, and notions themselves, that perhaps there is not any one thing that deserves more to be looked after." In all cases the mind should seek essential relations, and particularly the relation of cause and effect and that of individual and species. Necessary connection enables the mind to make deductions, and thus it acquires a sort of generative memory, so to speak—a memory which can deduce or develop from given data the other data that stand in relation to it. It is true that this is difficult with regard to certain classes of memory, as, for instance, the memory of proper names, or the memory of dates, or memory of words in general.

The memory of dates, names, or words in general can and should be cultivated to some extent without attempting association of any kind except that of sequence. The committing to memory of fine passages from poets and literary prose writers certainly cultivates a memory for words without detriment to thought. A memorized list of proper names, names of persons of historic note or characters in the great literary works of art, such as the plays of Shakespeare, the Iliad and Odyssey—the memorizing of these names will serve the double purpose of being at once very useful and a means of arousing into activity the faculty of remembering proper names—a faculty that grows torpid quite early in persons engaged in science, literature, and philosophy. Also the memorizing of paradigms in the study of language has the effect to cultivate this memory of words and isolated items. If the mind thinks at all in the process of memorizing these lists of proper names and the important dates of history or the paradigms of grammar, it considers the deeds and characters of the persons named, or the events associated with the dates, or the logical relation of the inflections to the verbs and nouns inflected. And such kind of thinking as this is positive and valuable. But in case of associating in accordance with certain mnemonic rules the names, dates, and inflections with arbitrary and fanciful suggestions, the thinking power is set moving on wrong lines.—If the discovery of Broca, generally recognised as the beginning of physiological psychology on the new basis, is to be understood in the sense that a certain convolution near the base of the brain is used by the mind in recalling words and associating them with ideas, it would seem that a cultivation of the memory of words should be undertaken in later life by all people who have an incipient tendency to aphasia. If a person finds himself forgetful of names, it is a health-giving process to take a certain portion of time in committing to memory words. If this is done by committing to memory new masterpieces of poetry and prose, or in committing to memory the words of a new language, there is profit or gain to the thinking powers as well as to the memory. Doubtless the cultivation of verbal memory, building up as it does a certain convolution in the brain, has a tendency to prevent atrophy in that organ. This contains a hint in the direction of keeping up in the later part of life the faculties which are usually so active in youth. The tendency is to neglect childish faculties and allow them to become torpid. But if this is liable to weaken certain portions of the brain in such a way as to induce hæmorrhage, ending in softening of the brain, certainly the memory should be cultivated if only for the health of the brain, and the memory for mechanical items and details should be cultivated on grounds of health as well as on grounds of culture. The extreme advocates of the rational method of teaching are perhaps wrong in repudiating entirely all mechanical memory of dates and names or items. Certainly they are right in opposing the extremes of the old pedagogy, which obliged the pupils to memorize page after page the contents of a grammar " verbatim et literatim et punctuatim " (as, for instance, the graduates of the Boston Latin School tell us, was the custom early in this century). But is there not a middle ground? Is there not a minimum list of details of dates and names which must and should be memorized both on account of the health of the nervous system and on account of the intrinsic usefulness of the data themselves? And must not the person in later life continue to exercise these classes of memory which deal with details for the sake of physical health? This is a question for the educational pathologist.

§ 120. We have seen in the preceding sections that in the order of the development of the so-called " faculties " of the mind sense-perception is the lowest, because the mind is relatively passive in its exercise. We behold or contemplate an object because it is presented to our senses. Remove the object, and our sense-perception ceases. We perceive only what is present, here and now. This is its limitation: it is dependent on the object. But with the memory we are not thus limited by what is external. We can call up at will our past perceptions when the objects are no longer present. In this we realize for the first time our power over time and space. We can create for ourselves objects which no longer exist. Memory to some degree makes the past now, and the far-off here.

§ 121. Memory is a sort of double self-activity as compared with sense-perception. In our third chapter we have stated that even sense-perception proves its right to a higher place than plant life or mere assimilation by the fact that the percipient reproduces within itself the form of the object, and by this act is able to perceive. Feeling and perception are forms of reproduction, while nutrition or assimilation is merely a destructive act which imposes its own form in place of another on the food consumed. But memory is an explicit reproduction of the object once perceived, and its freedom is clearly seen. We may say that perception is unconscious reproduction of the form of the object, while memory is the conscious reproduction of it. It has been pointed out that the reproduction called perception takes place only in the presence of the object, while memory is entirely independent of the object.

§ 122. Sense-perception if overcultivated can therefore prove detrimental to the development of the higher faculty, memory. The habit of occupy-

ing the mind only on what is present before the senses
arrests the growth of memory. But the more considerate power of perception which employs the memory
to re-enforce sense-perception is useful to both alike.
In Chapter X we have indicated the form under which
this takes place. In the first figure of the syllogism
we bring all that we have already learned to re-enforce
our perception by testing it and setting it to verify
or refute previous experience (see above, § 116).

The Pestalozzians who speak so often of the importance
of cultivating sense-perception in the school do not seem
to have ever considered the relation of perception to memory, for they make no mention of this radical difference of
activity, nor do they proceed to show how the higher
faculty may be made to assist the lower. A similar mistake is made by those writers on psychology who do not
discriminate the higher from the lower faculties, but treat
them all alike. They hold that the higher are built up
out of the lower, as though perceptions would grow into
thoughts when they have become sufficiently numerous.
They have no insight into the primary fact of psychology
—namely, that every higher faculty is an activity which
is negative to the lower activities, although it preserves
in a transfigured shape what was valid in the lower.

§ 123. "Memory is indispensable in all intellectual processes, and therefore must be trained and developed." Yes, but it is liable to prove destructive to
the other faculties (so called) and supplant them;
hence it must be restrained within its proper limits,
made auxiliary to the other faculties, and not allowed

to assume the chief rôle. It is a matter of everyday
comment that much memorizing deadens the power
of thought, verbal or statistical memory being " mechanical." But it is also equally true that memory
may paralyze the powers of sense-perception, imagination, and will. With an overactive memory we
suppose ourselves to see in an object what we remember to have seen in it before, and any new features
escape our superficial perception. This is true, too,
in the case of imagination, a power which ought to
be productive as well as reproductive, and by which
we ought to envisage not only real objects but possible ones, and thereby sharpen our powers of invention and discovery. Even the imagination may be
dulled by a too active memory, and degenerate into
a mirror of the past. The productive imagination
should belong not only to poets and artists, but to
all men, as a faculty of discovering ideals and emancipating us from the imperfect reality. It should give
us a tendency to invention and to aspiration. But,
under the weight of prescribed forms and the sway
of memory, a civilization crushes out self-activity on
the part of individuals and imposes the rôle of external authority upon all. Thus the will of the individual loses freedom, and settles down into passive
obedience to custom and prescription.

The important question to determine is the proper
amount of memory-cultivation. The Chinese education
fills the memory with maxims of Confucius and Mencius,
and the individual follows these because there is little
else in his mind: their lines are graven so deep that nothing else seems important. The antidote for this baneful
effect of memory is to be sought in a method of training
that associates effects with causes, and individuals with
species; that associates one idea with another through
its essential relations, and not by its accidental properties.
One must put thought into the act of memory. But the
special kind of memory that is weak should be cultivated
by itself and not attached to some other form of memory.
The simile of a magnet is to the point here. Load it
to-day with iron filings, and to-morrow it will support a
few more. The memory, if only strong enough to retain
a single item with effort, will grow stronger by the effort,
and will soon retain two items, and finally others in vast
numbers and without effort.

§ 124. It is a reasonable thing to correct special
defects in the lower orders of memory when they
become matters of serious embarrassment. Those special powers of memory should in that case be strengthened. It is a perception of this necessity that has led
to systems of mnemonics. The common device of
such systems has been association of the items of one
province of memory with those of another. The items
easily forgotten are fastened, so to speak, to items
easily remembered—names or dates, for example, to
places or events. As has been shown above, it often
happens that the items of one order are not related to

the other order by the principle of causality or genetic development, and it results that the mnemonic association by which memory of a particular kind is to be strengthened is merely an accidental relation of the items associated. Contiguity of space or accidental resemblance in sound is to assist us to remember. By mnemonics we cultivate a habit of consciously seeking such accidental relations, and we accordingly injure our power of logical thought by neglecting essential for unessential relations.

In § 119 we have already pointed out the dangers incident to the use of mnemonic systems. The following example will illustrate further this wrong method: Gregor von Feinaigle's New Art of Memory (London, 1812) says * that "the recollection of ideas is assisted by associating some idea of relation between them; and as we find by experience that whatever is ludicrous is calculated to make a strong impression upon the mind, the more ridiculous the association is the better." Think of an effort of the mind to discover absurd and ridiculous relations between ideas with a view to remember them! That would be to cultivate memory at the expense of sane, rational thought. The true method of cultivating and strengthening a defective memory is to practise it on the kind of items that it easily forgets. As already suggested, a few such items must be memorized and reviewed daily, adding a small increment to the list as soon as it has become perfectly mastered. A list with fifty items thus memorized will suffice to develop a habit of attention to such items and a power of recalling them which will grow steadily with such exercise as circumstances bring occa-

---

* Quoted by David Kay, Memory, p. 281.

sion for. By this method we avoid fantastic associations and correct the weak faculty itself, instead of fastening its work on another faculty. Pursuing the suggestions made above (§§ 119, 123), let the exercise be a list of dates valuable to retain for themselves, such, for example, as the dates of accession of the English kings; also of the Roman emperors; the founding and important events of the great cities of the world. Or, if it is names that one wishes to remember, select a list of important persons that furnish centres of historical information; such, for example, as the names of the Roman emperors, the French kings, the heroes of Plutarch's histories; or of typical personalities, such as the characters in Shakespeare's dramas or in Homer's Iliad—items of world-historical importance. A list of one hundred proper names learned in their order, as kings of France and of England, and the emperors of Rome, will furnish central nuclei to historic material, and the memorizing of such a list, or, indeed, a list half as large, will so discipline the memory for names as to permanently remove all embarrassment from this source. It is not the length of the list, so much as the thoroughness with which it is learned, that develops the memory. It is not well to go on beyond a hundred items, for the reason that such mechanical memory should not be made too strong. Idiots and semi-idiots may show prodigious powers of remembering numbers, and very feeble intellects may be exceptionally apt in remembering names and other words. Therefore, while there should be some special training to strengthen varieties of mechanical memory that have become too weak for the service required of them, they should not be overcultivated. Repetition and careful attention should be relied upon more than association in the cultivation of the mechanical varieties of memory, for the reason that association, though more showy and brilliant in its effects than repetition and attention, is not so much a correction of the special province of defective memory as a substitution of another province of memory for the defective one. Memory of places, for example, is substituted vicariously for memory of numbers or names. Physiological psychology has not thus far discovered much that is of practical value in the educational treatment of memory. Many psychical activities, it is true, have been located or partially located in the brain and nervous system, and diseases of the memory may with some degree of certainty be connected with accompanying lesions in the brain. But whether these lesions are causes or effects, or both, we are not able to cure an ordinary case of failing memory except by pure psychological means—namely, by attention, mental association, and repetition—doubtless affecting the brain thereby, but through free acts of the will. We can affect the brain through the effort of the will on the memory, but we can not as yet develop the memory through body-culture.

§ 125. Memory is not a simple homogeneous faculty or activity of the soul. It is an entire series of activities rising in a scale from the mere representation in the form of a picture of what has been seen up to a sort of creative memory which, recollecting the law or principle, deduces the picture or thought of the object with greater accuracy than the merely mechanical memory retains it. Thus there is memory of shapes, colours, places, times, and sense-impressions; then there is memory of numbers, and this is not a memory of sense-impressions, but of the mental acts of abstracting the quantity; then there is memory of causal action, and this is a very high order of memory. When we remember causal action, we possess a sort of rule or law by which we may create the results or effects, and do not need to learn them by the use of mechanical memory. The cultivation of one species of memory may assist or it may hinder another kind of memory, according as the mental activity by which the attention is fixed on one subject aids or hinders the mental activity of the other kind of memory.

The cases are rare in which a person has a weak memory in all directions. In considering the question of improving the memory, therefore, the individual must ask in what respect he is defective; is it dates, or names, or something else that he fails to remember? Moreover, it is necessary to ask whether it is important to remember those items that he forgets so easily—whether, in short, it is worth while to acquire a habit of remembering them. For instance, as children we remembered village gossip, personal remarks, actions, or things and events that are so trivial that we do not permit ourselves now to interest ourselves in them or recall them. Do we not find, in fact, our memories of those insipid things and events of childhood still too vivid? We are apt to speak of children, for this very reason, as having strong memories. But would we willingly have again our childish memories? Would it content us to notice trivial circumstances and overlook essential matters? If so, it is easy to gratify our desire by cultivating the childish form of memory. We may give our attention to the accidental features of an event, to the details of foolish gossip, and neglect the main issues and the causal processes. It will naturally result, then, that we shall remember as children remember, with the difference that we shall find ourselves able to do a far greater amount of superficial observation and recollection than children can do.

§ 126. Attention is regarded as the condition of memory, when we explain the loss of memory by the lack of attention to the event, or prescribe a habit of attention as the remedy for loss of memory. But such a habit does not strengthen general memory; it weakens it rather. For it implies a selection of a small province of the field before us, and a neglect of the rest; hence the training of attention implies also a cultivation of neglect. As we grow mature in our intellectual power we increase in our ability to seize the objects of our choice and to pass over without notice all others. The person without a well-developed power of attention is in a state of passivity toward invading external influences. He is a prey to impressions that come from his environment. Most of these " early impressions " of which we hear so much were received at a time when trivial things could seize upon us and absorb our powers of observation to the neglect of more essential things. Such passive impressibility, the condition of the childish memory, it is the object of education to eradicate. The pupil must learn to exclude and ignore the many things before him, and to concentrate all his powers of mind on the one chosen subject.

It follows that the discipline of attention makes the memory uneven or unequal. The study of relations weakens our memory of mere isolated data. The study of general ideas causes us to be careless in regard to specific details that naturally follow as effects. Our insight

15

into laws weakens our hold of special instances. Knowing the law of eclipses, we can calculate all past and all future instances, and we do not care to burden our memory with the historical record of eclipses. Our attention to the meaning of a word weakens our memory of its sound; attention to a person's character makes us less careful to remember his costume. While, therefore, it is a correct educational maxim that the memory must be trained on essential relations and causal processes, so as to strengthen the power of thought at the same time, yet there may be excess even in this direction. We find, accordingly, people whose memory of dates is so defective as to cause much waste of power; other persons are so forgetful of names as to be under constant embarrassment in conversation or in writing.

§ 127. Memory is therefore not a faculty of the soul which is to be desired on all accounts and cultivated always with assiduity. With the growth of culture of the higher powers it will occupy less and less place compared with the whole mind.

Aristotle's profound insight into the nature of the soul and its powers deserves more study. In his De Anima that philosopher places memory with the fantasy, the activity of sense-perception, and the discursive intellect, as together constituting the " passive reason " (Νοῦς παθητικός). He considers this part of the soul perishable or moribund. This thought of the perishability of such faculties in the onward career of the soul has quite another and deeper meaning than that usually attributed to it. Memory and sense-perception become less and less prominent factors in the human mind, and in some departments they already occupy a very inferior position. In arithmetic and geometry, for example, we deduce the special instance rather than observe it and memorize it. In each of the natural sciences an epoch of observation closes with an exhaustive inventory of its details, and there follows an epoch in which the whole compass of details is organized into a system by means of a discovery of the laws and modes of action of the organic energy that produces the facts. Each fact is then seen in the perspective of its history, or of its genesis, and thus thoroughly explained; but with such explanation the scaffolding of original facts that were inventoried and systematized falls away, and all observation of new facts in the province becomes a mere verification of the known mode of action of the energy. Agassiz, having learned the principles of biological structure, recognises a new fish from one of its scales, and can tell with confidence its structure and conditions of living. It is not a matter of memory, but of direct insight. So Cuvier can see the whole animal in one of its bones, and Lyell see in each pebble its entire history. Goethe's allegorical Homunculus * symbolizes this new achievement in the scientific mind. The little living being confined in a bottle figures the final career of induction which has arrived at insight or intuition. Having exhaustively surveyed its limited field, each special science seizes upon the organizing principle and can predict facts or recognise and explain them at sight. When we can see each immediate fact in the perspective of its genesis or history, we have no use for memory which preserves for us facts and events isolated from their producing and deducing causes. Memory is moribund, and in province after province it is losing its importance. A fact-producing principle is seized and the facts are kept no longer in vast storehouses, for they can be deduced when wanted, or, if encountered in our experience, they can be explained and dismissed. We look beyond them to their causes, and let sense-perception and memory of such facts both drop. The relative amount of activity of

---

* See the second part of Faust. Homunculus stands for Winckelmann, who attained such knowledge of Greek art that he could give the rules that would enable one to recognise the god or goddess by a small part of the face.

sense-perception, of memory, and of mere reflection on
accidental relations (νοῦς παθητικός) continually diminishes,
and the thinking on principles, causes, and organic processes (νοῦς ποιητικός) increases.

CHAPTER XXV.

From Perception to Conception: each Object seen in its Class.

§ 128. WE have already seen (§§ 116 and 117)
how the memory differs from recollection by making
its survey include not only the particulars recalled
by recollection, but also the entire process of recollection itself as a creative or producing unity of the
mind. This phase of memory makes it a faculty that
adds the general, the class, or species to the individual,
and thus elevates perception to conception, and makes
language possible.

(a) Nutrition implies foreign objects on which to exercise its energy. It manifests itself as a destruction of its
environment and the extension of its power by conquest.
If it could conquer all its environment it would become
a totality; but then its activity would cease for want
of food. The old Norse mythology conceived the tree
Yggdrasil—the world-tree which had digested its environment in this way.—(b) Sense-perception, on the other
hand, implies impressions from foreign objects as the
occasion of its activity of ideal reproduction. It can not

perceive without objects; hence its energy is always conditioned by energies independent of it. (c) Representation is reproduction without the presence of the senseobject; recollection and memory are forms of this. In the form of recollection the individual energy reproduces the activity of a past perception. The impression on the sense-organ is absent, and the freedom of the individual is manifested in this reproduction without the occasion which is furnished by the impression on the organism from without. The freedom to reproduce the image of an object that has been once perceived leads by easy steps to the perception of general notions; for, when the mind notices its mode of activity by which the former perception is reproduced or represented, it perceives, of course, its power of repeating the process, and notes that the same energy can produce an indefinite series of different images resembling one another. It is by this action of representation that the idea of the universal arises. It is a reflection on the conditions of recalling a former perception. The energy that can produce within itself the conditions of a former perception at pleasure, without the presence of the original object of perception, is an energy that is generic—that is, an energy that can produce the particular and repeat it to any extent. The universal or generic power can produce a class.

§ 129. With this consciousness of a generic energy manifested in the power of representation arises the recognition of generic energy manifested in the external world as the producer of the particular objects perceived, and each object is seen in its producing energy as one of an indefinite number produced by the continued existence of that energy. The consciousness of freedom of the Ego in this restricted province of representing or recalling former

sense-perceptions lies thus at the basis of the perception of objects as specimens of classes; hence representation or recollection, which is of special and individual objects, leads to the act of reflection by which
the self as representing power is perceived, and with
it the perception of the necessary generic character
of the energy at the foundation of every impression
upon our senses or at the foundation of every object
perceived.

§ 130. At this point the activity of perception
becomes Conception, or the perception of the general in the particular. The " this oak " is perceived
as " an oak," or a specimen of the class oak. The
class oak is conceived as an indefinite number of individual oaks, all produced by an energy which manifests itself in an organic process of assimilation and
elimination, in which appear the stadia of acorn,
sapling, tree, and crop of acorns—a continuous circle
of reproduction of the species oak, a transformation
of the one into the many—the one acorn becoming
a crop of acorns, and then a forest of oaks. It is the
energy, of course, that is the universal. It is not
a conscious thought in the sense of being a special
or abstract object of consciousness. But it is a part
of the unity of the conceived object, and we may find
it by analysis.

§ 131. We have already noted at several points in our progress the mistake of the psychological theory which thinks that universal terms are derived from particulars by abstraction. In Chapter XI it has been shown that the third figure of the syllogism discriminates subclasses, dividing the vague and general class which experience brings with it by a more minute observation. The fixing of the first object that the mind perceives is, of course, very inadequate. The object is empty and vague because the infant has no previous experience with which to apperceive or interpret the first sense-impressions of his new life. Differences of light and shade, of agreeable and disagreeable taste, of heat and cold, of pleasant and unpleasant movements, of soft and loud tones and noises, successively impress his senses, and he gradually parts his general or common sense into special senses, and after a time locates them in parts of his body and comes to know his body from its environment. His first general categories are existence and non-existence, and are divided into subcategories, something and something else, and change. This is on the surface of his intellect; but deep down are the vital instincts which are as unconscious as those of the plant. As consciousness awakes, it finds the self engaged in processes of spontaneous action, which are not guided by intellect or will. The plant life, the life of nutrition, is the basis of the animal life of feeling and instinct which has arisen. The infant gradually conquers this first life by a higher form of self-activity—higher because more nearly conscious and individual. He becomes conscious of his feelings, and gradually discriminates the products of his five senses, and later on can distinguish his body from the environment, and still later divides the latter into things and self-moving beings, persons, animals, plants, and inanimate beings. It is a descent from vague general categories to more specific ones by division, his analysis taking the form of the third figure. At first, one category does for the whole of his experience— *is* and *is not*.

§ 132. Concepts do not arise, however, until the infant mind has attained the power of comparing its recollection with the reality, and has transferred its thought of itself as maker of particular representations to the object as a particular example of a hidden producing generic cause. Each thing is then seen as one specimen out of an infinite number of possible specimens produced by the objective cause. Language becomes possible only on this condition. The object must be dislodged from its solidarity with Nature and made to stand out as a product distinguishable from its causal genesis.   Everything has a causal genesis, it will be admitted.   This act of separation individualizes or personifies in the infant mind, and he forms a concept every time he has a percept, and unites them by the second figure of the syllogism, identifying the particular with a class by some mark of class production.   A dog is thus identified as a cat from its resemblance to the already familiar animal; or, *vice versa*, if the dog is a familiar object, the new object, cat, is identified with dog.   Objects are identified in a class by the concept, which is an idea below the threshold of consciousness equivalent to *the-cause-that-produces-this-kind-of-appearances*.

"My little grandchild Florence was held in my arms asleep.   A distant locomotive sounded its whistle like a trumpet as it approached the town.   She aroused herself, and said softly, 'Tow' (for *cow*).   She had come from a ranch in the distant West and was familiar with the lowing of cows.   Hence she interpreted the particular of sense—the sound which came to her ear—as produced by a cow."

§ 133. The human characteristic is the knowing by universals.   Man recognises or sees all objects as specimens of classes.   He sees the particular in the universal.   Hence his act of cognition is more complex than that of mere sense-perception, which he shares with the animal.   Note that the sense-perception which sees classes as the background on which the particular is imaged implies self-consciousness. The soul has perceived itself as a free producing cause in the act of recollection, and it transfers unconsciously this idea of itself to the object, and now perceives with concepts.

§ 134. The rise of self-consciousness, or the perception of self-activity, and the perception of the general object in the external world, are thus contemporaneous. With the perception of the general energy the psychological activity has outgrown *representation* and become *conception*. With conception the energy or soul begins to be an individuality for itself—a conscious individuality. It recognises itself as a free energy. The stage of mere perception does not recognise itself, but merely sees its own energy as the objective energy, because its acts are entirely occasioned by the external object. In the recognition of the object as an individual of a class the soul recognises its own freedom and independent activity. Recollection (*Erinnerung*) relates to individuals, recalling the special presentation or impression, and representing the object as it was before perceived. Memory (like the German word *Gedächtniss*) may be distinguished as the activity which reproduces the object as one of a class, and therefore as the form of representation that perceives universals. With memory arises language.

§ 135. Imagination and fancy, or fantasy, are like recollection, free in the sense that they depend on the self. But they are freer than recollection, because they are not tethered to real events or things that belong to a past experience. They determine forms, shapes, situations, and actions entirely ideal, and without reference to actual existences, except in so far as the general laws of space and time, which logically condition fancies, as well as existences, demand. The freedom of imagination is therefore seemingly more perfect than that of recollection, or even memory. It is, however, only the abstract freedom as compared with the true freedom of ethical thought and action, as we shall see later on.

CHAPTER XXVI.

Language as the Distinguishing Characteristic of the Human Being.

§ 136. LANGUAGE fixes the knowledge of objects in universals. Each word represents an indefinite number of particular objects, actions, or relations. The word *oak* stands for all oaks—present, past, or future. No being can use language, much less create language, unless it has learned to conceive as well as perceive—learned to see all objects as individuals belonging to classes, and incidentally recognised its own individuality. All human beings possess language. Even deaf and dumb human beings invent and use gestures with as definite meaning as words, each gesture denoting a class with a possible infinite number of special applications.

Language is the means of distinguishing between the brute and the human—between the animal soul, which has continuity only in the species (which pervades its being in the form of *instinct*), and the *human* soul, which is immortal, and possessed of a capacity to be educated. There is no language until the mind can perceive general types of existence; mere proper names or mere exclamations or cries do not constitute language. All words that belong to language are significative—they " *express* " or " *mean* " something; hence they are conventional symbols, and not mere individual designations. Language arises

only through common consent, and is not an invention of
one individual. It is a product of individuals acting together as a community, and hence its use implies the ascent
of the individual into the species. By this expression is
meant that the individual in his particularity becomes conscious of his ego as producing cause—as self-active—hence
the individual recognises himself as a universal or species,
in recognising himself as an independent, original cause
of his acts and deeds, his thoughts, his feelings; for his
feelings are his reactions against alien being. He is the
common term to all his variety, and hence in this sense
species as well as individual. Unless an individual could
ascend into the species, he could not *understand* language. To know words and their meaning is an activity
of divine significance; it denotes the formation of universals in the mind—the ascent above the here and now
of the senses, and above the representation of mere images,
to the activity which grasps together the general conception of objects, and thus reaches beyond what is transient
and variable. Doubtless the nobler species of animals possess not only sense-perception, but a considerable degree
of the power of representation. They are not only able
to recollect, but to imagine or fancy to some extent, as
is evidenced by their dreams. But that animals do not
generalize sufficiently to form for themselves a new objective world of types and general concepts, we have a
sufficient evidence in the fact that they do not use words,
or invent conventional symbols. With the activity of the
symbol-making form of representation, which we have
named Memory, and whose evidence is the invention and
use of language, the true form of individuality is attained,
and each individual human being, as mind, may be said
to be the entire species. Inasmuch as he can form universals in his mind, he can realize the most abstract
thought, and he is conscious. Consciousness begins when
one can seize the pure universal in the presence of immediate objects here and now. The sense-perception of
the mere animal, therefore, differs from that of the human
being in this: The human being knows himself as sub-

ject that sees the object, while the animal sees the object,
but does not separate himself, as universal, from the special act of seeing. To know that I am I is to know the ego,
the most general of objects, and to carry out abstraction to
its very last degree, for what is of a higher degree of gen-
erality than the ego as determiner of itself, as subject
but not yet as object? It is the power to become any or
all thoughts, feelings, and volitions, but as subject it is
not any one of these as yet. And yet this is what all
human beings know, young or old, savage or civilized. The
savage invents and uses language—an act of the species,
but which the species can not do, without the participation
of the individual. It should be carefully noted that this
activity of generalization which produces language, and
distinguishes the human from the brute, is not the generalization of the activity of thought, so called. It is the
preparation for thought. These general types of things
are the things which thought deals with. Thought does
not deal with mere immediate objects of the senses; it
deals rather with the objects which are indicated by
words—i. e., general objects. Some writers would have us
suppose that we do not arrive at general notions except
by the process of classification and abstraction, in the
mechanical manner that they lay down for this purpose.
The fact is, that the mind has arrived at these general
ideas in the process of learning language. In infancy,
most children have learned such words as *is, existence,
being, nothing, motion, cause, change, I, you, he*, etc. They
do not contain all the experience that they will contain
late in life, but they are already used as general terms.
At the very beginning the child uses the third figure of
the syllogism in each discrimination of a difference, and
makes a definition of the new type which will include
an infinite number of examples if they can be furnished.
The definition will also do equally well for the one specimen under observation, if there are no more.

§ 137. Language is therefore the sign by which
we can recognise the arrival of the soul at this stage

of development on the way to complete self-activity. Hence language is the evidence of immortal individuality. In order to use language, it must be able not only to act for itself, but to act wholly upon itself. It must not only perceive things by the senses, but accompany its perceiving by an inner perception of the act of perceiving (and thus be its own environment). This perception of the act and process of perceiving is, as has been shown, the recognition of classes, species, and genera—the universal processes underlying the existence of the particular.

§ 138. Language in this sense involves conventional signs, and hence, as has been remarked above, is not an immediate expression of feeling, like the cries of animals. The immediate expression of feeling (which is only a reaction) does not become language, even when it accompanies recollection or free reproduction—nor until it accompanies memory and conception or the seeing of the particular in the general. When it can be shown that a species of animals use conventional signs in communication one with another, we shall be able to infer their immortality, because we shall have evidence of their freedom from sense-perception and environment sufficient to create for themselves their own occasion for activity. They would then be shown to react not merely against their

environment, but against their own action; hence
they would involve both action and reaction, self and
environment within each self. They would in that
case have selves, and their selves exist for themselves,
and hence they would have self-identity.

Take away self-identity, and still there may be persistence of self-activity; but it is only generic—that of the
species and not of the individual. The species lives, the
individual dies in such cases. If the same individual lived
on in another life, it would only be unconscious transmigration. The animal soul could not remember its former
life, because it did not know itself in the form of moral
feeling. It did not reach a sense of moral responsibility,
and hence did not feel itself as an independent cause,
originating changes in the world.

§ 139. These distinctions of self-activity or of
spontaneous energy which have been pointed out in
the stages of nutrition, feeling, sense-perception, and
recollection are often overlooked, or are accounted
as the direct product of the environment, and not
admitted as the reactions of individual energy. The
science that ignores the manifestation of energy in
the reaction of the individual assumes that all the
energy is in the environment, although the obvious
fact is that there is energy on each side—on that of
the individual and on that of the environment.

§ 140. In these lower stages of the activity of
individual energy we have individuality that can not

recognise itself because it can not recognise the universal, and therefore can not conceive of pure causal activity, but identifies it with special manifestation. Hence (as implied in § 137) the permanence of such individuality would not be the continuance of individuality in the sense of immortality any more than a perpetual sleep would continue it.

Even memory and the phenomena of language are not recognised by psychologists generally as being manifestations of the self-conscious individuality. Psychology, however, readily recognises the advent of universal ideas in the activity of reflection, and notes the self-activity of mind in forming such ideas and thinking with them. We have already noticed more than once that it is usual to account for the production of these universal ideas by supposing that the mind first collects many individuals and then abstracts so as to omit the differences and preserve the likeness or resemblance, and thus form the conception of class. It therefore makes reflection responsible not only for the recognition of the universal, but for its creation. But the act of reflection only discovers what had already been elaborated in the lower faculty of the mind. Besides, the mind does not first seize differences; it does not begin with the particular in all its particularity, but only with the identity, the likeness of each to everything else, and it admits differences only as they are forced on it; it descends from vague and shallow general ideas by experience to accurate and fully determinate ideas. Self-consciousness is not the cause of universal ideas, but the universal rises with the rise of self-consciousness as its condition (the perception of the universal being a perception of the self as producer behind the objects). Both appear at the same time as essential phases of the same act. The soul uses universals in lan-

16

guage long before it recognises the same as universal (its first recognition of the universal being only self-recognition). Reflection discovers that these ideas are general, but it has used them ever since human beings became human.

§ 141. Why do we hold individual immortality to begin with the perception of universals and of self-identity rather than with individual reaction in the plant, or in that of self-feeling in the animal, or rather with that of free self-activity in recollection? This question has been partly discussed already (§§ 137, 140), but its importance demands all the light that can be thrown on it from different points of reflection. Undoubtedly there is individuality wherever there is reaction. But mere reaction is not sufficient to constitute personal identity. The activity in reaction arises on account of the activity of another being, and hence is not entirely the activity of itself in the case of the plant or the nutritive form of life, or in that of the mere animal or the feeling and locomotive being. Were such individuality to be imperishable, it would be unconscious imperishability and devoid of memory that recognises its own being in the present and in the past. Mere recollection is not the recognition of the being of the self. A self must be universal, the unity of all its phases, and can in no wise be a mere particular thing or act such as can be recollected. The self is the principle of the process of reaction against the environment and of the activity of reproduction and synthesis.

§ 142. The individual, therefore, is not only a self—a universal—but also an entire sphere of particularity. The self can generate by the reproductive activity all that it has seen and heard, all that it has experienced, reproducing it as often as it pleases and entirely free from the presence of the objects perceived, and it can generate from itself the ideas of the general processes in which originated the special facts of sense-perception. Hence its particulars may be and in such cases are also general. Such a stage we call Memory, in the special and higher sense of the word, as corresponding to Plato's ἀνάμνησις—not the German meaning of *Erinnerung,* but of *Gedächtniss* —not the memory that recollects, but the memory that recalls by the aid of universal ideas and conventional signs. (Such memory is creative, as it goes from the general to the particular.) These general ideas are mnemonic aids—pigeon-holes, as it were, in the mind—whereby the soul conquers the endless multiplicity of details in the world. It refers each fact or event to its species, and saves the species under a name—then is able to recall by the name a vast number of special instances.

Hegel, in his Psychology (complete works, vol. vii, § 461), makes much of this distinction between recollection and memory by means of words and other signs as a very important step in the emancipation of the soul from the bonds of Nature. He shows the significance of names as making possible the higher stage of the soul, the thinking intellect.

CHAPTER XXVII.

Thinking as the Activity of the Understanding, including " Common Sense " and Reflection.

§ 143. In Chapter IV we have already discussed the three stages of thought. The first of these is entirely unaware of the mutual dependence of the things of the world, and supposes them all to be self-existent, without essential relations to their environments. This is called "common sense" when it begins to think metaphysically. It seems very clear to its mind that a thing either is or is not; that if it is, it makes no difference to its existence whether other things are or are not. " This tree, this stone, this piece of ice would continue to exist if you blotted out all the rest of existence." It holds that mere relativity, mere phenomenal being, is unthinkable and contrary to reason. For how can being be itself and at the same time dependent on another? Can an existence be in and through another? It carries the images of things of sense into metaphysics without the slightest misgivings of their absolute validity everywhere. Being is being, and there is no confusion of being and non-being to be tolerated. The principle of contradiction is taken in a superficial meaning: " a thing can not be and not be at the same time "; for, taken superficially, this would deny essential dependence. A depends on B in such a way that the being of B is the being of A. B is the noumenon, or essential being, and A is the phenomenon, or derivative being. The argument against motion or change rests on this superficial (and superstitious) application of the principle of contradiction: " a thing can not move where it is, and of course it can not move where it is not; hence it can not move at all." " A thing either is in one condition or another; if it is in any one condition, it is not changing, nor likewise if it is already in another; therefore a thing can not change." " A being either is or is not; if it already is, it is not becoming, and if it is not, there is likewise no becoming; hence there can be no becoming." In the same way consciousness can be proved impossible, for common sense can not think such a thing as a self that is subject and at the same time object to itself. (See Herbert Spencer's First Principles, 1864 edi-

tion, pages 63–65.) " The mental act in which self
is known implies, like every other mental act, a perceiving subject and a perceived object. If, then, the
object perceived is self, what is the subject that perceives? or if it is the true self which thinks, what
other self can it be that is thought of? Clearly, a
true cognition of self implies a state in which the
knowing and the known are one—in which subject
and object are identified—and this Mr. Mansell rightly holds to be the annihilation of both."

§ 144. In the discussion of Memory and Conception (Chapters XXIV and XXV) we have seen that
human sense-perception sees each object in its universal, and looks upon it as one of an indefinite number of examples of the class. There hovers in the
background an idea of a formative energy or process
by which the particular object has arisen: if it is a
pine tree, the pine-making energy made it; if it is a
table, the table-making energy, howsoever incarnated
in cabinetmakers, woodsmen, sawmill labourers, de-
signers that planned the form and size, human society that wanted the table and set to work the special
workmen that made it. Always back of the object
is projected a complex unity of energy that created
it and others of the kind, potentially or really. In
other words, a double order of existences is presup-

posed: first, the immediate, reached by the senses; and, secondly, a higher order of existence, a productive energy. Of this second order presupposed, the first stage of the understanding (or common sense) is not conscious. Hence it takes its particular beings, as if they were only particular and not indivisibly attached to a higher order, the generic energies that produce and shape the particulars of sense.

§ 145. On trying to think metaphysically, common sense, therefore, figures to itself an abstract world of individual beings, each one self-existent, an atomic world, in short. For it has never noticed that its perception is connected with concepts, that it perceives each and every object as a result of a process and thereby knows it in its class rather than as a unique individual.

§ 146. All that is necessary to refute this empty stage of thought is the discovery of essential relations—*relations of dependence*. Some of these are already known to common sense, but the fact has not attracted its distinct attention. It has not realized what they involve. Show that sense-objects are dependent on others, and that relativity is their essential condition, and common sense awakens to a deeper thought—that of phenomenal being as opposed to noumenal being. It sees that the principle of con-

tradiction does not strictly apply to sense-objects or
dependent beings, or to things that change or *become;*
for all such beings are only partial, and not entire
beings; they are not wholes or totalities. To make
them total, we must think them together with their
producing energies, and then the principle of contradiction will be true if applied to them. I call this
higher stage of the understanding *reflection,* to indicate a deeper and more conscious knowing than mere
" common sense."

As a human process, the knowing is always a knowing
by universals—a re-cognition, and not simple apprehension, such as the animals or other beings have that do
not use language. It is always apperception. The process
of development of stages of thought begins with *sensuous
ideas,* which perceive mere individual, concrete, real objects,
if common sense is correct in its views. In conceiving these,
it uses language and thinks general ideas, but it does not
notice this fact, nor is it conscious of the relations involved
in such objects. This is the first stage of the understanding. The world exists for it as an innumerable congeries
of things, each one independent of the other, and possessing self-existence. It is the standpoint from which atomism would be adopted as the philosophic system. Ask it
what the ultimate principle of existence is, and it would
reply, " Atoms." But this view of the world is an unstable one, and requires very little reflection to overturn
it, and bring one to the next basis—that of *abstract ideas,*
or ideas of what is only partially realized in itself and is
partly in and through another. When the mind looks carefully at the world of things, it finds that there are dependence and interdependence. Each object is related to something else, and changes when that changes. Each object

is a part of a process that is going on. The process produced it, and the process will destroy it—nay, it is destroying the object of our sense-perception by changing it now, while we look at it. We find, therefore, that things are not the true beings which we thought them to be, but processes are the reality. Science takes this attitude without being fully aware of it, especially when its disciples are in the " common-sense " stage of thought, and studies out the history of each thing in its rise and its disappearance, and it calls this history the truth. This stage of thinking does not believe in *atoms* or in *things;* it believes in *forces* and *processes*—called "abstract ideas " because they are negative, and can not be seen by the senses. This is the dynamic standpoint in philosophy. Reflection (the name we give to the second and mature stage of the understanding) knows that these abstract ideas possess more truth, more reality, than the " things " of sense-perception; the force is more real than the thing, because it outlasts a thing—it causes things to originate, to change, and disappear.

§ 147. This stage of reflection, with its doctrine of abstract ideas, or of negative powers or forces, finally becomes convinced of the essential unity of all processes and of all forces; it sets up the doctrine of the *correlation of forces,* and believes that persistent force is the ultimate truth, the fundamental reality of the world. This we may call a *concrete idea,* for it sets up a principle which is the origin of all things and forces, and also the destroyer of them all, and hence more real, more concrete, than the world of things and forces; and because this idea, when carefully thought out, proves to be the idea of self-determination—self-activity. Persistent force, as taught us by the scientific men of our day, is the sole ultimate principle, and as such it gives rise to all existence by its self-activity, for there is nothing else for it to act upon. It causes all origins, all changes, and all evanescence. It gives rise to the particular forces—heat, light, electricity, magnetism, etc.—which in their turn cause the evanescent forms which sense-perception sees as " things."

We have described three phases:

I. Sensuous Ideas perceive " things."

II. Abstract Ideas perceive " forces."

III. Concrete Idea perceives " persistent force."

IV. There is one step higher—namely, the Absolute Idea, which is perceived by the reason as self-determined (see Chapter XXVIII).

In this progress from one phase to another, the understanding advances to a deeper and truer reality at each step. Plato and Aristotle call this stage of thinking, which includes under it I, II, III of the above, the διάνοια; its name was " discursive intellect " at one time.

Hume, in his famous sketch of the Human Understanding (Book I, Part I, of his Treatise of Human Nature), makes all the perceptions of the human mind resolve themselves into two distinct kinds: *impressions* and *ideas.* " The difference between them consists in the degrees of force and liveliness with which they strike upon the mind, and make their way into our thought and consciousness. Those perceptions which enter with the most force and violence we may name *impressions*, and under this name include all our sensations, passions, and emotions, as they make their first appearance in the soul. By *ideas*, I mean the faint images of these in thinking and reasoning." In his maturer work, which he desired to take the place of his earlier Treatise on Human Nature, Hume divides ": all the perceptions of the mind into two classes or species, which are distinguished by their different degrees of force and vivacity. The less forcible and lively are commonly denominated *thoughts* and *ideas*. The other species, . . . let us call *impressions*, . . . by which I mean all our more lively perceptions when we hear, or see, or feel, or love, or hate, or desire, or will " (An Enquiry Concerning Human Understanding, section 2). "The identity which we ascribe to the mind of man is only a fictitious one " (Treatise, etc., Book I, Part IV, section 6). "What we call a mind is nothing but a heap or collection of different perceptions, united together by certain relations, and supposed, though falsely, to be endowed with perfect simplicity and identity " (Book I, Part IV, section 2). He builds the higher faculties on the lower, and assumes the superior truthfulness of what he calls "impressions." It is the *reductio ad absurdum* of the philosophy of Locke. The second or third stage of reflection, if consistent, would not admit the reality to be the object of sense-impressions, and the abstract ideas to be only "faint images." One who holds, like Herbert Spencer, that persistent force is the ultimate reality—"the sole truth, which transcends experience by underlying it "—ought to hold that the generalization which reaches the idea of unity of force is the truest and most adequate of thoughts. Herbert Spencer is therefore inconsistent when he holds substantially the doctrine of Hume, in the words: "We must predicate nothing of objects too great or too multitudinous to be mentally represented, or we must make our predications by means of extremely inadequate representations of such

objects—mere symbols of them" (page 27 of First Principles).

§ 148. The understanding, therefore, has two
phases, the earlier one being naïve and dogmatical,
and the later one " enlightened " and sceptical. The
so-called " rationalism " belongs to this second stage.
While the first looks upon the sense-world as composed of real, independent beings, co-ordinate with
man and God, the second looks upon all sensuous
things, all existence in time and space, as phenomenal,
as only the *show* of true being. The persistent force
is the noumenon of which all changes of matter and
all the transmutations of force are the manifestation
or phenomenon. There are many names besides " persistent force " for this noumenon; indeed, that cf
force is not a suitable designation, for the reason that
force implies an existent opposite; for there can be
no force except in a state of tension, although the cor-
relationists have not perceived this.

§ 149. The understanding in both of its stages
holds to the finite. In the first stage it mistakes the
phenomenal for the noumenal, taking perishable
things for imperishable; the second stage mistaking
the noumenal for the phenomenal, and taking even
the absolute for the relative. We have called the
former *common sense,* and the latter *reflection.* Re-

flection makes all things *relative;* we never get beyond the dependent and relative. The objects which we perceive by the senses are things, and all of them in a process of origination, change, and decay—all proceeding from the influence of the environment—from a beyond through the action of forces. If we go back of one of these, we come not to an absolute source, but only to a relative source—another thing as relative as the first. It is an infinite regress; we never come to the ultimate source. Reflection finds, therefore, no adequate source, but only a *transmitting link* of the causality beyond. This stage of thinking seems to be an ultimate and final one, but only because the mind figures to itself a world of separate things and forces beyond the object, a multitude that must be seized one after the other, and whose inventory can never be completed. The understanding supposes that it must approach the world of true being through the world of particulars from which it starts in its first stage—that of common sense. But this is not the case, as it soon sees when it begins to consider the results and the presuppositions of *reflection,* its second stage.

§ 150. Take the results of reflection: all the objects of the senses are relative. They are transitory, and have originated in the past from other, different

beings—in an endless series. They are changing
while we behold them, and passing on into other
beings—in an endless series. Each one is a manifestation of some phase of an essence that reveals itself
not in each, nor in any one of them, but only in the
entire series. Each is therefore not the whole of
itself, but only a fragmentary realization of its true
self, the essence that reveals itself only in the entire
series.

§ 151. Take the presuppositions of reflection:
The fact that the series of relative beings must proceed to the infinite, means that no term in the series
can possibly be anything but relative; no one of
them can be an original source of energy; no one of
them can be self-determined or self-active; for a
self-active being would be an original source of movement and formation, and that would end the series.
It follows that reflection presupposes the source as
entirely outside the series and distinct from it. The
source is different from and alien to the members of
the series. It produces them all, and causes also their
transmutation from one into another. It is a force,
but not a thing. It is not even a particular force,
but only the origin of the series of forces. It is regarded as a negative unity. A *negative unity* is that
which produces and destroys a series of results, being,

in itself, outside of and beyond the series in such a manner that the series can arise and pass away without involving any reaction or effect upon the negative unity. Such a *negative unity* is therefore *transcendent*, or existent apart from the series of things and forces of which it is the negative unity.

The East Indian thinking, particularly in the Sankya and Vedanta systems, conceives in the clearest manner this negative unity as transcendent, as above and beyond the series of beings in the world. It is not a creator even, for that would involve a transfer of true being to the world. The world is therefore a complete illusion, and is not even a manifestation or phenomenon; it is not the revelation or even the appearance of the negative unity or Brahma. When the night of Brahma comes, all particular existences, even the highest gods, are totally absorbed into him, and lose their being utterly. There is no description to be given of the negative unity except that it is indifferent to all that is finite. It has no quality, no quantity, no attributes of any kind. It is the simple negation of all that exists or can exist. For if we take away all limitation, all determinations, all special attributes, we have the utter denial of all existence. The absolute negative unity neither exists for anything else nor for itself; it is utterly distinctionless. It is the same as pure nothing. To this idea reflection mounts in its search for the explanation of relative beings. The abyss of nothingness discovered in an absolute negative unity has been mistaken for an unknown and unknowable object. But this is an inadvertence of reflection which knows full well all that there is in the negative unity—namely, perfect emptiness and vacuity. For if there is any causality, any creative power, even this gives existence and a series of particulars as the revelation or manifestation of its causal energy.

§ 152. The understanding as reflection arrives at a clearing up; the Germans call it an *Aufklärung*. It discounts the entire world of experience, the totality of human learning. All is a knowledge of phenomena, of vanity rather than of true being. The understanding feels a pride in its achievements; for it annuls not only the results of its sense-perception, but also of its moral and religious intuitions. The contents of the ethical world are a series of relations, and so, too, are those of the religious world—distinctions purporting to relate to the divine. The reflecting understanding sees that all distinctions belong to the world of phenomena, and not to the transcendent negative unity. Hence religion does not conceive in its idea of God any ultimate being. It is only an anthropomorphic concept. Hence agnosticism or atheism is the inevitable conclusion.

In the French Revolution and the epoch preceding it we have *the* Aufklärung *par excellence*. All ideas of the divine were attacked and all institutions of man were assaulted. Every attempt to reach a deeper foundation on which the state and the Church could be built more securely was destined to failure. The lowest depth was reached in the Reign of Terror, when each citizen became suspicious of every other. When no one can trust his fellow, death is the only remedy; one must destroy his neighbour, and society as a whole must commit suicide. But the mind when it first comes to this insight into the presupposition of the absolute relativity theory feels the exhilaration of free thinking—i. e., of thinking that can reach a transcendent principle above all experience. Herbert Spencer begins his book on First Principles with a presentation of the doctrine of the Unknowable, resting it on this insight into a negative unity beyond phenomena, or found to be the persistent force in which phenomena lose their individual being just as the particular waves sink to rest and obliteration in the surface of the sea. Spinoza reached this insight, and stated it in his doctrine of Substance. All being is lost in the empty substance conceived as the negative unity. The Sophists in Greece felt the same exhilaration as the emancipated freethinkers of the French Revolution. They had learned to think away all fixed beliefs and to annihilate in their arguments all certainty of being. Hence any moral or religious ideas could be overthrown by showing that they presupposed the certainty of objective being. The Eleatic philosophy, like Spinozism, reaches a negative unity— pure being, empty and passive; transcendent of the world of multiplicity. Plato it is who turns the current of human thinking, and by a more careful inventory of the presuppositions of reflection discovers the positive doctrine of the negative unity; for he sees that the negative unity is not the complete thought of the ultimate or absolute, but only the half thought of it. The ultimate principle is self-determination, and not simply determinationlessness. There could be no negative unity as a higher reality above phenomenon, or time and space illusions, unless it were a self-related negative. Unless it were a self-determined being it could not be, for a mere negation of phenomena would be, as above stated, a mere nothing.

§ 152. The insight into the negative unity is the highest reach of the understanding, and this is the insight into its own futility and the illusion lying at the bottom of all experience. The entire world of experience is merely relative and phenomenal being,

17

and all that the understanding can know is relative and transitory. It knows that the true being is the annulment of the entire world of experience. But with the aid of Plato's thought it now investigates this negative unity and finds that it, too, is a result, and not something primordial. It is only a phase of self-determined being. With the arrival at the idea of self-determined being we have left the understanding and arrived at reason, which knows the total and interprets all things in the light of the total.

CHAPTER XXVIII.

The Reason.

§ 153. THE stages of the understanding, which we have named respectively *common sense* and *reflection*, have been characterized by the views of the world which they presuppose. One's view of the world determines his knowing in all its details, strange and improbable as this may at first seem. Common sense assumes that experience has before it a world of complete individual things which either are or are not, and do not exist in a state of becoming or change, nor depend essentially upon one another. This assumption is not true, and common sense is therefore an incorrect species of knowing. It colours every judgment that it makes and every observation that it records with this false use of the principle of contradiction. Reflection, or the second stage of the understanding, assumes the falsity of the standpoint of common sense. It assumes that all immediate objects in our world of experience are in a state of becoming, or genesis and decay. Moreover, it conceives true being as a negative unity which is devoid of the multiplex distinctions that characterize the particular things and forces of experience. But its negative unity, being conceived as by itself and not in correlation with the particular forces and things which vanish in it, is a totality by itself, and hence self-existent. If it has no determinations, marks, or attributes, and does not receive them from anything else or originate them within itself, it is a nothing; for it has no distinctions within it or on it whereby it can be discriminated or can discriminate itself from nothing. And yet the highest thought of the understanding has traced all the existences of the world of experience into that negative unity as the ultimate source. Unless, therefore, the Absolute is cause of these determinations of the world of experience, as well as their destroyer, they can not have arisen at all, and

the work of the understanding, which everywhere has
to assume the distinctions (things and forces) of the
world as its subject-matter, is at once rendered a
nullity in all its stages. Hence the same premises and
the same course of reasoning which reflection uses to
establish the doctrine of persistent force, Spinozan substance, Eleatic being, East Indian Brahma, or whatever form the pantheistic doctrine of negative unity
takes, establish just as well and with the same logical
clearness a creative or self-determining unity. Self-
determining unity must be the basis of negative unity,
its logical condition.

§ 154. A self-active unity is therefore presupposed to make the negative unity of pantheism possible. Self-activity is negative unity in one phase—
namely, the self as subject of the act—the determiner
that determines itself—is as such undetermined. It
is passive only as determined—as the object, but not
as subject. Now, as subject it is entirely without
what we have called (in § 153) the determinations
of the world of experience; it is wholly transcendent. But as determined it is passive and multiple,
like the objects of experience. It contains, then, both
the factors with which the reflective understanding
deals; it contains the negative unity as the subject
considered apart from the object, the determiner as

apart from its determinations. The understanding makes only a regressive movement; it traces up the determinations to the determiner on which they depend, and finds it to be a negative unity, instead of an originating cause or determiner.

§ 155. The understanding arrives at a negative unity, which, if properly comprehended, is an original, spontaneous cause—a *causa sui*. This is self-activity. The analysis of self-activity finds self as subject and self as object; self as determiner and self as determined. The negative unity is the end of analysis, and as *causa sui* it is the beginning of synthesis; for a self-activity determines itself and produces distinctions within itself. It externalizes or makes itself objective. The understanding is a process of analysis, while reason begins with synthesis. The understanding explains by neglecting or annulling the determinations of the world of experience, while the reason explains by showing the objectivating of the determinations of the Absolute Self. All is a process of revelation of the divine.

§ 156. Memory and concept-forming activity convert the results of sense-perception into general terms. Their presupposition is that every object is one of a class that the object-making process has made, or will make, or might make. The understanding devotes its attention to the discovery of the concrete terms in which these generic processes are expressed. While the concept-forming activity merely asserts the existence of such generic process as the explanation of the object without examining what it is, persistently affirming each object to belong to a class and to be only one specimen out of many similar objects produced by the objective causal process, the understanding, on the other hand, ascertains the particulars and mode of action of the object-forming processes of the world. It ascertains the warp and the woof of human experience. In finding the relations which each object has to every other, it learns the forms of production, and becomes a real knowing of the energies that produce the classes that language expresses and memory retains.

The child asks for the name of each new object. To the superficial observer he seems to have a superstitious reverence for mere names; for he seems to be perfectly satisfied when he learns the name. But to the psychologist the name-learning process has significance as the manifestation of the concept-forming stage of the mind—the distinctively human stage. These names are empty bags, which will hold all the experience of after-life that will cluster round the class of objects named. The name will give unity to that thread of experience and observation. "What is this?" Answer, "An acorn." The word acorn will tie together, or hold like a bag or a pigeon-hole, all the perceptions and reflections that relate to the genesis of oak trees, their doings and relations to the rest of the world. Hence language is the basis of memory properly so called, for it aids memory by giving it the inestimable gift of classification. It enables it to divide and conquer. Memory aided by language can re-enforce its recollection by the causal insight added to each object—viz., that it is the result of a process that has made it, and is one of a class having the same characteristics because made by the same method of action. It can deduce from the cause or process, as well as recall its sense-impressions.

§ 157. The understanding in both its forms (common sense and reflection) presupposes the concept stage already attained. Each object is one of a class. Common sense has a firm conviction that each object is an independent whole, because it unconsciously adds to the object its universal process; for that addition does make it whole, but a whole as species though not as particular sense-object. The seeing of the particular in its process or its universal makes it an individual, and the thought that thinks this is common sense. But reflection follows next, and necessarily; for the activity of the mind, which sets up each object as a class or a cycle of objects, will begin to analyze and discover the relations of the object to its environment—not merely its environment in space, but in time—its antecedents and consequents—its origin and its destiny; how it has proceeded from the object-making cause, and where it will vanish in other stages of the causal process. The understanding, therefore, in both its phases depends on language, and language is the product of the phantasy in its several shapes of recollection, memory, and imagination joined to the concept-forming activity.

Sense-ideas through which common sense looks upon the world as a world of independent objects do not cognize the world truly. The next step, abstract ideas, cognizes the world as a process of forces, and " things " are seen to be mere temporary equilibria in the interaction of forces; " each thing is a bundle of forces." But the concrete idea of the persistent force sees a deeper and more permanent reality underlying particular forces. It is one ultimate force. In it all multiplicity of existences has vanished, and yet it is the source of all particular existence. This view of the world, on the standpoint of concrete idea, is pantheistic. It makes out a one supreme principle which originates and destroys all particular existences, all finite beings. We have already intimated above that it is the standpoint of Orientalism, or of the Asiatic thought. Buddhism and Brahmanism have reached it, and not transcended it. It is a necessary stage of unfolding in the mind, just as much as the standpoint of the first stage of the understanding, which regards the world as composed of a multiplicity of independent things; or the standpoint of the second stage of the understanding, that of reflection, which looks upon the world as a collection of relative existences in a state of process.

§ 158. The final standpoint of the intellect is that in which it perceives the highest principle to be a self-determining or self-active Being, self-conscious, and creator of a world which manifests him. A logical investigation of the principle of " persistent force " would prove that this principle of Personal Being is presupposed as its true form. Since the "persistent force" is the sole and ultimate reality, it originates all other reality only by self-activity, and thus is self-determined. But such a persistent force is possible only in the form of personality. Self-determination implies self-consciousness and personality as the true form of its existence.

These four forms of thinking, which we have arbitrarily called *sensuous*, *abstract*, *concrete*, and *absolute* ideas, correspond to four views of the world: (1) As a congeries of independent things; (2) as a play of forces; (3) as the evanescent appearance of a negative essential power; (4) as the creation of a Personal Creator, who makes it the theatre of the development of conscious beings in his image. Each step upward arrives at a more adequate idea of the true reality. *Force* is more real than *thing;* persistent force than particular forces; Absolute Person is more real than the force or forces which he creates. The fourth stage we name Reason; the others belong to the understanding. This final form of thinking is the only form which is consistent with a true theory of education. Each individual should ascend by education into participation—*conscious* participation—in the life of the species. Institutions—family, society, state, Church—all are instrumentalities by which the humble individual may avail himself of the help of the race, and live over in himself its life. The highest stage of thinking is the stage of insight. It sees the world as explained by the principle of Absolute Person. It finds the world of institutions a world in harmony with such a principle.

CHAPTER XXIX.

A Review of the Psychology of the Intellect.

§ 159. IT will have been noticed by the attentive reader that in the foregoing sketch of the systematic exposition of the intellectual activities there has been constant return to the beginning; there has been repetition and again repetition. Some readers will have seen that each repetition presents the subject in some new light, and aids to form an all-round view of the subject. On each new, higher level the region that has been traversed takes on new aspects. But the most important reason for so much repetition is the fact that each step is to be followed by many results. After expounding one line of result, it becomes necessary to expound another, and hence a new statement of the first step must be made and its connection with the second line of result exhibited. Another and another line of result follows. Each new restatement throws, or should throw, a new light on the method of procedure; for a system is a method applied in such a way as to unfold a progressive realization of a principle. Self-activity is the principle of psychology. It is a principle that contains a progress implied in it. For, let us presuppose an activity, it will produce something and will reveal a method or form of acting. Hence after setting up self-activity we are bound to see what it will do; thus the principle becomes method. Next, if the method is continued, it will grow to a system which is a more complete revelation of the principle and method than could have been seen at the beginning. A system makes each step or stage throw light on each preceding and each subsequent step. The plant's activity of assimilation throws light on the animal's activity of feeling; for feeling is the activity of assimilation without food to act upon; it is a going through of the activity with itself for its food. Each higher activity acts upon the form (but not on the content) of the lower. Each higher result is as form again the content of a still higher form. Hegel claims in his Logic to have discovered the true method, because he has found the principle of self-activity—a principle which is likewise a method, because it acts, essentially. He names it *Begriff*, as Plato named the same principle *Idea*, to indicate its identity with the self-activity which we observe in mind.* Fichte calls it subject-objectivity, for it is a self which is active in making itself its own object.

---

* See A. T. Ormond's Basal Concepts in Philosophy for a strong and valuable exposition of self-activity.

(*a*) On this scale of degrees we rise from plant to animal, and from animal to man. The individuality of each lies in its energy. The energy of the plant is expended in assimilating the external; that of the animal in assimilating and reproducing; that of man in assimilating, reproducing, and self-producing or creating. But it is a discrete degree rather than a continuous degree from plant to animal; more and more assimilation does not bring us nearer to feeling, but the contrary is the result; for feeling arrests assimilation and reflects on its form. The discrete degree that separates the plant from the animal is measured by the distance between destroying and reconstructing; the difference between the animal and the man is measured by the distance between reproducing and self-producing, or, in another form of statement, it is the difference in two kinds of perception—the perception of object as particular and the perception of object as universal. More and more feeling does not approach thinking, but the contrary; for thinking arrests the development of feeling, and reflects on the form of activity which constitutes feeling—namely, it reflects on representation or producing-in-self what is external, and thereby making an object of it. Thinking reflects on this, and adds to the represented object the process of reproduction which feeling constitutes, and thus attains to a higher and more perfect knowledge of the object, for it sees it as a product of a complex unity of causes, the universal that generates a class.

(*b*) It is comparatively easy to recognise the difference between nutrition and perception; indeed, one would say that the difficult part is the recognition of the essential identity of their energies. On the contrary, the identity of sense-perception and thought is readily acknowledged, but their profound difference is not seen without careful attention. Inasmuch as the difference between sense-perception and thought underlies such distinctions, as, for instance, that between individuality that can survive death of the body and that that can not survive death of the body, the discrimination of sense-perception and thought justifies a careful discussion.

(c) The majority of thinkers who have advanced or defended the doctrine of immortality of the human soul have drawn the line of individual survival between the activity of sense-perception and the activity of reflection and reason, the former activity being understood as that which perceives particular objects, while the latter perceives general or universal objects. These general or universal objects are, however, as we have often reiterated in the preceding chapters, not mere classes or abstractions, fictions of the mind for genera and species, but they stand for generic processes in the world—such processes in the world as abide while their products come into being and pass away. They stand, in each case of a noun used as a class name, for this complex unity of causes that produced the individuals named by that noun and still sustains them in existence; this is the universal or generic. This is the true thought that underlies the old doctrine of realism as opposed to nominalism. The universal or productive process is more real than its dead results. Plato's ideas were his technical expression for self-active process or universal. Aristotle renamed it "entelechy." The oak before me is the product of a power that manifests itself in successive stages as acorn, sapling, tree, crop of acorns, etc., these stages being successive and partial, while the energy is the unity whence proceed all these phases through its action on the environment. The energy is a generic process, and whatever reality the particular existence may get from it is borrowed from its reality. The reality of this acorn is derived from the reality of the organic energy of the oak on which it grew. The reality of that organic energy is at least equal to all the reality that has proceeded from it.

(d) In the two forms of the reaction of energy, or individuality, which have been discussed as nutrition and feeling, the former draws the object within itself and destroys its objective form, while in feeling the individuality recoils from the attack made on the organism and reproduces its symbolic equivalent. Both of these forms find the occasion of action in the contact with the external.

Without conjunction, without limitation of the individuality by the object, there arises neither nutrition nor feeling. This mutual limitation is the reduction of the two, the subject and object, to the form of externality—namely, to mutual dependence—and hence it is the destruction of individuality so far as this dependence exists. By the act of assimilation, on the one hand, the vegetative energy reasserts its own independence and individuality by annulling the individuality of the object. The sentient process, on the other hand, reasserts its independence by escaping from the continuance of the impression from without, and by reproducing for itself a similar limitation through its own freedom or spontaneity. It elevates the real limit, by which it is made dependent on an external object, into an ideal limit that depends on its own free act. Thus both nutrition and feeling are manifestations of self-identity in which the energy acts for the preservation of its individuality against submersion in another, and thus attains progressive stages of freedom.

(e) To explain this difficult point still once more: These attempts to preserve individuality which we see in nutrition and feeling do not succeed in obtaining perfect independence. Both these activities, as reactions upon the environment, depend on the continuance of the action of the environment. When the assimilation is complete the reaction ceases, and there must be new interaction with the environment before the process begins again; hence its individuality requires a permanent interaction with external conditions, and the plant and the vegetative process in animals is not a complete or perfect individuality. It is not entirely independent. Its process involves a correlative existence, an inorganic world for its food.

(f) The activity of mere feeling or sense-perception, too, is aroused by external impressions, and is conditioned by them. If there is no object, then there is no act of perception. Every occasion given for the self-activity involved in perception is an occasion for the manifestation of a self-activity that acts only on external incitation and is not yet separable from the body.

(*g*) The reproduction of impressions that we have described above as the essential function of feeling or sense-perception is not the reproduction known under the name of recollection or memory. Recollection is a reproduction of the perception, while perception is a reproduction of the impression. The so-called faculties of the mind rise in a scale, beginning with feeling. We have shown, in (*a*) above, that each higher activity is distinguished from the one below it by the circumstance that it sees not only the *object* which was seen by the lower faculty, but also the *form* of the activity of that faculty. Each new faculty, therefore, is a new stage of self-consciousness.

§ 160. From a study of the higher faculties of the soul one learns much in regard to the destiny of the lower faculties. It has already been pointed out that with the arrival at the use of language the soul has come to know itself as independent self-activity. But there are many grades of knowing in the cognition of a thing, feeling, sense-perception, memory, common sense, reflection, reason, each one of these having a more complete consciousness than the one below it, because it knows the content which the lower one knew, and, in addition, knows the form or method of knowing that appertains to the lower faculty. Permanent individuality may exist as low as the animals; indeed, it is probable that it does so exist, for the world seems to be a sort of cradle for the nurture of independent individuality. The plants and the animals, therefore, are important stages in this process of nurture. But moral individuality is the beginning of real immortality, because at that point alone comes in the consciousness of the self as a responsible source of action. Infants who die before they attain a sense of responsibility would never be able to remember their earth life, but doubtless their already permanent individuality would develop into consciousness without transmigration or rebirth.

The ascent above sense-perception and recollection indicates to us the subordinate place of those faculties, and also their moribund character. As Aristotle hinted, in his profound treatise on the Soul, these lower faculties are not immortal in their nature (although they will long outlast this earthly life). In thinking of such faculties in the lives of great men of science—like Agassiz, Cuvier, Lyell, Von Humboldt, Darwin, and Goethe—we see what this means. The first and crudest stage of mental culture depends chiefly on sense-perception and recollection. After the general has been discovered, the mind uses it more and more, and the information of the senses becomes a smaller and smaller part of the knowledge. Agassiz saw the whole fish in a single scale—so that the scale was all that was required to suggest the whole. Lyell could see the whole history of its origin in a pebble. Cuvier could see the entire animal-skeleton in one of its bones. The memory that holds types, processes, and universals, the condensed form of all human experience, the total aggregate of all that the senses have perceived of the universe and of all reflection on it—this constitutes the chief faculty of the scientific man, and sense-perception and mere recollection play the most insignificant part. This points to the complete independence of the soul as regards its outward experience. When the soul can think the creative thought, the theoretic vision of the world—ἡ θεωρία, as Aristotle calls it—then it comes to perfect insight, for it sees the whole in each part, and does not require any longer the mechanical memory, because it has a higher form of intellect that sees immediately in the individual thing its history, just as Lyell or Agassiz saw the history of a pebble or a fish, or Asa Gray saw all botany in a single specimen. Mechanical memory is thus taken up into a higher " faculty," and, its function being absorbed, it gradually perishes. But it never perishes until its function is provided for in a more complete manner. This higher faculty has been named by the Schoolmen angelic knowing.*

§ 161. Man is born an animal, but must become a spiritual being. He is limited to the present moment and to the present place, but he must conquer all places and all times. Man, therefore, has an ideal of culture which it is his destiny or vocation to achieve.

He must lift himself above his mere particular existence toward universal existence. All peoples, no matter how degraded, recognise this duty. The South Sea Islander commences with his infant child and teaches him habits that conform to that phase of civilization—an ethical code fitting him to live in that community—and, above all, the mother tongue, so that he may receive the results of the perceptions and reflections of his fellow-beings and communicate his own to them. The experience of the tribe, a slow accretion through years and ages, shall be preserved and communicated to each newborn child, vicariously saving him from endless labour and suffering. Through culture the individual shall acquire the experience of the species—shall live the life of the race, and be lifted above himself. Such a process as this tribal culture thus puts man above the accidents of time and place in

---

* See my booklet, The Spiritual Sense of Dante's Divina Commedia, § 38.

18

so far as the tribe or race has accomplished this. Whatever lifts man above immediate existence, the wants and impulses of the present moment, and gives him self-control, is called ethical. The ethical grounds itself, therefore, in man's existence in the species and in the possibility of the realization of the species in the individual. Hence, too, the ethical points toward immortality as its presupposition. Death comes through the inadequacy of the individual organism to adjust itself to the environment; the conditions become too general, and the body gets lost in the changes that come to it. Were the individual capable of adapting himself to all changes, there could be no death; the organism would be perfectly universal. This process of culture that distinguishes man from all other animals points toward the formation of an immortal individual distinct from the body within which it dwells—an individual who has the capacity to realize within himself the entire species. Immortality thus complements the ethical idea. In an infinite universe the process of realizing the experience of all beings by each being must itself be of infinite duration. The doctrine of immortality, therefore, places man's life under the form of eternity and ennobles his earthly career to its highest potency.

CHAPTER XXX.

The Will and the Intellect.

§ 162. The highest step of knowing is self-knowing; not mere consciousness, but the recognition that reason is not only in me, but also beyond the world, or in its innermost, as its cause. Completed self-determination is not only intellect, but will. Imperfect will and imperfect intellect are not identical. But new light may be thrown on the ascent from sense-perception to reason by considering the interaction of will and intellect. It will be seen that the will combines with the intellect to produce the higher orders of knowing.

§ 163. It is usually taken for granted that the mind is at its lowest stage of self-activity in sense-perception—that is to say, when it is simply receptive of the impressions of the senses. The moment it attempts to guide these impressions, or to reflect on them, the mind ascends to higher forms of activity, and limits the scope of its passivity. When at this lowest point of activity, the infinite manifold of objects before the senses engrosses the entire attention. One object succeeds another in controlling the focus of attention. This condition of mind is very nearly that of the idiot, who is successively attracted by one object after another, and never reflects, or connects these objects by the thought of causality, or attempts to guide his perceptions and make them a consistent whole. The contents of his mind are therefore a mass of sense-perceptions, without connection between them.

§ 164. Intellectual culture begins when the will

first commences to act on the senses. Its first action produces what is called attention. Attention selects one object out of the manifold and collects the various impressions made upon its senses, while it wilfully neglects the multitude of other objects that are in its presence—it inhibits the consideration of these others. Attention, then, may be regarded as the name of the first union of the will with the intellect. It turns the chaos of sense-impressions into a system by connecting them about a focus arbitrarily chosen.

Intellectual training begins with the habit of attention. In this activity will and intellect are conjoined. The mind in this exercises its first self-determination. It says to the play of sense and idle fancy: Stop, and obey me; neglect that, and notice this. The infinitely manifold objects always present before the senses vanish, and one object engrosses the mind. This is the *sine qua non* of intellectual culture. All the grades of intellectual power that follow are successive stages of strength to concentrate the mind, and exclude extraneous objects. Hence attention becomes analysis, and this deepens to reflection, or the perception of other objects implied in the one before the mind. Continued analysis discerns in the isolated object the influence of other objects, and hence its (the object's) relativity, its connection and interdependence with other things; and this is properly named reflection, because it is the discovery of the object in what seemed extraneous to it—namely, the discovery of the being of its object in the being of the environment. Reflection is (etymologically) a bending back of the mind, and in the discovery of essential relations one finds in what is outside of or beyond the object that which bends him back to the object which he started with.

§ 165. Attention gathers, one after the other, the sense-impressions that proceed from the particular object, and it discriminates these; and by this discrimination it separates the object from other objects and defines it. Hence the first product of attention is analysis, and we may therefore call analysis the second product of the union of the will and the intellect. All specialization of the attention is analysis. By analysis the sense-impressions are properly grouped and carefully discriminated, and through them the object is defined. Continued analysis discerns in the isolated object the influence of other objects and its influence on them. To recapitulate: The object is isolated by attention; analysis discriminates and defines its properties and qualities. Analysis is composed of repeated acts of attention. The will isolates the object and excludes others from it; then again it selects a portion of this object for its minuter attention, excluding the rest of the object; again and again narrowing its attention down to more and more limited fields of observation, it approaches the simplest elements. Such is analysis. But in taking account of the simplest elements of the object, it discovers its (the object's) complication with other objects. It notes the reaction of other objects upon the object it has chosen for its attention; it notes evidences within the object of reaction upon other objects. It thus traces the object into its unity with other objects. Hence the result of repeated analysis is synthesis. It appears that we have analysis as the result of repeated acts of attention, and that we have synthesis as the result of repeated acts of analysis.

The activity which we have defined as reflection is therefore the ultimatum of analysis and the beginning of synthesis. The mind, analyzing, abstracts and isolates, but at length discovers the relativity of the isolated object, and finds reflected in it other objects, and, thus synthesizing, it comes to define the isolated object as a bundle of relations to the rest of the universe. Attention, analysis, and reflection result in generalization, because they discover community of being between the object and its environment. These stages of reflection, analysis and synthesis, belong to the understanding. Perception deals with isolated properties; the understanding with abstractions and relations, the realm of relativity; the reason deals with totalities or wholes.

§ 166. Synthesis, then, is the discovery of connections, of reciprocal actions, of the action of the object upon other objects, and of the reaction in turn of these objects upon it. Synthesis, then, results in the discovery of relativity—a system of relations which connect the object with other objects. The continuation of this process is called reflection. Reflection consists of analysis and synthesis—the descent to the elements and the ascent to the complex interrelations which form the constitution of the object.

Here I use analysis and synthesis only in their application to objects of experience. This activity of reflection and of its separate elements of analysis and synthesis is called the understanding.

Naming these in a different way, we can say that these are the potencies of the mind, the first potence being attention simple; the second potence being analysis; the third potence synthesis; the fourth potence reflection. Still further, if we regard the essential personality as will power, we can describe the various stages of growth thus far considered as the directing of the will or personality upon its intellect, overcoming its passivity, and directing it actively toward the mastery of the world. In this study the transition from mere attention to the stage of analysis is involved. Analysis is attention, but carried to a higher power. Attention simple should be the concentration of the activity of the mind on an object. Analysis concentrates the activity on the results of attention, and is thus in a certain sense self-related, for herein attention notices itself—it uses itself as an instrument. Again, in reflection, as synthesis, self-activity concentrates on the results of its own work in the stage of analysis; it perceives *relations*, and thus retraces its analysis, and connects the object with the elements that were excluded in the first act of attention (hence reflection is a self-activity twice self-related). There are two kinds of attention: that which relates to the environment, and that which follows a process of thought; the former is critical alertness and the latter absorption; these are opposite and mutually exclusive. The former kind of attention is spoken of here.

§ 167. There is another step of the intellect above that of reflection just described. We may call it insight, or philosophic knowing. Just as each of the

other stages of knowing arises from the persistent
and systematic use of the lower orders of knowing
by the will, so the highest, or insight, arises from
the systematic use of reflection through the will. Reflection follows out relations of dependence, and acknowledges relativity as its highest category. Its
doctrine is that each thing depends on everything
else. It holds that all knowledge is relative because
all things are relative, existing in a system of mutual
dependence. The final result of this process of reflection is to reach a whole of mutually dependent
beings. This is evident if one considers that, when
reflection arrives at the conclusion that dependence
is everywhere present among things, it is able to state
its principle in a universal form; and hence it now
has before it a whole—to it there is one system of
interdependent things in time and space. This is the
summit of the understanding. But now it becomes
possible to discern some facts regarding the whole as
a whole. This order of knowing is called reason by
some psychologists. For illustration of the character
of its knowledge, take as an instance, first, the insight
that the whole can not be dependent on another whole.
The whole must be independent. Second, it follows
that the whole must be self-active, because it can not
by any possibility receive its attributes and properties

from another; and, on the other hand, it must originate activity within itself, because there is within it
a constant process of dependence and interrelation,
causing changes or metamorphoses of integration and
disintegration.

This predicate of self-activity, applied to the whole,
is the most important conclusion reached in this higher
kind of knowing. It is very important to get this clear.
And yet it must be noted as a fact that the scientific stage
of mind, which may be called the analytic and synthetic
or reflective stage, holds itself back determinedly from
thinking the totality. It inhibits that thought. Those, on
the other hand, who reach this thought of the self-activity
of a total have definitely adopted the method of philosophical thinking.

§ 168. The following review of the points named
will assist in making clear the necessity of this insight into self-activity.   Interrelation or dependence
among all objects in time and space necessarily implies the unity of the whole.   The whole is one being.
Destroy any portion of it, and you change all the
constituent parts by shutting out a portion of influence
that exercised an effect upon these.   Secondly, bearing in mind that the whole is not dependent upon anything else, one may see that it is essentially the originator of the movement of action and interaction going
on between the beings which compose this whole.

If one should attempt to avoid this by supposing that
simple mechanical interaction, a sort of persistent motion

or persistent force, is constant and eternally active within
the whole, then consideration must be invited to the character of this kind of perpetual motion. Any force, as we
know it, is a running down of some tension that has been
wound up. Any force is therefore essentially dependent
upon an opposite force. The correlation of forces therefore as a whole has the form of a series in which the running down of the first force (the same being transmitted
to each successive member of the series) finally winds up
the last force into action, and that one winds up the first.
It is a contrivance of such a kind that the running down
of a force effects its own winding up, although through
a long series of other forces. Now such a thought as this is
absurd from the standpoint of a relativist, and he ridi-
cules the theory by telling the story of the man who took
hold of the straps of his boots and lifted himself over a
fence. He sees clearly that perpetual motion is impossible
from a mechanical point of view. He does not see, however,
that for this very reason all mechanical motion must have
arisen in a will-force. But it is an admission, nevertheless, of self-activity as the principle of the whole. Self-
activity can always reproduce a new tension of force—
that is to say, it can forever wind up its tension when
collapsed. The doctrine of correlation of forces therefore
has (coiled up in it as an implication) the idea of self-
activity to make it possible. Hence the stage of knowing
which deals with the nature of a whole regards self-activity as the principle of explanation, if it is logically consistent.

§ 169. To recapitulate briefly, the will unites with
the intellect to produce attention, analysis, synthesis,
reflection, and insight. We have sufficiently discussed
the necessity of the will to the first three of these
activities. It is obvious enough without further discussion that reflection is possible only by holding back

through the will the mind from the action of impressions upon the senses. It inhibits direct sense-perception, and confines itself to the analyzing and combining of past sense-perceptions recalled by the memory. But the action of the will upon the intellect is most manifest in that order of knowing to which we have above given the name " insight." The inhibition of the lower and relatively passive orders of knowing by the will is here most complete and thoroughgoing, for the will drops the entire field of experience, together with its data of sense-perceptions, out of sight, and commences from the other extreme of the orders of being. It inquires what must be the nature of a whole or total, and finds the categories of independence and self-activity. It uses these, and applies them to the contents of experience as ultimate explanations.

Our division here, whether into three, four, five, or six steps, is somewhat arbitrary. Three is, on the whole, most convenient, and is used in Chapter IV. In Chapter XXVII we have subdivided the second step, the understanding, into common sense and reflection; also the stage of sense-perception is divided into that of mere impressions which are represented in feeling and that of perceiving objects as members of classes. Here we base our classification on the will. First we note simple passive reception of impressions without the action of the will; second, the first direction of the intellect by the will, producing attention; third, the second action of the will, using attention repeatedly and guiding its successive acts

—analysis; fourth, the third intention of the will, which, through analysis, discovers relations to other objects or beings, and thus discovers relativity or the relation of dependence upon other things. This last is called synthesis. The general name, reflection, is given for the union of synthesis and analysis, and this is our fifth step; each being used to produce its opposite—analysis to discover community of the object with other objects (which is synthesis), and synthesis to discover the necessity of a series of objects to realize the entire being of the object; as, for instance, the synthetic process of the life of the oak requires the analytic stages of the isolated acorn, sapling, tree, leaves, blossoms, and a crop of acorns. Up to this point we have traced the orders of knowing from the simplest sense-perception up to the highest scientific knowing. There is a sixth order of knowing, which considers the action of independent beings or wholes and formulates the necessary truths concerning the totality of relative beings which belong within it. We may note that the steps called attention, analysis, synthesis, and reflection all belong to what we have called reflection in Chapter XXVII, or the second stage of knowing in Chapter IV. Aristotle includes all these four steps under discursive thinking (διάνοια). But he also includes all these, and the imagination, memory, and sense-perception, under the passive reason (νοῦς παθητικός). To the passive reason Aristotle opposes the active reason (νοῦς ποιητικός), including under this what we have called insight. He calls this elsewhere θεωρεῖν. Thus we may have only two steps, the first one including the first five steps and the second the sixth step. It is important that the student shall see that all these steps are real, and that he may discern still other phases which may function separately, but that he may group them all in three, or even in two, classes of activity.

§ 170. The most important thing to be noticed in the theory here presented is, that the will as a self-determining power, uniting itself with the intellect in the ascending series of attention, analysis, synthesis, reflection, and insight, approaches at each step nearer and nearer to an adequate knowledge of itself. In fact, insight, the completest order of knowing, may be said to have as its object pure will; for a self-active whole is precisely a will. Hence insight is self-consciousness in the full meaning of that term, for the self as will perceives will, or a self, as the fundamental being and final explanation of things. It is only this kind of knowing (which may be called theistic knowing) that can recognise truly what is involved in freedom and responsibility. The lower order of knowing, here named reflection, which deals with analysis and synthesis, and arrives at nothing beyond universal relativity, can not consistently admit the idea of freedom or responsibility. It does not entertain the idea of a whole or a self-active being, and hence can not conceive of such a thing as will.

Science may ascertain that a thing is, and expound its interrelations with other beings, but philosophy and theology have not explained an object until they have shown its place in the purposing will of the Absolute First Principle, or God—that is to say, philosophic knowing begins with the *highest presupposition* of a being, and not with its immediate presentation to the senses. Science thus proceeds from the incomplete to the more complete and toward the absolute, while philosophy and theology proceed from the complete toward the incomplete, following the creative purpose.

§ 171. We have seen already, in Chapter XXVI, that feeling may be considered as the embryonic form of both will and intellect. On the side of desire, feeling moves toward the will; on the side of sensuous impressions, feeling relates itself to intellect. It is evident that feeling can not be educated directly in itself, but only mediately through the intellect and the will. The will is trained by forming habits; the intellect is trained by developing higher orders of knowing. When a habit is formed, and a theoretical view is reached by the intellect which corresponds to that habit, it will happen soon that feeling will come to contain the contents of the willing and knowing in the form of immediate impulse or unconscious tendency. Therefore the feeling can be cultivated, and is cultivated, in fact, by producing the growth and development of the intellect and will.

§ 172. This progressive series of stages of knowing, arising from the action of the will upon the intellect, would at first be supposed to lead away from reality toward abstraction; or, in other words, from the concrete to the abstract. But, in fact, it is otherwise. The higher members of the series of knowing are more adequate, and reach the concrete truth, while that kind of knowing which merely knows impressions, without taking cognizance of relations, is an abstract knowing, because it deals with mere dependent things, properties, and qualities, without seizing them in their true relations, whereas the reflective knowing seizes things in their causal relations, which make them possible and sustain them in being (compare § 158). It is a more concrete kind of knowing, therefore. But the kind of knowing which I call insight (θεωρεῖν)—which explains the dependent things by the independent whole—is philosophic or theologic knowing. Its aim when realized enables one to see each thing in God's final purpose in the universe. Hence what we call insight, or the knowing of the Reason, deals with moral purposes.

§ 173. It is true that the psychological theory of these kinds of knowing is apart from and unnecessary to the realization of the kinds of knowing themselves. That is to say, a person may be engaged in analysis without knowing that it is analysis, and without any special information regarding the nature of analysis. Physiology and hygiene give one an insight into the processes of digestion and respiration, but are not necessary for the performance of those functions. One breathes and digests quite as well without a scientific knowledge of the nature of the process; but such scientific knowledge is indispensable to the pathologist. So, too, one pays attention, analyzes, reflects, and reasons without knowing scientifically what is involved in such acts; but the science of psychology is necessary for settling all questions of educational criticism. To see the complexity of the physiological process of digestion or breathing astonishes us. Still more does it astonish the psychologist when he for the first time traces out the complexity of the most ordinary mental processes. The accumulation of one act upon another, each higher one acting upon a lower one, is a continued process of involution which seems at first wholly incomprehensible. But complete self-knowledge implies this knowledge of mental processes.

Psychology explains; it does not make. To explain the purposive movements of life is not to say that these are conscious. The actions of a plant indicate the adaptation of means to end, but not a conscious adaptation. So the greater part of the movements of animals are purposive, but not conscious. The animal does not reflect upon them. It is a shallow, first thought of the reader of psychology to suppose that his author undertakes to give an account only of conscious processes. Fichte was the first among thinkers to trace out these subtle evolutions, and his works form the classics of psychology, defective though they are in ontology. Attention to an object, analysis of its properties, reflection upon its relation to other things, are very ordinary intellectual activities, but they differ widely in significance. The lower activity never comprehends the higher; it is limited, but knows not its limit. Things seem to it impossible which are perfectly easy to the stages of thinking above it.

THIRD PART.

PSYCHOLOGIC FOUNDATIONS.

251

THIRD PART.

PSYCHOLOGIC FOUNDATIONS.

§ 174. In Part I of this volume the method of psychology has been illustrated by various inquiries based on introspection. In Part II the intellect and the will are examined in the light of the principle of self-activity, and a genetic deduction attempted of the higher activities from the lower activities or faculties of the mind.

A genetic deduction derives the later forms from the inherent growth of the earlier forms. The earlier forms are found to have certain constructive activities, which through their own changes will result in the later forms. By this the later forms are explained and the earlier forms are better understood, inasmuch as their destination and goal are revealed.

§ 175. In Part III an application of psychology will be made to solve the most important of the live problems of education. All human activities have a psychologic side. There is a mental coefficient to each (see § 8). What the mental action or reaction may be, and what its ultimate effect may be on itself, must be demanded by pedagogy in regard to each act and each situation of the soul; for it is the chief concern in pedagogy to inquire into the educative factor of the doings and sufferings of humanity. Hence in this last part of the book I inquire into the psychologic foundations (1) of society and its institutions, and of reactions against them; (2) of the national ideas that have successively appeared in the world history; (3 and 4) of art and religion and their history; (5 and 6) of science and philosophy; finally, of the school, (7) its course of study, (8) its division of the curriculum into elementary, secondary, and higher education.

CHAPTER XXXI.

The Psychology of Social Science.

§ 176. As a mere individual, isolated from the community, man can not ascend above savagery. What small portion of the earth and the heavens a mere individual can apprehend with his unaided five senses is only sufficient to bewilder him with problems. He can not attain to any solution of them. It is only when man comes to avail himself of the aggregate observations of mankind that he is placed in a position to get an inventory of the world of some value. What one individual can not do, the organized labour of mankind can do—continuous as it is through space and time—handing from one generation to the next, sacredly preserving the heritage of experience, and adding to it the small accretions of discovery made from time to time by the constituent members. Man, as an individual, is an insignificant affair; as social whole he constitutes a living miracle. By participation the individual is enabled to re-enforce himself with the sense-perceptions of all, the thoughts and reflections of all, the life experience of all. He reaps what others sow, he avails himself of the lives of others without having to pay the heavy price of first experience. All the mistakes made by others enter as so much positive experience, and are bequeathed as so much wisdom by the race to each individual. He is saved the trouble of trying over again what has been found to be error, and hence is saved also the pain which comes from it.

Human society is founded on the deep mystery of vicarious atonement which is announced in the creeds of Christendom. The social whole suffers for the first cost of its experience, dividing up the pain among the myriads of human beings who contribute this experience. But it delivers its entire lesson to each new person who comes into the world without the necessity of his living over again the life of toil and pain which has furnished the lesson. The race thus lives vicariously for the individual, and it is this vicarious living of all for each and of each for all, made possible by the institutions which form the network of society, that makes human nature divine.

(*a*) Man is not only an animal having bodily wants of food, clothing, and shelter, but he is a spiritual being existing in opposition to Nature. Man, as a child or a savage, is an incarnate contradiction; his real being is the opposite of his ideal being. His actual condition does not conform to his true nature. His true human nature is Reason; his actual condition is irrational, for it is constrained from without, chained by brute necessity, and lashed by the scourges of appetite and passion. Thus there is a paradoxical contrast between Nature and human nature; between Nature as spread out in time and space— existing in mineral, vegetable, and animal—and human nature, or realized reason. Nature in time and space consists of beings limited by each other, and not of self-limited beings. Thus fate everywhere prevails in Nature, and each natural thing is constrained by its circumstances, and can not change itself, can not realize an ideal of its own—in fact, has no ideal and is no self. Man, as he begins his career, is such a natural being. His human nature is then only a possibility to him. Human nature must be made by the activity of man in order to exist.

(*b*) As man ascends out of Nature in time and space into human nature, he ascends into a realm of his own creation, and therefore into a realm of freedom. The world of material nature is not self-limited. The chief attribute of matter is exclusiveness. Impenetrability is an essential quality of it. Two bodies can not occupy the same place, nor can one body occupy two places. Hence the material necessities of life—food, clothing, and shelter —are essentially brute necessities, having selfishness or exclusiveness as their basis. The food, clothing, or shelter appropriated by one human being can not be likewise appropriated by another at the same time. If participation exists in regard to material supplies, it exists through division and diminution of shares. But it is the opposite of this in spiritual things, in things of the mind. Spiritual blessings always increase by being shared. In fact, they do not exist except in and through participation. It is through combination of man with man that the individual is able to achieve a rational existence. By combination each one is able to participate in the life of every other, forming a vast organism of institutions called human society, wherein each helps all and all help each.

§ 177. The only possibility of amelioration for the natural man lies in the principle of combination. The individual must feel or perceive a common interest with other individuals. He must adopt for his own ideal the ideal of others. Then dropping his exclusiveness, he works for others, and through others for himself. He learns to recognise his own essential aims and purposes in those of others, and more and more to make a common ideal the object of his strivings and endeavours. Through this process arise the institutions of civilization—the family, civil society, the state.

These institutions are the secular forms of combination, and are the direct means by which man, the animal, is freed from his naturalness and the thraldom consequent upon his wants and necessities. Coincident with the development of these institutions of civilization, and in reciprocal interaction with the same, arise three other forms of combination—æsthetic art, religion, and science. These are spiritual modes of combination, while the former are secular. The visible Church is the institution in which religion is realized. The invisible Church contains also art and literature, and also philosophy and science—the

entire realm of the true, the beautiful, and the good.
While the secular institutions serve to provide man with
food, clothing, and shelter, and to protect and defend him
against physical violence and suffering, the spiritual combinations have for their end the evolution of man's absolute ideal and the elevation of the natural individual into
such participation in the life of the social whole that he
achieves independence of the temporal and finite and comes
to live a divine life.

§ 178. In the first province of the secular—the
family—natural affection seems to be the strongest
tie, and one might instance examples from the animal
kingdom to prove that mere instinct is sufficient to
found the family.   In like manner ants and bees could
be cited as furnishing examples of civil society and
the state founded on mere natural impulse.   Civil society would seem to be founded on greed or selfish
desire.   But the realm of instinct or mere natural
feeling does not include the ethical element, although that element must be regarded as essential to
all human institutions.   In fact, the forms of spiritual
combination—art, religion, and science—are to be
looked upon as underlying and conditioning even the
secular institutions of man.   The higher is the necessary condition for the existence of the lower; no
unconscious nature without an absolute, self-conscious, personal cause; no human institutions without insight or wisdom, the primitive form of all sci-

ence. Wisdom is the insight into the ideal of man, the totality of his potential nature and the ideal laws which govern its realization.

Thus while the secular forms of combination are negative in the sense that they provide merely food, clothing, and shelter, the spiritual forms of combination are positive in that they concern immediately the world of rational intelligence. The secular institutions likewise indirectly but necessarily have a function in the spiritual growth of man, especially in that they introduce mediation everywhere between the direct animal appetite and its gratification (that is to say, separating the appetite from its food by a process of labour for others). In civil society each man is given a special vocation. In this he must toil not directly for himself, but to produce commodities for society, receiving in return for his labour not the goods he wishes to consume, but only money—the general symbol of social obligation, the general solvent of property. His own wants are in turn to be supplied through the labours of other individuals in the social whole, which he procures for money. Thus, while he offers in exchange an amount of labour which, if applied directly for himself, would afford him a pitiful subsistence, yet by devoting it to others he secures access to the rich stores of human society, and cotton, silk and linen, tea, coffee and sugar, wheat, corn and spices, coal, wood and iron—whatever of luxuries or comforts that go to feed and clothe, protect and shelter man, are collected for him from all parts of the world. His animal wants are more than gratified, and yet the animal semblance of this gratification has been so completely removed—eliminated by the social alembic of combination—that even the most avaricious and grasping of our human fellows clothes his endeavours with the appearance of devoted solicitude for the welfare of his neighbours and for society in general, for he labours early and late to produce the commodities wanted by his fellows. In proportion to the perfection of the institution of civil society this direct serving of others becomes more conscious, cultivates with greater effect the humane sentiments of the individual, and binds him closer to the general mass.

§ 179. Civil society is distinguished from the state through this: While it is a social combination like the state, it does not exercise directive power upon the individual, and assume the functions of a will-power like him. But the state always assumes the control of the individual for the benefit of the social unit. Against this social unit he has no substantial existence. In civil society, on the other hand, an organization is formed which seems to be for the individual, and not for itself, like the state. The most important phase of civil society is its organization of the industry of man in the form of division of labour. Civil society seems to be an organization of the social unit for the use of the individual, while the state is the social unit in which the individual exists not for himself, but for the use of that unit, the state. In civil society the whole exists for each; in the state each exists for the whole.

§ 180. The state sifts out from man his selfishness and naturalness more effectually than the family or civil society. Against the greed and cruelty of animal passions it is indeed, as Hobbes called it, " the leviathan," or constraining might which subdues brutal impulse in order that the rational may hold sway. The state organizes the world of human passions and desires, of human arbitrariness and caprice, into a temple of justice wherein the fragmentary will of each individual is pieced out and complemented by the organic will of the whole community, and thus made to reflect the divine will. It organizes human combination with the idea of justice as its supreme principle.

Justice implies responsibility or free will, and undertakes to return to each actor the fruition of his deed. If his deed is rational, he shall not be deprived of its benefits through the violence of others; if he conspires against the freedom of others, his deed shall still be his own, although its return upon him may place him behind prison bars or even deprive him of his life. The state is the highest realization of the ideal of man in the secular world. It sets up the principle of responsibility or pure freedom, and this is the absolute ideal of man. It however remains purely secular in this, that it confines its cognizance to overt acts, and does not penetrate within the sacred circle of personality to take account of the subjective realization of the absolute ideal. It leaves this to conscience and the Church. It would be impossible for the state to retain the principle of justice as its standard and still attempt to enter the province of the private will except where that will has externalized itself in overt acts; for it presupposes freedom and responsibility, or else it could not punish. It says to the criminal: "Your deed is your own; take its consequences upon yourself." Conviction, opinion, thought, so long as unuttered, do not belong to the secular world, can not be arraigned by a secular power without a confusion which would destroy the secular world altogether. The state may return only his deed on the doer. What has not yet become a deed, but remains only a thought, is not yet sent out or externalized, and hence can not be returned.

§ 181. In the institution of the Church man essays to actualize in himself a reconciliation of his being with the divine ideal. Worship and sacrifice constitute the two essential elements of religion. In devotion or worship the soul concentrates itself upon the infinite and eternal ideal—the Absolute Person—and refuses to occupy itself with the particular concerns of life. Whether it is in joy or sorrow, success or misfortune, it is all the same; with its one privilege of communion with God all finite, secular things are as naught. Worship is the negative act of the religious intellect, annulling the world in the presence of the Absolute; sacrifice is the negative act of the religious will: the soul practically accomplishes in this what it theoretically acknowledges in the form of worship. That the soul, even when immersed in the distracting cares of the secular, or when its ideal is obscured by ignorance and superstition, still is capable of union with its ideal through sacrifice and worship, is the momentous reality which religion involves. Its doctrine of the True Personality—that it, because it is universal, involves the recognition of itself in others (as expressed in the symbol of the

Trinity)—is the central light of theology, and the same doctrine in scientific form is to be regarded as the first principle of speculative philosophy.

The great fundamental truth which has come out of social science is that of the serial nature of man's self. He is not simply a single self, as individual, nor is his race only a vast number of individual selves; but as individual he is one self, and then he exists in a series of selves ascending above him, each one a higher revelation of the nature of his self—a more complete realization of his ideal self. There is, besides the individual, the first self above him in the shape of the family to which he belongs. He is member of this higher self, and also, at the same time, one of its conscious centres; for in these higher selves the individual is not only a part, but he is at the same time the whole. This, indeed, to some extent is true of the humblest individual in society. Above the family there is the larger self of the community in which the individual lives. It is an industrial and civil unit. In this unit he is still more strikingly a subordinate member, a co-operating link; and, besides this, a more complete individual, a more perfect, self-determining being. In the state, in the Church, the individual finds new selves. To know one's self, then, means to know also society; to know not only the particular individual self which I am, but my universal self, realized above me in a series of vast colossal forms. To rise into higher selves, and to know himself in these higher selves, is the destination of man.

CHAPTER XXXII.

The Institutions that educate.

§ 182. EACH of these cardinal institutions exercises on the member of society its peculiar education. It forms his mind through action and reaction. This fivefold form of education (counting the school as a separate institution) begins with man as an infant— a mere animal with no spiritual growth as yet, but with the possibility of infinite unfolding and achievement of the spiritual attributes of intellect, will-power, and affections.

The first stage of this educative process we call that of nurture. It lasts from birth to the age of five or six years, and is the education which the family gives the child. The parents and other relatives of the child during this period impress on him his first lessons in human life. He learns obedience and courtesy toward his elders and superiors, personal habits relative to taking food, sleeping, recreation, cleanliness of clothing and person, the sense of shame, some degree of self-control and of consideration for others, and, above all, the use of his mother tongue. He learns to symbolize to some extent the life of the family, as far as he sees it, by means of the activity of play. His playthings are imitations, repetitions in miniature, of the objects with which the serious occupations of life are carried on by his elders: whether dolls with their outfits of cradles, carriages, culinary and laundry utensils; whether hobby-horses, water-wheels, dog-carts, miniature boxes of tools, or the more general games (less imitative and more deeply symbolic) with which he engages in later years of childhood.

§ 183. When the child outgrows the narrow circle of family life and comes to the period where his interest centres on learning the ways of society outside of the family, its occupations and its forms of combination in the industries, and its means of intercommunication, then comes the period of the school, whose object is to initiate him into the technicalities of intercommunication with his fellow-men, and to familiarize him with the ideas that underlie his civilization, and which he must use as tools of thought if he would observe and understand the phases of human life around him; for these phases of human life—all that relate to human institutions, all that relate to the science of society, and to the moral structure of civilization—are invisible to the human being who has not the aid of elementary ideas with which to see them.

The infant and the savage do not and can not see social relations: they can see only things, but not relations; they can not see forces, powers, processes, institutions, but only the dead results of such activities, and consequently they do not know of any whence and whither with which to explain the *what* that is before them. The school performs a very important function when it provides a knowledge of the technics of intercommunication, and makes familiar the elementary ideas of human institutions.

§ 184. After the school comes the education of one's special vocation. The business pursuit, be it trade or profession, is an education in which the individual man learns to limit himself to a narrow sphere of activity, so that thereby he can gain skill of production; and with this he learns to depend on his fellow-man for the supply of his many wants through exchange. He contributes the products of his own industry to the market of the world, and receives in return a share in all the productions collected for redistribution in that great market.

The dependence of the particular individual upon his race, and the reciprocal participation of each in the productions of the labour of all, are the great lesson of one's vocation in life. By the division of labour, the mere selfishness of man, as an animal or brute, is sifted out, and he does not take the food, clothing, and shelter for the gratification of his wants directly from Nature, but indirectly through the mediation of society; he gets them from his fellow-men, purchasing them in the market of the world. So what he uses involves this transaction with his fellows, wherein all parties are free agents, and the deed is one of courtesy rather than of compulsion or of animal greed. By the division of labour the productivity of man is so much increased that the civilized man goes well clothed, housed, and fed, and educated; while the savage or the wild man, who is his own food-provider, his own tailor and shoemaker, his own mason and carpenter, goes houseless and naked, and at times is half starved, and never fed with a palatable variety.

§ 185. The influence of the constitution of the state, and of its transactions with other states in peace

and war, weaving the web of world history, is known
to be more powerful in educating the individual and
in forming his character than any of the three phases
of education mentioned, for it underlies them and
makes possible whatever perfection they may have.
Without the protection of the state no institution can
flourish, nothing above savage or barbarous human
life can be realized.

In a despotic state, the family life, the school life, and
the life of society are capable only of arrested growth,
and they remain of necessity in their first rudimentary
stages. In a free nation, governed by a written constitution, those subordinate forms may unfold into completeness of development. The state is the essential condition
for history; history deals with states and nations, and not
with mere individuals. History commences with the evolution of man's substantial self and its realization or em-
bodiment in a state. The ideal even of the most despotic
state or the most rudimental form of the state, as well
as the freest and most perfect state, is that of justice.
The state exists in order that the deed of the citizen may
be returned to him in kind, and thereby that he realize
self-determination and freedom. Responsibility to the will
of the state is the great reality which educates the citizen,
and in whose presence he becomes ever more conscious
of the reflection of his own deed, returning upon himself
from society to bless or curse him, according to its nature
as he sent it forth, a good deed or a deed of malice.

§ 186. In the presence of the state the individual
feels that he has entered a different relation from
that which he holds to the world of industry and
the division of labour.

20

While in his vocation or special business (art, profession, or trade) each individual is served by the entire world of productive industry, and he commands for his own productions a share in the total product of the labour of man in every clime under the sun, and it comes to pass that the organization of society seems to exist solely for the comfort and enjoyment of the individual; on the other hand, in the state the citizen comes to recognise his responsibility to a higher self, and to feel his utter lack of substantiality as compared with it. To his substance as it exists realized in this higher self in the state he must yield ready obedience, and be at all times willing to sacrifice for it his wealth and possessions, and even his very life itself—the sacrifice of the unsubstantial self for the substantial self. Thus the state educates the citizen into a higher realization of human selfhood or personality than he has learned in the family and civil society.

§ 187. Neither property nor individual life in the body is essential to the existence of the human soul; and it is this higher substantiality of the individual as immortal soul, responsible to a Personal God, which transcends the state and all subordinate institutions. This higher substantiality is taught to man in the fifth form of education—that which man receives through the spiritual institutions growing from art, religion, and science, and especially through the institution of the Church, which makes them possible. In the education of religion man learns to know himself as a being that transcends Nature in all its forms —even the highest form of Nature, which is that of organic life. He comes to realize the infinite character of his will and its acts, of his intellect and the truth it cognizes, of his affections and their Supreme Personal object.   Theology as enunciated by the Church expounds the fundamental ideas which underlie the whole life of man; and therefore it happens that the form of religion confessed by a people is all-important in determining the degree of development of each and every other form of education, whether of the state, of social economy, of the school, or of the family nurture.

In the development of the consequences of a religious principle, or of any general principles, it does not signify whether this or that person is conscious of it. Few are conscious of principles, theoretically—i. e., few see all or even many of the logical results that follow their application—but each one touches its application on some one side of it, and on the whole the nation or people will in a series of years draw out of a dogma every one of its implied conclusions. If the absolute is held to be an unconscious unity, all particular individuality, all immortality for particular men, and all freedom of political institutions, will ultimately go to the ground among the people whose priesthood hold that doctrine. If the absolute is held to be a conscious person, quite a different history will result, and everything will be favourable to the development of the individual, through education, into the type or image of the absolute self-conscious person.

CHAPTER XXXIII.

The Psychology of Nations.

§ 188. THERE are three nations of ancient time that stand to modern civilization in the relation of teachers in an eminent sense of the term, and these are Greece, Rome, and Judea. The nations of Europe and America to-day recognise this debt to Judea by setting apart a learned profession—the highest and most sacred of all professions, the clergy—to master the divine message revealed through the highly endowed spiritual sense of the Hebrews, and in turn to make the whole people, high and low, acquainted with that message and able to govern each his own life in accordance with it. This education in revealed religion demands and receives one day in seven set apart for its exclusive purpose, besides its daily recognition.

§ 189. Again, our civilization sets apart a learned profession to master the laws by which justice is secured between man and man. The protection of life and property and the punishment of crime, the ordinances by which individuals combine to form social aggregates for the prosecution of business, to provide for the welfare of towns, cities, counties, states, and the nation—all these proceed from a Roman origin, and were, in the first instance, taught by the Roman prætorian courts that followed in the wake of Roman armies and made secure their conquests by establishing Roman jurisprudence in the place of the local laws and customs that had before prevailed; for the Latin mind had pondered a thousand years on the forms of the will, discovering, one by one, the limitations of individual caprice and arbitrariness necessary to prevent collision of the individual with the social whole.

The Latin lesson to the world teaches us how to frame laws and guide the individual in such ways as to make all his deeds affirmative of the purpose of his community and nation, and cause him to inhibit all such deeds as tend toward trespass or injury of others. This goes to make each person strong through the corporate will of his community and nation. It prevents the collision of each with all—a collision which reduces to zero all reasonable action. The modern system of education in Europe and America places the study of Latin in all secondary and higher education as a first essential side by side with mathematics in the school studies. This secures for youth from three to seven years' daily occupation with the workings of the Latin mind. The boy or the girl gradually becomes permeated with the motives of that serious-minded people. He comes to realize the special significance of those words that express the ideals of Roman character (and the ideals of all character)—words which we have preserved in our translation into English—gravity, soberness, probity, honesty, self-restraint, austerity, con-

siderateness, modesty, patriotism. Rosenkranz* says:
"The Latin tongue is crowded with expressions which
paint presence of mind, the effort at reflection, a critical
attitude of mind, the importance of self-control."

§ 190. But there is a third people and a third
language which we recognise in secondary and higher
education. We place the Greek language before the
pupil for its influence on his mind in opening it to
the vision of science, art, and literature. The Greeks
invented the chief poetic forms—epic, lyric, and dramatic. They transformed architecture and sculpture
into shapes that reveal spiritual freedom. They discovered, in fact, the beautiful in its highest forms
as the manifestation of freedom or self-determination. Besides the beautiful, they also found the true,
and explored its forms in science and philosophy.
Science and æsthetics treat of the two forms of the
intellect just as jurisprudence treats of the forms of
the will. Thus Greece educates all modern nations
in forms of art and literature, while Rome educates
them in the forms which make secure life and property.

.   In the beginning Greece is only æsthetic, worshipping
beautiful individualities, the gods of Olympus. From the
beginning it prizes its athletic games as a sort of worship of the beautiful by realizing gracefulness and phys-

---

* Philosophy of Education, vol. i of this series, p. 232.

ical freedom in the body. Later it fixes in stone and
bronze the forms of its athletes as models, and sets them
up in temples as statues of the gods. Gracefulness is well
said to be the expression of spiritual freedom in bodily
form. The soul is represented as in complete control of
the body, so that every movement and every pose shows
the limbs completely obedient to the slightest impulse of
the soul. There is other art than the Greek: we have
Egyptian and East Indian, Chinese, Persian, and Etruscan,
but no art that has any success in depicting gracefulness
or individual freedom. Even Christian art in Italy, Germany, and France does not attain to supreme gracefulness as does the Greek; for, while Greek art succeeds in
representing freedom *in* the body, Romantic art represents freedom *from* the body, or at least a heart-hunger
for such freedom. The martyr saints painted by Fra Angelico, and the dead Christs of Volterra, Michel Angelo,
and Rubens, all show an expression of divine repose, having in view the final liberation from the body. Religion in
its essence is a higher form of spiritual activity than art.
Christianity is superior to the Greek and the Roman religions; but Christian art is not so high a form of art as
Greek art, because it represents freedom only negatively
as separation from the body rather than positively as full
incarnation in the body, like the Olympian Zeus or the
Apollo Belvedere. Inasmuch as art is the consecration
of what is sensuous and physical to the purposes of spiritual freedom, it forever piques the soul to ascend out of
the stage of sense-perception into reflection and free
thought. To solve the mystery of self-determination in
the depths of pure thinking is to grasp the substance of
which highest art is only the shadow. Thus the glorious
career of Greek philosophy from Thales, through Heracli-
tus, Pythagoras, and Anaxagoras to its consummation in
Socrates, Plato, and Aristotle, is the process by which
inner reflection attains the same completeness and perfection that art had attained under Pheidias and Prax-
iteles. Art has, moreover, a link connecting it with philosophy. The dramas of Æschylus and Sophocles grapple

with the problems of Greek life, the relation of fate to freedom, the limits of human responsibility, and the motives of Divine Providence. Thus art prompts to thought on the questions of ultimate moral import, and, in a word, to " theology, or first philosophy," as Aristotle names his treatise on metaphysics.

§ 191. These three historical nationalities have for modern peoples the highest interest, because they furnish the three strands which have been united in the civilization of the dominant races that have entered history in recent times. The psychology of these peoples may be briefly characterized: (*a*) The Greek contribution is the perception of the beautiful as the manifestation of personal freedom in physical form; this is gracefulness, the subordination of things to the soul; next, the freedom of thought in science and philosophy. (*b*) The Roman is the perception of the freedom of the will; its contradiction of its own freedom through trespass on property or violence against life and liberty; the forms necessary to protect the individual in his rights of property and the development of his freedom, even to the point of arbitrary choice or caprice; the security of the social whole, as city or empire; the necessity of the individual to devote his person and property to the safety of Rome; *salus populi suprema lex.* (*c*) The Hebrew is the insight into the nature of the Absolute as a person; justice ("righteousness") and mercy ("goodness" or "loving-kindness") as the essential characteristics of the true God; justice, implying responsibility, freedom, and independent existence on the part of the creature; mercy, implying immaturity, error, and sin, but the choice of God to endure the imperfect for the sake of the growth toward perfection of his creatures ("long-suffering," "tenderness," "pity of a father for his children"); perfect altruism of the Absolute (Old and New Testament). The last of these national ideas is the deepest power in civilization.*

Other nations have contributed important ideas, although not so essential as these three:

(*a*) China has worked out the idea of the family, making it the foundation of the state (a parental government), of its religion (the worship of ancestors), of its philosophy (having, instead of one first principle, two—*yang* and *yin*, a male and likewise a female first principle), and of all its learning; for in the family the subordination of all its members to the patriarch and the paternal affection of the latter toward the former are essential. Hence etiquette becomes the chief thought or ruling idea in the Chinese mind. The writings of Confucius and Mencius are devoted to its exposition. Education with the Chinese consists chiefly in fixing the maxims of this etiquette firmly in mind.

(*b*) India makes caste the supreme thing, as if it apotheosized civil society and its division of labour, just as

---

* Hegel's Philosophy of History and Rosenkranz's summary of its ideas furnish the basis of this chapter, and also of much else in this book.

China the family. The observances of one's caste, its duties of action and withholding from action, fill up life. Even the philosophy of the East Indian is only a reaction from this all-prevailing caste idea; for the Sankhya system teaches the escape from all distinctions, ceremonies, deeds; from all manifoldness, even consciousness of self, by persistently thinking of the abstract unity and inhibiting all thought of individual things. This is emancipation— escape from caste and from its eternal demands for this or that ceremony. The *Bhagavad Ghita* is a good compend of East Indian philosophy, which is agreed on this fundamental point, but differs in many superficial points.

(c) Buddhism is this emancipation from caste realized in a religious life, which strives to attain the extinction of self-interest as well as interest in others. It furnishes a key to the psychology of the Thibetans, the people of southern India, Farther India, nearly one third of the Chinese, and a large part of the Japanese. It conceives the absolute not as a person, but as an empty unity devoid of all multiplicity (what we have called a " negative unity " in §§ 143-152). It is a phase of thought that crops out perpetually in history whenever there is a revolt against the existing religion.

(d) The Persian psychology is in sharp antithesis to the East Indian. (1) In Persia we have a new religious principle, that of the distinction between good and evil. Hence we have a negative power within the divine; for not good alone is supreme, but the good is limited by evil, and both are eternal, or at least real and actual in the present world. The East Indian did not acknowledge the reality of evil; it was all "*maya*," or illusion. The whole world of Nature, as well as the world of humanity, was a dream that exists only in human consciousness, and which is to be got rid of by abstraction, penance, and mortification of the flesh.

(2) When the Indian Yogi has tortured and misused his body until he has benumbed and paralyzed it to a degree that it can not feel or perceive, then he is no longer haunted by the things of the world; they do not any

longer flow into his mind through his senses, and he becomes divine, or like Brahma, who has no distinctions whatever, and hence no consciousness. For consciousness is a distinction in the *ego* or *me*, which divides it into subject and object—*I* and *me*—nominative and objective cases. The Hindu (or East Indian) will not regard evil as divine, or as a part of the highest principle, nor even admit any distinction in it; for (he thinks) is not all distinction or division a limitation? and is not limitation in God the destruction of his infinitude? It will not do, therefore, to think God as a this or that, or as not this or that, for that would be to limit him. He must be, therefore, pure unity, without distinction; yes, he must be even above all unity, above all thought. We see why the Hindu does not permit the ideas of goodness or righteousness to be applied to Brahma.

(3) But the Persian does not hold a similar view. He believes that there is Ahura-Mazda (Ormuzd), the lord of all good, and opposed to him is Angra-Mainya, or Ahriman, the lord of all evil. The Persian insists on this dualism. Both principles are real; the evil is real, and the good is real. Both are in perpetual conflict. This religious principle is the cause of the great differences in the character of the two peoples. The Persian is an active people, making war on surrounding nations, fighting for Ahura-Mazda and helping him gain the victory over Angra-Mainya. The Hindu believes that evil is only an illusion or dream of fallen creatures that have consciousness like man, and that Brahma is elevated above all opposition or conflict of good and evil, as well as all other conflicts. Hence the Hindu, in his education, cultivates abstract contemplation and meditation, and teaches the nugatoriness of all things. The child must be taught how to attain blessedness by passivity and repose. No active duties and struggles to overcome Nature, but he must be mild and spare animal life, even in tigers, serpents, scorpions, and vermin.

(4) The Persian education fits the youth for a career of active warfare against wild beasts and all unclean ani-

mals. All animals are unclean if they are not useful in extending the kingdom of Ahura-Mazda, because the Persian conceives them to be in the service of Angra-Mainya and to be inhabited by evil spirits. The principle of good and evil originated in the principle of light and darkness—a physical distinction being converted into a moral distinction by the great teacher Zoroaster. The religion of the Brahmans must have been the same as that of the Persians before their migration from the high table-lands of Bactria to the Indus Valley in the southeast. But a divergence took place—the Brahman thinking out a supreme unity that formed the ground of his Vedic gods of the sky, while the Persian preserved the distinction and held it to be more substantial than the principle of unity.

(5) Persian education trains the youth to speak the truth. This is before all things the highest duty, because truth is akin to clearness and light, and is, therefore, the mental activity akin to Ahura-Mazda. Next to truth-speaking is the practice of justice, for justice treats every one according to his deeds; it returns like for like, and thus treats each one's will as real. Truth-speaking is the worship of reality. If events and things are only a dream, it is of no consequence to pay so much respect to them as to be scrupulous of veracity in regard to them. Hence the Indian makes monstrous fables about things and events, and lets them become the sport of his imagination. Thus we see how deep-reaching the religious principle is, and how widely different the educations based on two principles such as the Hindu and Persian.

(6) The Chinese revere the past, and make their education consist in memorizing with superstitious exactness the forms of the past—the maxims of Confucius and Mencius—even the vehicle of literature (the alphabet) requires prodigious efforts of memory to acquire it. Do not exercise your spontaneity, but conform to the past. Be contented in repeating the thoughts which were original twenty-five hundred years ago, and make no new paths, plan out no new undertakings. The Persian is not content with the past. He must assist Ahura-Mazda in the

great fight with evil, and hence he must hurry to the front. The man who is content to remain within the domain already conquered is a craven, and does nothing for the realm of light and goodness, but allows the realm of darkness and evil to hold its own defiant position. Besides truth-speaking and justice and faithfulness to one's pledge, the Persian lays great stress on physical education, or gymnastics. The riding on horseback, and the use of the bow and arrow, the spear, and the javelin, were taught with the greatest painstaking. While the East Indian Yogi, on the other hand, mortifies his body, paralyzes his senses, and tries to lose his power of discrimination, the Persian wishes to put his conscious will into his muscles.

(e) While farther Asia conceives the individual to be lacking in substantial and eternal elements, western Asia sets aside this idea and makes decided progress toward the idea of the conscious personality of God, which the "chosen people" finally attain. The Persian idea is that of the struggle of light and darkness, of good and evil; that of the Euphrates Valley civilizations, of pleasure and pain as belonging to the divine nature. These feelings are subjective; hence to attribute them to God is to insist on his having subjectivity. Babylon and Assyria are thus advanced beyond Persia in this respect, that they have overcome its dualism of good-and-evil first principles. The Hercules myth and that of Adonis show a further advance over the Euphrates Valley idea, for labour and suffering are seen to be means of purification by which the mortal becomes divine.

(f) The psychology of the Egyptians shows a further ripening of the idea of death as mediatorial for the attainment of the divine. The elevation of mind to the point of seeing Nature with its returning cycle as the symbol of the soul, whose consciousness is a constant return into itself in self-recognition; this is the arrival at the idea of individual immortality as an essential attribute of the soul. In Asia it had been regarded as accidental; the East Indians had sought how to discontinue the series of new births. The Egyptian celebrates his insight into immor-

tality in manifold ways. His sphinx (Har-em-Akhu, or
the sun at its rising) was the symbol of resurrection.
Osiris dies, but still lives. The death court decides on the
merits of the life of each individual, and thus sets up a
standard of living for the population of the entire land.
The leading idea of Egypt is preparation for death and care
for the future life of the soul.

(g) The Phœnicians, a commercial people, stand in
contrast to the Chinese in regard to the principle of the
family. The children were trained to neglect the family.
They were weaned from their love of home by cruel family
customs. They learned irreverence for their parents, and
could sail away on adventures in far-off countries without
the feeling of homesickness. The fearful worship of the
fire god—which required the mother to give up her first-
born son to " pass through the fire to Moloch," repressing
her cries even when she saw him laid in the red-hot arms
of the idol—was a means of educating the parental and
filial indifference necessary to produce a population of
commercial adventurers.

(h) The Teutonic peoples possessed a nature which
had for its peculiarity an inordinate desire for personal
recognition. Tacitus noted this characteristic on his first
acquaintance with them. We, too, may notice the same
characteristic in the most remote descendants of these people as we find them in the cowboys of the American bor-
der lands; for we see one of these wild men approach
a settlement and announce his presence by daring the
whole village population out to fight him. He ends his
appeal to their recognition by asking them all to drink
with him. His love of recognition is " daimonic," as Rosenkranz calls it, using Goethe's word to describe it. " Other
peoples," says Hegel, " have definite objects in which they
seek supremacy. They seek wealth or beauty or abstract
right, or power, or caste distinction, but the Teutonic race
seek the satisfaction of the heart " (or *Gemüth*, as he calls
it). There is no religion except that of the Old Testament that has the element of divine recognition for the
satisfaction of this heart-hunger. The Psalms of David

are the eternal expression of this longing, for all ages and all peoples. Christianity, however, is far more explicit in its terms of fulfilment. It extends its offers to all nations, and is the first religion for all mankind. It offers to the man desiring recognition the highest possible satisfaction. The Goths and Vandals and Franks had their own religion. They had gods like Odin and Thor. They learned from Greeks and Romans of Zeus, Ares, and Apollo, or Jupiter, Mars, and Saturn. But they were not attracted by such mythologies. Indeed, they cared very little for their own native religion. Tacitus said of them, " They are *securi adversus deos*." But when the Christian missionaries came to them we may imagine them profoundly impressed with the news of such divine condescension and such complete recognition. " This new god is the very one we have always felt the need of."

CHAPTER XXXIV.

Reactions against the Social Order.—Play and Crime.

§ 192. THIS social order, realized in the institutions of civilization, described in Chapters XXXI and XXXII, appears to be a sort of fate surrounding the individual. If he rebels against it, it crushes him. Also, if he obeys it implicitly and passively, it crushes him still. Progress from Asiatic tyranny to European and American democracy consists in improvements in the method of securing the social order

through the free choice of the individual instead of
by mere external authority. More and more, society invents ways by which the individual can feel
his own selfhood fully recognised in the requirements
of social order. Education is the process of adoption
of this social order in place of one's mere animal
caprice. But it is the adoption of a consistent course
of action instead of a self-contradictory one, and
hence it is a renunciation of the freedom of the moment for the freedom that has the form of eternity.
The methods of recovering one's sense of freedom,
in this passage from impulse to obedience to social
order, are many. Some of them are social, like festivals and holidays, national ceremonies and celebrations, and some are individual, like plays and games.

If one would make himself acquainted with the character of a people, he must closely observe not alone their
political proclivities, their industries, their literature and
plastic art, but he must look especially to the manner and
matter of their festivities on holidays; for a people celebrates its deepest conviction on such occasions of mad
joy and revelry. It celebrates, in the most external way
perhaps, the very innermost phase of its civilization. A
symbol-making activity * seems to be the especial characteristic of humanity, as distinguished from brutes; for,
while the apes and certain birds, such as the mocking-

---

* Aristotle in his Poetics doubtless means by μίμησις
the act of embodying one's nature in symbols—that is, the
act of portrayal.

bird and the parrot, possess the gift of imitation to a high degree, they do not indicate in any way the existence of that correspondence between external manifestation and internal state of feeling or idea which is essential to the symbol.

(a) *The Significance of Play.*—Work and play belong to the same antithesis of conceptions. In work, the individual surrenders himself to the service of a universal want or necessity of society, which has created a vocation or calling. Man gives up his particular, special likes and desires in work. He sacrifices ease and momentary convenience for rational (universal) ends. He adopts the social order. In play, on the other hand, he gives full rein to the individual whim or caprice. In play, his activity is wholly turned toward his own immediate gratification. After work, in which he sacrifices his private, particular inclinations for society and for rational ends, comes play, in which he returns to his individuality and relaxes this tension of work. He regains his feeling of self in play, because in play immediate inclination alone guides his activity, and thus the particular self is the impelling principle, and also the immediate object of it.

(b) *The Play Idea in Greek Art.*—It has been pointed out that the games of the Roman people adumbrated the principle of their civilization. This, too, was the case among the Greeks. Gymnastic celebrations presented the visible spectacle of the human body perfected as a work of art. This spectacle for the Greeks had something of a divine or religious significance. The Olympians manifested their presence to the Grecian people in the form of beautiful incarnations. Personality seems or appears in the beautiful —i. e., in matter so completely under the immediate sway of personal being that it offers no resistance, but is pervaded with it. Not a line or lineament of the Greek statue but is full of grace—in other words, expresses free control of the spirit—hence classic repose, dignity, and self-possession.

(c) *The Roman Arch and Dome.*—The Romans, however, had a different national principle and different divinities

21

to celebrate. All is a dualism—a gigantic struggle—with
the Roman. He sets up the contradiction of private gain
over against the social order. He does not delight in the
immediate manifestation of the beautiful, but demands a
deeper and truer revelation of personality than beauty
affords, for in his consciousness there has dawned the
idea of the just and of law. The will is, accordingly, the
principle which the Roman symbolizes and enjoys in his
spectacles. The history of the will in man is the history
of the victory over one's self, of the struggle between I
want and I *ought*, between caprice and obedience to law,
civil and moral. Not moral but civil law was the Roman
contribution to humanity. They went no further than
the idea of the just, and for this reason did not fully realize even it. The moral law, and especially the immediate
and internal union of the human and divine in the innermost depths of the soul—for this a new national idea was
demanded, and it also came in the "fulness of time."
But the fierce struggle of the Roman national life to realize the supremacy of the state under whose sway the
world should be subordinated to one principle is the significant phase of Latin civilization. Its architecture hit
upon the happy expression of this principle in the Pantheon. Its dome is the highest and most perfect realization of the arch in architecture; the arch was so rounded
with itself as to make a complete building. In the arch
each component stone supports all the rest, and is in turn
supported by all the rest; each is thoroughly subordinated to the whole, and through this subordination each
is supported by the entire strength of the whole structure.
The dome is the same principle applied in all directions,
not merely lengthwise, but transversely. This makes it
possible to have, instead of the keystone, a complete circular opening or double arch at the top, which gives a
skylight. In the dome we have the image of the broad
heavens realized in stone. As under the heavens all people
breathe alike the common air, and "the rain descends
upon the just and the unjust," so in the Pantheon shall
be placed all the divinities on the same footing. The gods

of the several nations, subdued and brought under the yoke of Roman law, shall be here protected and co-ordinated under the sheltering dome, fitting symbol of the Roman state and its civil law.

(d) *Roman Games.*—In the Colisseum the Romans crowded to behold the contests of gladiators with each other and with wild beasts. The daily lesson of sacrifice of the individual for the will of the state made him delight in the spectacle (even in his games) of the sacrifice of individuality. For here he felt his own freedom; it was his arbitrary will, and not external necessity, that created the spectacle. Hence the clash of opposing individual might and its destruction had a power to delight the Roman heart. It gave enjoyment to see portrayed what he felt as his highest principle.

(e) *The Saturnalia.*—Illustrations of this principle are found in the Saturnalia and Lupercalia, in the Dionysia and Panathenæa, in the Eleusinian mysteries, and the like. That feature of the Saturnalia wherein the slaves were relieved from all ordinary toil and were permitted to wear the *pileus*, the badge of freedom, and granted full freedom of speech—were allowed to partake of a banquet, attired in the clothes of their masters, who waited upon them at the table—suggests the interpretation of this class of popular celebrations. The presentation of wax tapers (*cerei*), used in the Saturnalia as the tapers (*moccoletti*) are used in the carnival, points in the same direction. In Rome was realized the idea of the abstract equality of man before the law; for Roman law endowed each living being with rights peculiar to its social and political sphere, and protected each one in his station. Even if the rights of the father extended to the privilege of taking the life of his children, and even if the master could put his slave to death, nevertheless the father and master could do this only to their own, and the child and the slave were protected against similar violence from others. Now this recognition by the formal institution of civil rights for the child and the slave is a fact to be celebrated in the Saturnalia. From the most abstract and fundamental standpoint, that of the Roman state, all are recognised as having rights; even the relation of master and slave is not essential, and may be reversed. There is in each potentially the rights and privileges of all. Indeed, one day in each year they shall celebrate this equality before the law by the ceremony of the *pileus* and masquerade supper.

(f) *The Carnival.*—Under Christianity the corresponding conviction has become deeper. Before the awful reality of the incarnation of the divine in the human form, and the consequent equality of all men in the substance of their personality, how superficial become these social and political distinctions! There shall be enacted the spectacle of the nugatoriness of these distinctions annually. Just before the long days of fasting, previous to the celebration of the resurrection of the Son of Man, there shall be a carnival (in New Orleans "the Mardi Gras," in St. Louis the "Veiled Prophets," etc.), and in this all shall realize for a brief time this consciousness of the equality of men in the substance of their manhood. The vestments and insignia of caste and power shall become for the time masks, and each one shall choose for himself what rôle he will play in the human world. Rank and station are only garments that the human soul puts on, and in them masquerades for a brief season. Social distinctions are shams in the presence of the soul. This conviction shall rule the hours of the carnival.

(g) *The Higher Sense of Freedom.*—The reason for the diminished interest in the carnival in Great Britain and the United States arises from the fact that their political forms are freer, and it is possible for man to realize for himself to a greater extent whatever he desires to be. The Anglo-Saxon seeks adventures on the border-lands. Hence he is not forced to resort to the masquerade to realize for a brief hour his possibilities. In the land of civil equality the career opens to the talent, and talent unfolds with education. Man is not bound by caste; the doors open before his resolute endeavour. He may know that he is his own fate, and that his own intelligence alone limits and conditions him, and this sort of fate he can himself form and control. Hence man under a free government is under the constant influence of this fact. It does not come upon him spasmodically, exciting him to the wildest joy and the utmost abandon. It is the conviction of the everyday working world. But this can be said only with some reservation. Wherever the organization of civil society is such that a working class is formed who do not enter into participation with the intellectual consciousness of the nation by means of the printed page of the book and newspaper, there we are certain to find this pent-up feeling of selfhood, which must get vent in some sudden eruption and burn itself out in a brief period of madness and fury.

(h) *The Newspaper.*—The permanent and healthy cure for this pent-up feeling of selfhood is the daily newspaper, in which every morning the man lifts himself above the consciousness of his vocation into the life of the world, and beholds the spectacle of universal humanity in its eternal process. With this power of lifting the veil that shrouds from view the universal (a veil woven of remoteness and lapse of time), the commonest labourer and the man of lofty station go into their narrow spheres of vocation (for vocation is narrowing, no matter what kind it is) without murmur or complaint. In the midst of the special limitations of daily toil they feel the possibility of the universal, which they can and do realize daily. Goethe remarks: " For the narrow mind, whatever he attempts is still a trade; for the higher, an art; and the highest, in doing one thing, does all; or, to speak less paradoxically, in the one thing which he does rightly he sees the likeness of all that is done rightly." The daily realization of one's identity with the " grand man," or humanity, is essential to living a life of freedom. Any vocation whatever becomes a galling slavery unless relieved by the spectacle of the whole of society. It will, if pent up, burst forth in the wildest orgies.

(i) The novel, too, is the sociological means invented by the civilization of the nineteenth century to secure for the individual the consciousness of his identity with the social whole, it being only his greater self.

§ 193. Wherever there is much pressure laid on the individual, there the reaction is most violent. The pupils in a strictly governed school must have their forms of reaction. The school recess should be an outdoor one, and should be devoted to spontaneous play in the open air, so as to rest the will from its tension. In the college, where the pressure of prescription is far greater, the reaction produces secret societies, college songs, hazing, initiations, pranks on the citizens, etc.

(a) *Students' Pranks.*—The study of a dead language, abstruse mathematics, and disciplines far removed from the ordinary life of the age, produces what is called " self-estrangement " (*Selbst-entfremdung,* a word used by Hegel in his Phenomenology of Spirit to describe a phase of the reaction against authority and traditional faith, which belonged to the French Revolution). The study of the classics and pure mathematics, the effect of foreign travel, of the isolated life of students at universities, of wearing gowns and hoods to distinguish them from the outside world, all produces self-estrangement. The student by and by becomes at home in what was at first alien, and has enlarged his selfhood. But he preserves his elasticity in the meantime by forming Greek-letter societies, wherein he caricatures his daily studies, mocks them with inextinguishable laughter, and forms for himself the consciousness of a new life, a college life of his own creation. He " hazes " the members of the lower class, and initiates them into his artificial college life by rites well planned to shock the traditions of civil order.

(*b*) *Self-estrangement.*—The process of self-estrangement and its removal underlies all education. The mind must fix its attention upon what is alien to it and penetrate its disguise, making it become familiar. The student's reason must find the reason underlying the objective world. Wonder is only the first stage of this estrangement. It must be followed by recognition. The love of travel and adventure arises from the instinct in man to discover his own reason in the external world. When he has been through his self-estrangement, he has gained power to objectify his immediate feelings and impulses, and can understand what was before obscure in himself. (See Rosenkranz, Philosophy of Education, §§ 23 and 24.)

§ 194. When the reaction against the social order fixes itself permanently and seriously, it passes beyond the limits of play and becomes crime. In play, the serious recognition of the social order as something substantial and in rightful authority remains underneath the mask. But when the individual in all seriousness attacks the authority of the social whole, he becomes a criminal.

(*a*) Crime is the attack made by the individual against the social whole—the attack made against the higher self of human nature by the lower self. Life is not worth living for man unless he can participate in the life of the race, and thus partake of infinitude. For by this participation he uses the sense-perceptions of innumerable beings like himself, past and present; he uses the results of their thinking over the problems of the world and profits by the fruits of their experience. The individual, thus reenforced by the entire race past and present, is, as we have named it, made infinite. The criminal would by his act destroy this great process of collecting from all and distributing to each; for he refuses to obey the necessary laws that make society possible.

(b) *Sin and Crime.*—There are two attitudes of the individual who puts his lower self in hostility to his higher self—these attitudes are called sin and crime. The institution of the Church takes cognizance of sin, while the state takes cognizance of crime. The Church looks at the disposition of the man, while the state looks at the overt act. The attitude of hostility to the higher self in the depths of the soul—in the innermost disposition—is deadly sin, and, whether accompanied with overt acts or not, is immeasurable in its deserts of punishment. Only repentance can undo the sin—no amount of external deeds will restore the sinner to holiness. But the state must not regard the mere disposition; it must wait for the overt act. The overt act can be measured, while the disposition can not be measured. The state can attempt to measure out its punishments and fitly adapt them to each case. The overt act, the actual deed, can be measured, but the internal disposition is immeasurable. If met by justice, it must suffer annihilation. Grace will meet it if it repents, and save it from punishment and eternal death.

(c) *Church and State.*—This distinction between crime and sin has been growing clear for many centuries, and by its light the nations are coming to see the necessity of the separation of Church and state. If the two standards are mixed, we should have the state undertaking to punish individuals not for overt acts, but for supposed intention to commit such. This produced in France a " reign of terror." The Church, on the other hand, does not treat sin as though it were crime, and offer forgiveness for sin as an equivalent for the performance of some work of penance or for the suffering of some temporal inconvenience. The Church must not measure sin, nor the state omit to measure the overt act.

(d) *The Measurement of Crime.*—In the course of the ages of human history the state has learned how to secure justice—that is to say, how to measure crime and inflict due punishment. It has discovered that this can be done by returning the deed on the doer. It does this symbolically rather than literally. It says to the murderer: "You have taken the life of a fellow-man; your act shall come home to you, and you shall take your own life either on the scaffold or in prison with a life sentence." Or it says to a thief: "Your act was to take away property which is man's means of independence; you shall lose your independence as a consequence of the deed coming home to you, and you shall sit in a jail."

. (e) *Poetic Justice.*—What the state has devised has also been celebrated in the literatures of all lands. In fact, the supreme task of literary art has been this: to show how human deeds come back to their doers in spite of the struggles of the criminal to escape their consequences. Literature has shown this so clearly that it furnishes the wisdom of the race in its most accessible form. The great poets—Homer, Dante, Shakespeare, and Goethe—have created for us personages whose inner dispositions and overt acts are perfectly transparent to us, and their fates square the account of justice. These literary forms are so much clearer to us than any historical characters can be that in them we realize the saying of Aristotle—that poetry is truer than history. In history we are ever at a loss to determine the relation between the overt act and the disposition or motive of the doer. But we are in no doubt whatever as to this relation in the case of such as Macbeth, Othello, King Lear, Ulysses, Agamemnon, Achilles, or Faust. The logical connection between the deed and its reward is portrayed by these great literary artists in order to reveal man's higher self—the social self. But more than this is done: it is shown that the individual is so made in his innermost nature that he can not exist as human apart from the institutions of society. Hence his punishment overtakes him for his crimes even when there is no punishment done on him by the state.

§ 195. Man, as we have said, has two selves. The primal self is largely a product of Nature. There is

heredity, which gives the person his outfit of dispositions and impulses—the body that he lives in and
must use as an instrument to act with. He may in-
herit strong passions or a weak nervous organism, or
a tendency to any one of the seven mortal sins. This
does not, however, destroy his freedom, nor can the
surrounding circumstances which form the second element of fate next after heredity annul his transcendental freedom. He is free to withhold from all
action—he can utterly suppress the natural factor
attached to him, by suicide—this is the transcendental
character of his will. If he permits passion, or interest, or impulse to have sway, it is he that consents and
is responsible.

(a) *The Psychology of Dante's Inferno.*—Dante has devoted his great threefold poem to this internal relation
of the soul to its deeds. There are seven mortal sins or
states of hostility within the soul to its higher self, as
realized in institutions—there are lust, intemperance, avarice, anger, indolence, envy, and pride. Dante shows us
by symbolical pictures in his Inferno how the sin itself—
the very disposition in which the sin originates—is itself
a punishment of hell.

(1) To him, the soul in the lustful frame of mind is
driven about by tempestuous gusts through the darkened
air without a star. The lustful souls fly in long flocks
like cranes. Lust darkens the air and shuts out the light
of truth. The intemperate lie on the ground, beaten upon
by storms of hail and foul water, their bodies preventing
their intellectual souls from partaking of the higher spiritual food, the wisdom of the race. So, too, the avaricious

are shown to us rolling heavy weights to and fro, heaping pelf and squandering it, but not using it for independence of bodily wants or for the diffusion of a knowledge of the higher self. The angry are represented by Dante as swimming about in thick, putrid mud gurgling in their throats—an apt symbol of the effects of wrath on the soul's power of insight. The indolent are driven furiously about, running after a giddy flag. Having no reasonable purpose of their own, they are driven about by the goadings and stings of outside circumstances.

(2) The envious are punished in the different ditches as perpetrators of as many different kinds of fraud. The hypocrites, for instance, wear heavy cloaks of lead, gilded on the outside to look as if of gold. They have to endure the hard task of sustaining two different characters—first their own, and second of the one they assume. The soothsayers and fortune-tellers, who open the book of fate and make the future known in the present, have all suffered a paralytic stroke, and their necks are so twisted around that their faces look backward, as if Dante had said: The effect of knowing the future, or of supposing that we know it, is to paralyze our wills in the present, and prevent us from acting and trying like reasonable beings to do our best to make the future better than the present. If we believe the fortune-teller, all is now already determined and irrevocably fixed before we have acted. All time, in fact, is converted into a past, and we can only stand with our hands folded and look at the future as if already gone by. Our necks are so paralyzed and twisted that we look back upon all as past and only past.

(3) Pride is the deepest of the mortal sins, because it strikes at the very fundamental principles of all institutions. It wants no bond of union with its fellow-men or with the Creator. It says, "I alone by myself am sufficient for myself." Dante therefore punishes pride as four different kinds of treachery, freezing the proud traitors in ice, to symbolize the effect of unsociality in chilling the activities of the soul. The sins of incontinence—lust, intemperance, avarice, anger, and indolence—do not strike

against society and institutions directly, but indirectly through their ultimate effects. But envy with its ten species of fraud attacks the social bond itself; for fraud assumes the forms and ceremonies of society to work the ruin of social ends and aims. The individual, seeing that fraud is done in the forms of society, hesitates to trust society. Thus envy strikes against the social bond direct. But envy does not equal pride in its negative effects. Pride says, " I do not want either the goods of my fellow-creatures or their society." Envy says, " I wish all your goods given to me and you deprived of them."

Dante has in the second part of his poem shown the sort of pain that the soul suffers in its struggles to purge itself free from these seven mortal sins. The Purgatory differs from the Inferno, therefore, in the quality of its pain and suffering. The state of mind which is in the Inferno persists in retaining its sinful purposes and doing its deeds against the institutions of society. It supposes that its sufferings are undeserved, and due to the hatred and unjust persecution of its fellow-men and of God. It does not see that its state of torment is due to its own deeds—to the atmosphere of those of its deeds which strike against the existence of its own higher self.

(b) *The Psychology of Dante's Purgatory.*—But in the Purgatory the soul sees that mortal sin brings with it its own atmosphere of torment, and it strives to eradicate from itself all tendency to sin, and for this purpose it welcomes the pain that comes as a means of purification. If the mortal sin had not been accompanied by hellish torments, the soul would not have been able to discover the true nature of its deed, and might therefore have never known the paradise of the higher self—the life in subordination to institutions. Punishment is thus seen in the purgatorial state of the soul to be a tribute of recognition on the part of the Creator—a recognition of the freedom of the will. Man is recognised as responsible for his acts, as owning his deed. Punishment by imprisonment on the part of the state is a high compliment to the individual criminal, for it assumes that the individual is free in doing his deed.

CHAPTER XXXV.

The Psychology of Infancy.

§ 196. For the first four years of the child's life the family education has been all in all for him. He has learned in his first year to hold up his head, to clutch things with his hands, using his thumbs in contraposition to his fingers, to follow moving objects with his eyes; he has learned smells and tastes, sounds and colours, and the individuality of objects. He has learned to move himself, using his limbs somewhat as a turtle does in crawling. In his second year he has learned to stand alone and to walk; to use some words and understand the meaning of a great many more. His recognition of colours, sounds, tastes, and touch-impressions has increased enormously. He has acquired his first set of teeth and can use them.

The scientific observations of Professor Preyer have taught us how important is the epoch when the human infant ceases to clutch objects only with the four fingers like most of the ape family, and learns to use his thumb over against his fingers. This contraposition of the thumb began, in the case he records, about the twelfth week of the infant's life—at first a sort of reflex action without the will, and then soon after produced by the will, so that contraposition of the thumb was quite attained by the fourteenth week. The infant rejoices in each new power gained, and incessantly practises it with voluntary attention until it by degrees sinks into a habit. The first look of attention on the part of the child of Preyer was given to some swinging tassels on the thirty-ninth day. In the ninth week it noticed and gave attention to the ticking of a watch. Other important epochs mentioned in his Mind of the Child are the following: 1. Holding up its head by the act of will in the eleventh week. 2. Standing alone in the forty-eighth week. 3. Walking in the fiftieth week. 4. Recognition of its mother on the sixty-first day. 5. Recognition of its own image in a mirror in the sixth month—stretching out its hand to the image—also recognising its father's image, and turning to look at the real father and compare him with the image. 6. In the seventeenth week is noticed the first recognition of self, indicated by attention to his own hand; and six weeks later an elaborate series of experiments of touching himself and foreign objects alternately. 7. The discovery of itself as cause when it can produce sound by rattling a paper, or by striking one object with another, or tearing asunder a piece of paper—this is a most delightful discovery to the child. 8. But imitation, which begins about the fifteenth week and by and by develops into the use of language, is the most interesting evidence of the growth of the intellect. This glance at infant life reminds us that in education things that are very trivial at one epoch are of great moment at another. In cases of arrested development the educational value of such matters as the contraposition of the thumb, the exertion of the will in supporting the body erect, and in imitation, is coming to be well understood, as one may see in recent schools for the feeble-minded. But the order of development of these things is all-important. An act is educative when first learned, and then only. After it has become habit it is a second nature—a new nature produced by the will, and is no longer educative. Man as a bundle of habits is a self-made being. Professor Preyer's child was so delighted with the discovery that it could put a cover on a box, that it deliberately took it off and replaced it seventy-nine times without an interval of rest. It was an educative step in its development—a step in the discovery of its selfhood as an energy, as well as a step in the discovery of adaptation in the external world.

§ 197. Imitation precedes the acquisition of language. In his third and fourth years the child's knowledge of the external world has progressed steadily, powerfully aided, as it is now, by the acquisition of language; for by language the child has become able to use the senses of other people as well as his own. He listens to their accounts of what they have seen, and asks questions incessantly to draw out the experience of his parents, old brothers and sisters, attendants and acquaintances. Not only does he learn to see and hear through other people—that is to say, get information of the results of older people's observations—but he begins to use their reflections and inquires eagerly for explanations. It is a great delight for him to discover that things and events are little sections in endless chains of things and events—little beads, as it were, strung on a long thread of causal relation—each thing or event being the effect of some antecedent thing or event, and likewise destined to be the cause of other things and events to follow it. The world seems very wonderful to the child when the principle of causality begins

to act in his mind, and he wishes to know the why
of things and events, wishes to learn in what sense
they are means to something else, in what sense they
are results of something else.

Through imitation of sounds and the effort to attach
a meaning to them, language has arisen, and now the child
has enlarged his educative possibilities infinitely; for he
can, as we have just seen, learn the results of the sense-
perception of older and wiser people than himself, and
also the results of their thoughts and reflections. A
miraculous change takes place in the child's sense-perception in learning to talk. Before he learns the use of language each thing or event is looked upon as all in all by
itself. Hence he does not see its relations and can not
" apperceive " it. But just as soon as he learns language
he sees every object, every single event or thing, as an individual of a class, as one specimen of an indefinite number of possible specimens (see Chapter XXV). In other
words, the use of language implies that the child has
begun to use universal terms, words for classes, and to
think all objects as specimens of classes. It is a note-
worthy thing, therefore, in the second year of a child to
hear him call the name of an animal or thing upon seeing
it. He has ascended above his previous state of development. To him the particular object seen and named is
one individual seen on a background of infinite possibility
of the production of such individuals. It is evident that
language implies a causal view of the world, and, more
than this, it implies a world of genera or species and particular individuals. Finally, it implies that the classes or
species or genera are not mere results of picking out similar individuals and arranging them together in classes. He
assumes that each object has a producing process of some
kind behind it, and this concept is the idea of a true universal. The child, therefore, begins to ask the names for
all things and events. He tries the patience of his elders

by his persistence. Why does he lay so much stress on mere names? they ask. The reply is found in what we have just now considered—the child's sense-perception has arisen above the plane of animal sense-perception, and he now and forever after sees each thing, and will see it, as a specimen of a class. Classification is effected by naming. It is the primary condition for putting the mind in an attitude of re-enforcing his present observation by all its own experience and all the experience of his fellows. He therefore wants a name for the class, so that he may forthwith begin to store up the different possibilities of form, shape, size, colour, and other varieties of type that he may find in future experience.

§ 198. The place of imitation in the development of civilized man is beginning to be recognised.* Not only does imitation give rise to language, but it leads to the formation of institutions, the family, civil community, the state, the Church—those greater selves which re-enforce the little selves of isolated individuals. Imitation is social in its very nature, for it is the repetition by the individual within himself of the deeds of his fellows. The study of imitation leads to the discovery of the modes by which the individual man repeats for himself the thinking and doing

---

* Mr. G. Tarde, Les lois de l'imitation étude sociologique, Paris, 1890. Prof. Mark Baldwin, of Princeton University, articles on The Psychology of Imitation, in Science, 1891, 1892; in Mind, 1894; his book, Mental Evolution in the Child and the Race, 1895. Prof. Josiah Royce, of Harvard, article on The Imitative Functions and their Place in Human Nature, in the Century for May, 1894.

22

and feeling of his fellows, and thus enriches his own
life by adding to it the lives of others. Thus (as
shown in Chapters XXXI and XXXII) his own life
becomes vicarious for others, and he participates vicariously in the life of society. The psychology of
imitation explains the mode in which the individual
man unites with his fellow-men to form a social whole.

(a) What are manners and customs but imitated forms
of doing, that preserve the results of successful experience
in dealing with Nature or in co-operating with one's fellows? What is fashion, with its apparently capricious
changes, but the method of emancipating individuals from
the tyranny of old customs and usages that insist on
minute punctilios in matters that are unimportant except
as symbols of our membership in the social whole? Thus
one kind of imitation supplants another as more progressive. The fashions of the semicivilized and savage people
last without change from generation to generation—and,
indeed, it is likely for hundreds and even for thousands
of years—because the savage intellect can not as yet attain the strength to discriminate between moral and indifferent actions. The savage has only two kinds of deeds,
moral and immoral; while the civilized man has three
kinds, moral, immoral, and unmoral. Thus that form of
imitation which we all despise as mere fashion has significance as the means of emancipating us from that heavy
yoke of ceremonial that once prescribed the forms of our
indifferent actions as though they were of moral or religious import.

(b) Imitation develops, on the one hand, into habits,
or customs and morals, and this is the will side of the
human mind; and, on the other hand, it develops into
perception, memory, ideas, and insights, this being the
intellectual side. It is evident that the pedagogic interest in psychology is the evolution of the higher facul-

ties out of the lower. It is all-important for us to understand this progressive step by which free moral action develops in the place of mere unconscious use and wont. We must discover how mere external memory of borrowed ideas gives place to insight. It is necessary, first of all, to discover the most elementary forms of imitation. In this research the students of psychical phenomena have greatly aided. The discovery of the fact that a small percentum of people are so sensitive to the mental influences about them that they can, without the intermediation of words, read the thoughts of others, has been made and verified in numerous instances. The study of hypnotism has taken up this fact into a class of related facts belonging not only to the intellect, but to the will and the emotions as well. The phrase "hypnotic suggestion" has come to play a great rôle in elucidating the rudimentary facts of imitation. The hypnotizer suggests an idea, which the hypnotic subject takes up and carries out in feeling or action. The rapid progress of scientific investigation in this field of psychic research promises to throw light on all social thought, feeling, and action. It will help us to understand much that has been obscure in the rise and spread of popular beliefs, the genesis of social tornadoes, like the Crusades, the French Revolution, the Tartaric invasions of Europe, or even such local affairs as strikes and mobs.

§ 199. To see the significance of imitation in the child-mind, we must look upon it not as a comparatively feeble and mechanical effort, as something determined by outside influences, but as a phase of self-activity which is engaged in emancipating the self from heredity and natural impulse. We must not lose sight of this essential fact, that shows itself even in the most rudimentary of the phenomena of imitation. There can be no imitation whatever except on the part of self-active beings—in other words, only souls can imitate. "Imitation," says M. Compayré, "is the reproduction of what one has seen another do." It is therefore always to some extent an act of assimilation. Even if we extend the meaning of imitation so as to include unconscious mimicry and all phenomena akin to hypnotic suggestion, still it is self-activity that does the imitating. What is beheld as an act of another is converted by adoption into an act of self. The pride and pleasure that the infant exhibits on the occasion of his first conscious imitation has its root in this, that he has made something his own—has proved himself equal to imitating in himself a movement by his will—he has revealed his selfhood to some extent. This is the significance of play, which is chiefly imitation, that the undeveloped human being is learning to know himself by seeing what he can do. He is revealing himself to others and to himself, and getting strength in his individuality.

(a) Thus we see that there is an element of originality in the most mechanical phase of imitation. The self is active and assimilative. It sees an external deed which it proceeds to make its own deed by imitation. The child proves itself to possess a human nature identical with the one whom it imitates.

(b) Originality grows by progressive deepening of the

insight into the causes and motives of the thing imitated. The lowest stage of imitation superstitiously imitates all the details, because it has no insight into the grounds and purposes of the action imitated, and but little comprehension of the means employed. When it understands the means and the motives, it strikes out for itself and makes new adaptations. It modifies its imitation to suit differences of circumstances.

(c) Originality grows with this ascending comprehension of means and purposes. There comes a time when the imitative child comprehends the principle as well as does the master whom he imitates, and then he is emancipated from all imitation in this part of his education. If he keeps on and comprehends the genesis of the principle from deeper principles, he emancipates himself from even the "hypnotic suggestion" of the principle itself, and all external authority has become inward freedom.

(d) M. Tarde, in his great book on the Laws of Imitation, speaks of self-imitation, as in the case of habit (page 83), which he defines as a sort of "unconscious imitation of one's self by one's self." Here, in the stages of originality, where the person has learned to comprehend what he once imitated, and now understands it in its causes and in the reasons for its existence, is self-imitation, if we are to speak of imitation at all. It is no longer an activity at an outward suggestion, but purely spontaneous. It has vanquished the external object by ascending to its causes.

(e) It is worthy of note that this book of M. Tarde is a French study of sociology. In the French Revolution the thought of Rousseau produced individualism, and the social whole was denied a valid existence in the shape of the state, except in so far as it appeared as a free contract between individuals. It was not considered that a contract always implies the pre-existence of state or government, a social whole to give validity to the contract. It is well that this new movement in psychology, which proves the substantial basis of mental evolution to lie in social institutions, should receive its great impulse from a Frenchman. Rousseau's influence in behalf of individualism has extended to all nations that read books. M. Tarde is the anti-Rousseau. With Rousseau the individual is from "the hand of Nature," while the institutions of society are man-made, artificial, and without binding reality. Over against this doctrine of individualism the tendency of M. Tarde is to set up the doctrine of the social whole as all in all.

§ 200. Imitation in its purest and simplest form —that of mechanical repetition of the actions of another person—is, by common consent, placed at the bottom of spiritual achievements. A monkey or a parrot can mimic actions or speech, and to call the action of a human being parrotlike repetition or a process of aping is to express reproach and contempt for it.

(*a*) This proves the felicity of a study of the psychology of education which makes imitation its corner stone. What teacher is there that does not despise mere verbal repetition in his pupils? Can there be a greater paradox in educational psychology than the theory which sets out with the function of imitation and attempts to show that all forms of intellectual and moral activity are only varieties of this despised mode of action? If there is an attractive method of bringing psychology to the attention of teachers, surely it has now been found. The sheer audacity of the theory that places the stone which the teachers had rejected for the head of the corner will fix the attention alike of the primary schoolmistress and the professor in college.

(*b*) The profoundest thinker of the human race, Aristotle, hits upon this subject of imitation in his Poetics, making it the basis of his philosophy of art. What he says in the fourth and ninth chapters on the subject of Mimesis, or imitation, leads us rather to see a deeper meaning in the word than mimicry or mechanical repetition. It seems almost to mean symbol-making. "Man is the most imitative of animals, and makes his first steps in learning by aid of imitation," he tells us. Man is a symbol-making animal always in whatever he does; making a symbol of what he is in his essential nature; always repeating in himself the symbols of the existence and actions of all other beings.

(c) Leibnitz, the philosopher who translated Aristotle's ideas for modern readers, has told us in his Monadology that each soul is a monad which, by its self-activity, repeats for itself, or represents, the whole universe. This is imitation on a grand scale—imitation transfigured, we might say—that by self-activity assimilates the whole universe. The monad creates for itself the world that it perceives. Here, we see, is the harmony of freedom and authority. The soul is not determined by what lies outside it, but determines itself (see Chapter XXII) so as to reproduce the beings and the causes that are outside it. Here, too, is the social man again of M. Tarde; for each man has this one destiny, to sum up in himself the life and deeds of the race.

(d) The great world poet, Goethe, in his Wilhelm Meister, treats the problem of culture or education, in its widest sense, in connection and contrast with the problem of dramatic art—how to make an actor. The individual sees ideals above him, and impersonates them; loves them and imitates them; wears them as a player acts his part. Gradually he acquires as a second nature his ideals, and must keep growing on into new and higher ideals. The mere actor (he shows) must be able to assume quickly all characters, and yet possess no character himself; he must be a sort of professional wig-block, to hold one after another all kinds of wigs, but to have not even a scalp of its own. Goethe's favourite characters are those who react against their environments by internal development. They always press beyond imitation toward

the indwelling principle of that which is imitated, and
thus attain freedom. In contrast to these, he draws us
pictures of characters who have hardened into habit and
become fixed in all their imperfections.

§ 201. In the acquirement of language the child
has come into possession of the most powerful instrument of self-education that exists, and he has acquired a new faculty of mind—the faculty of seeing
each object before the senses in the light of its universal—that is to say, he sees the real with a margin
of ideal possibilities all around it. Ever after he will
see any example or specimen that comes under a
class name with a reflection that the previous specimen differed from it in some respects of size or colour
or shape. He will think of the other possibilities
not realized whenever he sees any given real specimen of a class. Here, therefore, begins the child's
perception of ideals; right here, when he begins to
use language. Seeing possibilities or ideals, the child
now begins to have will-power. Before ideals or motives are seen, the will-power has not yet risen out of
blind impulse or instinct. Now as he sees objects he
thinks of their unrealized possibilities, and at once he
has a motive to act. To act gives him a consciousness
of his own power to create; for to change a possibility into a reality, to actualize a motive, is to create
a new form; it is to cause that to exist which was

mcrely ideal before. Thus in process of learning language the child is unfolding genuine will-power, learning to see all things as results of processes which are active universals, and getting true self-consciousness. The recognition of the self as causative, or creative of new forms, is self-consciousness, the recognition of one's own individuality.

(*a*) This recognition of ideals, when one comes to see the individual object on the background of the universal or class, has a significance for science. Science is, in fact, the systematic statement of what unconscious experience has found in the object; for this purpose science begins with an inventory which gleans all the individual observations and preserves them. All the phases of the object are necessary to its complete revelation. Then science can see in each phase all the others as helping to explain it.

(*b*) The first step above brute instinct begins when man looks beyond things as he sees them existing before him, and commences to consider their possibilities; he begins to add to his external seeing an internal seeing; the world begins to assume a new aspect; each object appears to be of larger scope than its present existence, for there is a sphere of possibility environing it—a sphere which the sharpest animal eyes of lynx or eagle can not see, but which man, endowed with this new faculty of inward sight, perceives at once. To this insight into possibilities there loom up uses and adaptations, transformations and combinations in a long series stretching into the infinite behind each finite real thing. The bodily eyes see the real objects, but can not see the infinite trails; these trails are invisible except to the inward eyes of the mind.

(*c*) What we call directive power on the part of man, his combining and organizing power, all rests on this power to see beyond the real things before the senses to the ideal possibilities invisible to the brute. The more clearly man sees these ideals the more perfectly he can construct for himself another set of conditions than those in which he finds himself.

§ 202. The period of infancy is dominated by what may be called the symbolic stage of mind. We have seen * that even in feeling there is a reaction within the animal soul, the same being a reproduction for itself of the object felt in the environment. The representation, unconscious in feeling, becomes conscious in recollection and memory. In fancy and imagination it becomes free from the external. These forms of activity all deal with images or pictures in the mind. There is an ascending series of these, from the fixed image in the perception of an immediate object, toward the image of the productive or creative imagination. More and more the image is accompanied with thought, which defines relations of cause and effect, of genus and species. Thought is non-picturable, but the image furnishes illustrations for the causal relations seized by the thinking process. Think any object by definition, and it must be thought as an individual of a species; the general includes the process by which the individual is originated, and the individual is a result of that process. The result can be imaged. The mental pictures that accompany

* Chapters xxii to xxv.

thought are thus representations of some of the results of the process thought out in conceiving a genus or species. But it is long before the mind becomes aware of the relation of its images to its thoughts. It takes for granted that the mental pictures include all that there is in its thoughts; whereas, in fact, they include only termini, and not the process that lies between those termini. The first suspicion that the mind gets of the inadequacy of these mental pictures leads to symbolic thought. In the symbol the object is seized in its identity with some other object and made to stand for it. The difference is kept in the background of the mind, but not lost. The symbol has great advantage in dealing with thoughts that can not be imaged. The Latin word for soul, *anima*, means breath. The ideas of *invisibility* and *pervading* belong to both, and the material breath becomes symbol for the immaterial self-activity, soul. The symbolic stage is the identification of the natural with the spiritual, and likewise the beginning of a discrimination of them. All objects are conceived as containing a spiritual meaning.

§ 203. The symbolic phase of mind is not analytic so much as synthetic. If it analyzes its object, it comes at once on differences, and more numerous differences than identities. Air differs from soul in very many ways; it resmbles it in two, or perhaps three, ways. The more mature analysis differentiates (using the third figure of the syllogism, Chapter XI), while the earlier synthetic activity identifies (using the second figure, Chapter IX) and catches analogies. The symbol is consequently one-sided and equivocal. It may be understood in a different sense from that intended, and will be so understood by the person lacking poetic sense.

§ 204. There must be distinguished the following stages of symbolism:

(*a*) Personification: the placing of a soul in a thing; animism.

(*b*) Metaphor: the elevation of thing to a spiritual meaning (thing to soul, as personification makes soul to thing).

(*c*) Play: one thing substituted for another: " Make believe that this stick is a horse "; " I have built a house with these blocks "; " This is the way the farmer mows his grass."

(*d*) The unconscious symbolic in poetry and mythology. It uses typical characters, shrouding the human in the forms of animals in fairy stories and fables. It uses typical characters in their proper personality in poetry. The particular is taken for the general class.

(a) The child delights in fairy tales because they sport with the fixed conditions of actuality, and present to him a picture of free power over Nature and circumstances. Thus they to some extent prefigure to him the conquest which his race has accomplished and is accomplishing; it is made to appear as the exploits of some Aladdin or Jack the Giant-killer. "To modify, change, or destroy the limits of common actuality," as Rosenkranz says, is the perpetual work of the race. It moulds the external world to suit its own ideas. Play is the first education that the child gets to prepare him for this human destiny.

(b) How what is symbolic becomes conventional is perhaps the most interesting question in the psychology of early education. Conventional studies, like the alphabet and orthography, can not well be taken up until the child has reached this conventional epoch of growth. In the old hieroglyphic system the letter A represented the face of an ox, and was symbolic. Since the Phœnicians carried the alphabet to other peoples, A has been a conventional sign for a particular sound, and its original meaning forgotten.

§ 205. The step from the image of a material object by symbolism to a spiritual relation shows a progress. At first the object (e. g., breath) is conceived, and, next after, it becomes symbol (viz., of the soul). But the more familiar this step becomes the less time is occupied in imaging the material object, and the accent is placed more sharply on the thought of the spiritual object. By and by the image of the material object drops away almost entirely, and the word becomes a conventional sign for the spiritual thought and the mind forgets the sensuous meaning. This is the passage from the symbolic to the conventional stage of the mind, and takes place at a well-defined epoch in the life of the child in modern civilization. In savage life it is never reached. The mind remains at the myth-making or symbolic stage.

(a) A great poet converts all things and events lying familiar about him in the world into tropes or similitudes, so that they lose their imposing airs of actuality, and become transparent images of ideas and spiritual truth. If he accomplishes so much as this by means of his tropes and personifications, he accomplishes far more than this by means of his entire poetic structures, for the individual tropes are only the brick and mortar of the poetic edifice. What the scientific principle is to isolated facts and events, the poetic structure is to the separate tropes and personifications. It organizes them into a whole. It connects them with a central unity which stands to them in the twofold relation of efficient and final cause, and is at once their origin and the final purpose for which they exist.

(b) It may be said that the supreme object of a great poetic work of art is the production of a myth. A myth furnishes a poetic explanation for a class of phenomena observed in the world. The poet that can see tropes in natural objects sees his way lighted by their converging rays to an underlying unity. Under tropes of small compass lie more extensive tropes, which unite the former into a consistent whole. And as the poet's fundamental insight into the world is this, that the things and events of the world are means of spiritual expression, themselves moved and shaped by spiritual being, which they both hide and reveal, it follows that his combination of these poetic elements produces a whole structure that is spiritual throughout, and a revelation of human nature such as he has conceived and fitted to the world he has created.

(c) The poet is eyes to the blind and ears to the deaf. He is intuition and reflection for all. For he furnishes his people a view of the world in which they can all unite and build cities and civilizations. His inspired myth is recognised as the highest possession of the race, and implicit faith in it is demanded of all men. While it is permitted to deny the reality of existing facts and events, it is never permitted to deny the truth of the poetic myth which unites a people in one civilization.

(d) Not only in poetic art, but in all art—sculpture, painting, music, and architecture—there is a seeking after rhythm, or after regularity, symmetry, and harmony, and a delight in them simply as such, as though they constituted indubitable evidence of a rational cause identical in nature with the human mind that beholds it. What is consciousness but the rhythm of subject and object continually distinguishing and continually recognising and identifying? In this are regularity and symmetry, and also harmony. There is the repetition involved in self-knowing—the self being subject and likewise object—hence regularity. The shallowest mind, the child or the savage, delights in monotonous repetition, not possessing, however, the slightest insight into the cause of his delight. To us the phenomenon is intelligible. We see that his perception is like a spark under a heap of smoking flax. There is little fire of conscious insight, but much smoke of pleasurable feeling. He feels rather than perceives the fact of the identity which exists in form between the rhythm of his internal soul-activity and the sense-perception by which he perceives regularity.

(e) The sun-myth arises through the same feeling, illuminated by the poetic insight. Wherever there is repetition, especially in the form of revolution or return-to-itself, there comes this conscious or unconscious satisfaction at beholding it. Hence especially circular movement, or movement in cycles, is the most wonderful of all the phenomena beheld by primitive man. Nature presents to his observation infinite differences. Out of the confused mass he traces some forms of recurrence—day and night, the phases of the moon, the seasons of the year, genus and species in animals and plants, the apparent revolutions of the fixed stars, and the orbits of planets. These phenomena furnish him symbols or types in which to express his ideas concerning the divine principle that he feels to be First Cause. To the materialistic student of sociology all religions are mere transfigured sun-myths; but to the deeper student of psychology it becomes clear that the sun-myth itself rests on the perception of identity between regular cycles and the rhythm which characterizes the activity of self-consciousness. And self-consciousness is felt and seen to be a form of being not on a level with mere transient, individual existence, but the essential attribute of the Divine Being.

(*f*) Here we see how deep-seated and significant is this blind instinct or feeling which is gratified by the seeing and hearing of mere regularity. The words which express the divine in all languages root in this sense-perception and in the æsthetic pleasure attendant on it. Philology, discovering the sun-myth origin of religious expression, places the expression before the thing expressed, the symbol before the thing signified. It tells us that religions arise from a sort of disease in language which turns poetry into prose. But underneath the æsthetic feeling lies the perception of identity, which makes possible the trope or metaphor.

(*g*) In the poetic myth there is a collection of those phenomena which have astonished the primitive consciousness of the race, and impressed on the soul a deep feeling of awe. The activity of the mind with its regular and symmetrical recurrence or rhythm—the vibration between subject and object, its alternation of seizing an object at first new and unknown, and then recognising in it what is already become familiar, the alternation of subject and predicate, its self-estrangement and its removal—have not been recognised by primitive man as the characteristics of mind, but these phenomena of return-into-self have excited his attention, and suggested first the far-off questions of the cycle of the soul reaching beyond this life into the hereafter.

(*h*) Of all nations, the Egyptians were the most inclined to study these analogies of Nature. Because of the fact that the supreme natural circumstance in Egyptian life is the Nile, and its cycles of rise and fall alternating with seedtime and harvest, this attention to cycles finds its natural occasion and explanation. The calendar and the signs of the seasons of the year became objects of the utmost solicitude. By and by the poetic faculty seized on these phenomena and the doctrine of immortality was embodied in a myth for mankind. There is the still world of *Amenti* where the good Egyptian goes to dwell with Osiris. But the most highly gifted of all peoples in poetic insight were the Greeks. They possessed supreme ability in the interpretation of Nature as expression of spirit. All educated peoples since the Greeks have used their poetic myths in literature and art, and these have become conventional means of representing the life experiences of the soul.*

§ 206. When the child possesses language and begins to inquire for names, begins to see ideals and to act to realize them, he can be helped greatly by the kindergarten method of instruction. It should be used first in the house by the mother and the nurse, and afterward in the school. The kindergarten wisely selects a series of objects that lead to the useful possession of certain geometric concepts and numerical concepts that assist in grasping all things in their inorganic aspects. It provides for his new perception of possibilities or ideals by setting him to work at building. It has a series of occupations—

* *Cf.* my Spiritual Sense of Dante's Divina Commedia, pp. 122-128.

23

building, stick-laying, drawing, perforating paper, embroidery, joining sticks by soaked peas, modelling in clay, weaving, etc. In all these the child finds relations to the fundamental geometric shapes that he has learned to know, and he sees with clearness and precision how to realize ideals. The kindergarten, in using the gifts and occupations, however, does not use the highest and best that Froebel has invented. The peculiar Froebel device is found in the plays and games. Froebel himself wrote the Mutter- und Koselieder, and explained them with his subtle philosophy. The child here in the plays and games, in which all join (pupils and teachers), ascends from the world of Nature to the world of humanity; from the world of things to the world of self-activity; from the material and earthy to the spiritual. In the gifts and occupations he becomes conscious of his will as a power over matter to convert it to use and to make it the symbol of his ideals. But in such work he does not fully realize his spiritual sense, because he does not find anything in it to make him realize the difference between his particular self and his general self. In the plays and games he becomes conscious of his social self, and there dawns the higher ideal of a self that is realized in institutions, over against the special self of the particular individual.

(a) In the songs and pantomime the child uses his self-activity to reproduce for himself the doings of the world of society. He produces a reflection of this world of human life above him and repeats to himself its motives and its industries, putting himself in the place of the grown-up citizen and mimicking his mode of thinking and acting. By this he attains the new consciousness of a higher self acting within his particular self and dictating the customary usages, the conventional forms of politeness, the fashions set for him to follow, and, above all, he begins to have a conscience. The conscience demands unconditional obedience, the sacrifice not only of possessions but of life, too, in its behest. Here the child climbs up through his symbolic pathway through play to the absolute mind. He sees the ideal laws that are absolutely binding above all temporal considerations; he sees the moral law. The moral law is an entirely different thing from the laws of matter and motion. The latter relate to dead, inorganic substances moved from outside, and under fate. The former is the law of activity of spirit, the living, the human, the divine. It is the law of self-activity. No self-active being can retain its freedom or self-activity except by conforming to moral law.

(b) The kindergarten does well when it teaches the gifts and occupations, for it deals with the world of means and instrumentalities, and helps the child to the conquest of Nature. It does better with the plays and games, because these are thoroughly humane in their nature, and they offer to the child in a symbolic form a first version of the experience of the race in solving the problem of life. They make children wise without the conceit of wisdom.

(c) The first self-revelation of the child is through play. He learns by it what he can do, what he can do easily at first trial, and what he can do by perseverance and contrivance. Thus he learns through play to recognise the potency of those "lords of life" (as Emerson calls them) that weave the tissue of human experience—volition, making and unmaking, obstinacy of material, the magic of contrivance, the lordly might of perseverance that can re-enforce the moment by the hours (and time by eternity). The child in his games represents to himself his kinship to the human race—his identity, as little self, with the social whole as his greater self.

(d) The child is always outgrowing his playthings, always exhausting the possibilities of a given object to represent or symbolize the occupations and deeds of grown-up humanity in the world about him. Were the child to arrest his development and linger contented over a doll or a hobby-horse, the result would be lamentable. Hence *unmaking* is as important as *making* to the child.* His destructive energy is as essential to him as his power of construction—a point often missed by kindergartners who have not penetrated Froebel's doctrine of inner connection in its third degree.

(e) True inner development or education should proceed from the symbolic to the æsthetic or artistic, from art to science, and from science to philosophy; for true art (including also poetry) is a higher form of "inner connection" than the merely symbolic, which constitutes the spiritual side of play. Again, science and philosophy are more advanced than art in the fact that they seize the inner connection directly and simply, while the symbolic form is only a suspicion or intimation of an inner connection, and art is only a personification or an illustration of it.

§ 207. After the symbolic comes what is called the conventional. In his first stages of using language the child is just in the symbolic stage of culture, and the kindergarten is exactly the kind of

---

* Goethe has indicated this in his.Wilhelm Meister by showing how the father, by a puppet show and a wrong policy in regard to it, made a lifelong impression on the mind of Wilhelm, and nearly arrested his growth at the puppet stage.

instruction best adapted to him. At the age of seven years, or in the beginning of the seventh year in some cases, the child has acquired this sense of higher individuality. Just as in the first attainment of the gift of speech the child learns to see all things as specimens of their universals, and to desire names for all things, so four or five years later he has acquired the humane culture which it was the object of the plays and games of Froebel to teach, and he now regards himself as a member of a social whole—in fact, as an individual having special duties to perform in the life of the whole. With the beginning of this consciousness the symbolic bent of the mind begins to yield place to a higher and more conscious form of intellectual and moral activity, and the child is ready for the methods of the primary school. The child, in fact, has arrived at a point where he needs instruments of self-help; he needs to master the conventionalities of human learning; he needs to learn how to read and write, and how to record the results of arithmetic.

(a) The human race uses arbitrary characters to represent elementary sounds and combines them into words, a process of analysis and synthesis quite difficult for the child of the symbolic period of culture to master. With the acquirement of these arbitrary means of indicating speech the child will have a new means of self-help altogether more wonderful than anything that he has before learned. He will be able now to appeal from the oral and desultory statement or narrative to the printed page, which contains the well-considered and exhaustive results of all human experience near and remote. Once acquired, the child is emancipated from dependence on the leisure of others; he can now, at his own leisure, consult the experience of the race in so far as it exists in his language and in so far as he can master its special form of exposition.

(*b*) This must be done by individual industry, and is an ethical deed quite distinct from the work of the child in the kindergarten. The child now feels the impulse of duty. Self-subordination to reasonable tasks is no longer play. He has arrived at the transition from play to work. He can now begin to be responsible to authority for the performance of them. Here we have the contrast of play and work. In play the child exercises his caprice. He sees possibilities and transforms things according to his arbitrary will. In this he learns his own power, the power of his selfhood, and thereby develops his individuality. When he acts under the direction of another he does not realize what is peculiarly his own causal energy. It is not *his* ideal, but the ideal of another that he realizes.

(*c*) It is very important not to force on the child, in the symbolic stage of his culture—say from four to six years of age—the ideals of others in the details of his work, for that will produce arrested development, and he will not have the vivid sense of personality that he ought to have. The kindergarten method encourages spontaneity, and thus protects the fountains of his originality.

(*d*) At the age of seven years the average child begins to tire of mere caprice, having gained, through play, the essential development of his originality. It is now attracted toward work or the exercise of the will along the lines of rational activity, or prescribed by established authority. This is work. While the kindergarten should lay stress on the form of play, and give the child opportunity to develop his spontaneity, the primary school must lay stress on the form of work, and lay down definite tasks for the pupil to perform by his own industry.

(e) By language the child rises from an animal individuality to a human individuality. By realizing his membership in society and conforming his deeds to the general standard, he develops a higher spiritual individuality. This, as we have seen, is the object of the kindergarten plays and games. When it is achieved, the method of play gives place to the method of work; the symbolic yields to the conventional; the kindergarten methods to the methods of the primary school. (See Dr. N. M. Butler, on The Meaning of Infancy and Education, Educational Review, 1897, p. 73.)

CHAPTER XXXVI.

Psychology of the Course of Study in Schools, Elementary, Secondary, and Higher.

§ 208. In the elementary course completed in the first eight years of school life (say from six to fourteen years of age) the pupil has acquired the conventional branches of common English. Reading, writing, arithmetic—the so-called " three R's "—grammar, geography, and United States history, furnish him the necessary disciplines that enable him to take up the rudiments of human experience; they give him a mastery over the technical elements which enter the practical theories of human life.

(*a*) There are five windows of the soul, which open out upon five great divisions of the life of man. Two of these relate to man's comprehension and conquest over Nature, the realm of time and space. Arithmetic furnishes the survey of whatever has the form of time; all series and successions of individuals, all quantitative multiplicity being mastered by the aid of the art of reckoning. Through the geographical window of the soul the survey extends to organic and inorganic Nature. The surface of the earth, its concrete relations to man as his habitat and as the producer of his food, clothing, and shelter, and the means of intercommunication which unite the detached fragments of humanity into one grand man—all these important matters are introduced to the pupil through the study of geography, and spread out as a panorama before the second window of the soul.

(*b*) Three other departments or divisions of human life lie before the view. Human life is revealed in the history—civil, social, and religious—of peoples. The study of the history of one's native country in the elementary school opens the window of the soul which looks out upon the spectacle of the will power of his nation. In the language of a people are revealed the internal logical laws or structural framework of its intellect and the conscious realization of the mind of the race, as they appear in the vocabulary, grammatical laws, or syntax. Grammar opens to the child his view of the inner workings of the mind of the race, and helps him in so far to a comprehension of his own spiritual self. Literature, finally, is the most accessible, as well as the fullest and completest expression of the sentiments, opinions, and convictions of a people; of their ideals, longings, aspirations. The fifth window of the soul looks out upon this revelation of human nature through literature. The study of literature commences with the child's first reader, and continues through his school course, until he learns, by means of the selections from the poets and prose writers in the higher readers, the best and happiest expression for those supreme moments of life felt and described first by men of genius, and left as a rich heritage to all their fellows. Their less gifted brethren may, by the aid of their common mother tongue, participate with them in the enjoyment of their insights.

(c) The studies of the school fall naturally into these five co-ordinate groups: first, mathematics and physics; second, biology, including chiefly the plant and the animal; third, literature and art, including chiefly the study of literary works of art; fourth, grammar and the technical and scientific study of language, leading to such branches as logic and psychology; fifth, history and the study of sociological, political, and social institutions. Each one of these groups should be represented in the curriculum of the schools at all times by some topic suited to the age and previous training of the pupil.

§ 209. The first stage of school education is education for culture, and education for the purpose of gaining command of the conventionalities of intelligence. These conventionalities are such arts as reading and writing, the use of figures, technicalities of maps, dictionaries, the art of drawing, and all those semi-mechanical facilities which enable the child to get access to the intellectual conquests of the race. Later on, when the pupil passes out of his elementary studies, which partake more of the nature of practice than of theory, he comes in the secondary school and the college to the study of science and the technique necessary for its preservation and communication. All these things belong to the first stage of school instruction whose aim is culture. On the other hand, post-graduate work and the work of pro-

fessional schools have not the aim of culture so much
as the aim of fitting the person for a special vocation.   In the post-graduate work of universities the
·demand is for original investigation in special fields.
In the professional school the student masters the
elements of a particular practice, learning its theory
and its art.

It is in the. first stage, the schools for culture, that
these five co-ordinate branches should be represented in
a symmetrical manner. On the other hand, a course of
university study—that is to say, what is called post-
graduate work—and ,the professional school should be
specialized. But specializing should follow a course of
study for culture in which the whole of human learning
and the whole of the soul has been considered. From
the primary school, therefore, on through the academic
course of the college there should be symmetry, and the
five co-ordinate groups of studies should be represented
at each part of the course—at least in each year, although
perhaps not throughout each part of the year.

§ 210. All activities of man have a psychological
coefficient.   There is some special category of the
mind employed in each operation.   In forming the
course of study experience has discovered, one after
another, the branches of study needed to open the
five windows of the soul.   The psychology of education should point out the categories involved in
each of these studies, as well as show their objective
scope and significance.   First, the categories of qual-

ity and quantity are used in the two Nature studies, arithmetic and geography. In quantity, the first stage of the understanding is active (see Chapter XXVII), and abstract equality and difference are seized, but in quality the second stage is active; for quality (in the philosophic sense) means dependence on others, or relativity—thing as determined through its environment (see § 146). In grammar, introspection is the chief mental operation; one must go behind the form of the word to its meaning, and then go behind the particular meaning to the part of speech—that is to say, behind the content of the meaning to its form; and both content and form of meaning are objects of introspection alone; they are concepts and categories. While grammar deals with the category of self-activity as revealed in language, history deals with it as will, and especially as the will of the social aggregate. Literature and art also deal with the same category in its third phase—namely, its symbol-making activity.

(a) Commencing with the outlook of the child upon the world of Nature, arithmetic or mathematical study furnishes the first scientific key to the existence of bodies and their various motions. Mathematics in its pure form as arithmetic, algebra, geometry, and the application of the analytical method, as well as mathematics applied to matter and force, or statics and dynamics, furnishes us the peculiar study that gives to us, whether as children

or as men, the command of Nature in this its quantitative
aspect. Mathematics furnishes the instrument, the tool
of thought which we wield in this realm. But useful, or
even essential, as this mathematical or quantitative study
is for this first aspect of Nature, it is limited to it, and
should not be applied to the next phase of Nature, which
is that of organic life. That needs another category; for
we must not study in the growth of the plant simply the
mechanical action of forces, but we must subordinate
everything quantitative and mathematical to the principle of life, or movement according to internal purpose
or design. The principle of life, or biology, is no substitute, on the other hand, for the mathematical or quantitative study. The forces, heat, light, electricity, magnetism, galvanism, gravitation, inorganic matter—all these
things are best studied from the mathematical point of
view. The superstitious savage, however, imposes upon
the inorganic world the principle of biology. He sees the
personal effort of spirits in winds and storms, in fire and
flowing streams. He substitutes for mathematics the
principle of life, and looks in the movement of inanimate
things for an indwelling soul. This is the animistic
standpoint of human culture—the substitution of the bio-
logic method of looking at the world for the quantitative
or mathematical view.

(*b*) The second group includes the study of whatever
is organic in Nature—especially studies relating to the
plant and the animal—the growth of material for food
and clothing, and in a large measure for means of trans-
portation and culture. This study of the organic phase
of Nature forms a great portion of the branch of study
known as geography in the elementary school. Geography
takes up also some of the topics that belong to the mathematical or quantitative view of Nature, but it takes them
up into a new combination with a view to show how they
are related to organic life—to creating and supplying the
needs of the plant, animal, and man. The mathematical
or quantitative appears in geography as subordinated to
the principle of organic life. For the quantitative—name-

ly, inorganic matter and the forces of the solar system—appear as presuppositions of life. Life uses this as material out of which to organize its structures. The plant builds itself a structure of vegetable cells, transmuting what is inorganic into vegetable tissue; so, too, the animal builds over organic and inorganic substances, drawing from the air and water and from inorganic salts and acids, and by use of heat, light, and electricity converting vegetable tissue into animal tissue. The revelation of the life principle in plant and animal is not a mathematical one; it is not a mechanism moved by pressure from without, or by attraction from within; it is not a mere concourse of atoms or an aggregation, or anything of that sort. In so far as it is organic there is a formative principle which originates motion and modifies by its self-activity the inorganic materials and the mere dynamic forces of Nature, giving them special form and direction, so as to build up vegetable or animal structures.

(c) The first study relating to human nature, as contrasted with mere organic and inorganic nature, is literature. Literature, as the fifth and highest of the fine arts, reveals human nature in its intrinsic form. It may be said, in general, that a literary work of art, a poem, whether lyric, dramatic, or epic, or a prose work of art, such as a novel or a drama, reveals human nature by showing the growth of a feeling or sentiment first into a conviction and then into a deed: feelings, thoughts, and deeds are thus connected in such a way as to explain the complete genesis of human action. Moreover, in a literary work of art there is a revelation of man as a member of social institutions. Its theme is usually an attack of the individual upon some one of the social institutions of which he is a member—namely, a collision with the family, the state, civil society, or the Church. This collision furnishes an occasion for either a comic or tragic solution. The nature of the individual and of his evolution of feeling into thoughts and deeds is shown vividly upon the background of institutions and social life. The work of art, whether music, painting, sculpture, or architecture, belongs to the same group as literature, and it is obvious that the method in which the work of art should be studied is not the method adopted as applicable to inorganic nature or to organic nature. And, too, the physiology of a plant or an animal, and the habits and modes of growth and peculiarities of action on the part of plants and animals, are best comprehended by a different method of study from that which should be employed in studying the work of art. The work of art has a new principle, one that transcends mere life. It is the principle of *responsible individuality* and the principle of free subordination on the part of the individual to the ordinances of a social whole. It is, in fact, the exercise of original responsibility in opposition to social order, and the consequent retribution or other reaction, that makes the content of the work of art. Arithmetic and geography are not substitutes for literature. A purely mathematical treatment, or a biological treatment, of a work of art would be inept. Such methods can enter into a consideration of works of art only in a very subordinate degree. It would be equally absurd to attempt to apply the method in which a work of art should be studied to the study of an organic form or to the study of inorganic matter and forces.

(*d*) The next co-ordinate branch includes grammar and studies allied to it, such as logic and psychology. In the elementary school we have only grammar. Grammar treats of the structure of language; there is a mechanical or formal side to it in orthography. But one can not call grammar in a peculiar sense a formal study any more than he can apply the same epithet to one of the natural sciences. Natural science deals with the laws of material bodies and forces. Laws are forms of acting or of being, and yet by far the most important content of natural science is stated in the laws which it has discovered. Thus Nature studies are formal. So in the studies that relate to man the forms of human speech are very important. All grammatical studies require a twofold attitude of the mind: one toward the sign and one toward the signification; the shape of a letter or the form of a word or the peculiarity of a vocal utterance, these must be attended to, but they must be at once subordinated to the significance of the hidden thought which has become revealed by the sign or utterance. The complexity of grammatical study is seen at once from this point of view. It is a double act of the will focusing the attention upon two different phases at once—namely, upon the natural phase and the spiritual phase—and the fusion of the two in one. Looking at this attitude of the mind, at this method of grammatical study, we see at once how different it is from the attitude of the mind in the study of a work of art. In grammar we should not look to an evolution of a feeling into a thought or a deed; that would be entirely out of place. But we must give attention to the literal and prosaic word, written or spoken, and consider it as an expression of a thought. We must note the structure of the intellect as revealed in this form. The word is a part of speech, having some one of the many functions which the word can fulfil in expressing a thought. Deeper down than grammatical structure is the logical structure, and this is a more fundamental revelation of the action of pure mind. Logic is, in fact, a part of psychology (see Chapters IX, X, XI). Opening from one door toward another, we pass on our way from orthography, etymology, and syntax to logic and psychology. All the way we use the same method; we use the sign or manifestation as a means of discovering the thought and the classification of the thought. The method of grammar leads to insight into the nature of reason itself; it is this insight which it gives us into our methods of thinking and of uttering our thoughts that furnishes the justification for grammar as one of the leading studies in the curriculum. Its use in teaching correct speaking and writing is always secondary to this higher use, which is to make conscious in man the structure of his thinking and expression. Important as it is, however, when it is substituted for the method of studying art it becomes an abuse. It is a poor way to study Shakespeare, Milton, Chaucer,

and the Bible to grammatically parse them or analyze
them, or to devote the time to their philological peculiarities, the history of the development of their language, or
such matters. Nor is the proper method of studying the
work of art a substitute for that in grammar; it does not
open the windows of the mind toward the logical, philological, or psychological structure of human thought and
action.

(e) There is a fifth co-ordinate group of studies—
namely, that of history. History looks to the formation of
the state as the chief of human institutions. The development of states, the collisions of individuals with the
state, the collisions of the states with one another—these
form its topic. The method of historic study is different
from that in grammatical study, and also from that
in the study of literary and other works of art. Still
more different is the method of history from those employed in the two groups of studies relating to Nature—
namely, the mathematical and biological methods. In biology the whole animal is not fully revealed in each of his
members, although, as stated in Kant's definition, each
part is alike the means and the end for all the others.
The higher animals and plants show the greatest difference between parts and whole. But in history it is the
opposite: the lower types exhibit the greatest difference
between the social whole and the individual citizen. The
progress in history is toward freedom of the individual
and local self-government. In the highest organisms of
the state, therefore, there is a greater similarity between
the individual and the national whole to which he belongs.
The individual takes a more active part in governing himself. The state becomes more and more an instrument
of self-government in his hands. In the lowest states
the gigantic personality of the social whole is all in all,
and the individual personality is null except in the supreme ruler and the few associated with him. The method
of history keeps its gaze fixed upon the development of the
social whole and the progress which it makes in realizing
within its citizens the freedom of the whole. This method,

it is evident enough, is different from those in literature and grammar, different also from the biological and the mathematical methods. In history we see how the little selves or individuals unite to form the big self or the nation. The analogies to this found in biology—namely, the combination of individual cells into the entire vegetable or animal organism—are all illusive so far as furnishing a clew to the process of human history.

(*f*) It has been asked whether drawing does not belong to a separate group in the course of study, and whether manual training is not a study co-ordinate with history and grammar. There are a number of branches of study, such as vocal music, drawing, manual training, gymnastics, and the like, which ought to be taught in every well-regulated school; but they will easily find a place within the five groups so far as their intellectual coefficients are concerned. Drawing, for instance, may belong, like music, to art or æsthetics on one side, but practically it is partly physical training with a view to skill in the hand and eye, and partly mathematical with a view to the production of geometric form. As a physical training its rationale is to be found in physiology, and hence it belongs in this respect to the second phase of the study of Nature. As relating to the production of form, it belongs to geometry and trigonometry and arithmetic, or the first phase of Nature, the inorganic. As relating to art or the æsthetic, it belongs to the third group of studies, within which literature is the main discipline. But besides literature there are architecture, sculpture, painting, and music to be included in the æsthetic or art group of studies. Manual training, on the other hand, relates to the transformation of material, such as wood or stone or other minerals, into structures for human use. It is clear enough that the rationale of all this is to be found in applied mathematics; hence manual training does not furnish a new principle different from that found in the first or the second study relating to Nature. But it has an important psychological coefficient so far as it relates to the preparation for one's vocation

24

and the ability to support one's self in economical independence (see § 184).

(*g*) School instruction is given to the acquirement of techniques—the technique of reading and. writing; of mathematics; of grammar, geography, history, literature, and science in general. One is astonished when he reflects upon it, at first, to see how much is meant by this word *technique*. All products of human reflection are defined and preserved by words used in a technical sense. The words are taken out of their colloquial sense, which is a loose one, except when employed as slang; for slang is a spontaneous effort in popular speech to form technical terms. The technical or conventional use of signs and symbols enables us to write words and to record mathematical calculations; the technical use of words enables us to express clearly and definitely the ideas and relations of all science. Outside of technique all is vague hearsay. The fancy pours into the words it hears such meanings as its feelings prompt. Instead of science there is superstition. The school deals with technique in this broad sense of the word. The mastery of this technique of reading, writing, arithmetic, geography, and history lifts the pupil on to a plane of freedom and self-help hitherto not known to him. He can now by his own effort master for himself the wisdom of the race. By the aid of such instruments as the family education has given him he can not master that wisdom, but only pick up a few of its results, such as the customs of his community preserve. By the process of hearsay and oral inquiry it would take the individual a lifetime to acquire what he can get in six months by aid of the instruments which the school places in his hands; for the school gives the youth the tools of thought.

§ 211. Secondary instruction in high schools and academies continues the traditional course of study on the lines marked out already in the elementary schools.

(*a*) The five provinces which a rational insight into
the world of Nature and the world of man discovers are
represented, as we·have seen, in the course of study in
the elementary school. They are also carefully provided
for in the high school. Arithmetic and geography, sciences that relate to Nature (organic and inorganic), are
found in the common school. The high school continues
these by more advanced studies following in the same
line: algebra and geometry, physical geography, and natural philosophy (or physics). The mathematical studies
treat of time and space, the abstract possibility of existences in Nature. Arithmetic and algebra concern the form
of time; geometry that of space in general; trigonometry, the measurement of space by means of the triangle.
Physical geography, so named in the current text-books
for high schools, gives a survey of organic nature in
general, being a compend of ethnology, zoölogy, botany,
geology, meteorology, and astronomy; the total complex
of Nature viewed as an organism or systematic process.
Natural philosophy and chemistry (physics, molar and
molecular), take a survey of the elements and the forces
and their quantitative manifestation.

(*b*) Besides the two divisions of the world of Nature
into organic and inorganic, there are three divisions of
the world of man or human life, as we have already seen.
These three divisions of the world of man are represented
in the high-school course by universal history, and some
study of the framework of constitutional government,
for the will side of man; the study of Latin, Greek, some
modern language, rhetoric, mental or moral philosophy,
for the theoretical side of man; the study of the history
of English literature, of Shakespeare, and other standard
writers, and the literary contents of the Latin, Greek,*

---

* In Chapter XXXIII the reason has been given for
the extended study of Latin and Greek in secondary and
higher education. Our civilization is derivative from Rome
and Greece, and must be studied in its genesis (its " em-

French, or German languages selected, and perhaps some general or special study of the history of the fine arts, architecture, sculpture, painting, and music, for the æsthetic side of man.

§ 212. Higher instruction continues on the five lines marked out for elementary and secondary instruction, taking up such branches as (a) higher mathematical studies and their applications in physics; (b) the several sciences that contribute to a knowledge of the processes of the earth and of organic beings (geology, biology, meteorology, etc.); (c) ancient and modern languages, comparative philology, logic, philosophy; (d) political economy and sociology, moral philosophy, philosophy of civil history, constitutional history; (e) philosophy and history of art, literature, and rhetoric.

(a) The elementary course of study is adapted to the first eight years of school life, say from the age of six to that of fourteen years. That course of study deals chiefly with giving the child a mastery over the symbols of reading, writing, and arithmetic, and the technical words in which are expressed the distinctions of arithmetic, geography, grammar, and history. The child has not yet acquired much knowledge of human nature, nor of the world of things and forces about him. He has a tolerably quick grasp of isolated things and events,

---

bryology ") in order to be understood. If we do not comprehend the origin of the network of customs and usages in which we live, we yield to it a blind obedience, whereas insight converts it into a rational obedience.

but he has very small power of synthesis. He can not combine in his little mind things and events so as to perceive whole processes. It is the business of the school to induct him by easy steps into. these things. He can not perceive the principles and laws underlying the things and events which are brought under his notice. He consequently is not able to get much insight into the trend of human affairs, or to draw logical conclusions from convictions or ideas. It is a necessary characteristic of primary or elementary instruction that it must take the world of human learning in fragments, and fail to give its pupils an insight into the interrelation of things. It is the constant effort of good teaching to correct this defect. But, after all, the beginnings must have this character, because they are beginnings. The child's immaturity is not the only reason. Even adults, on commencing a study, get but a few elements at first, and only later come to see each element in the light of the whole. But there is a great difference between the teacher who requires only isolated details of his pupils and the one who directs their attention toward the relations and interdependencies from the beginning. The true teaching aims always to strengthen the power of seizing relations. It cultivates the power of thought.

(b) The education of high schools, academies, and preparatory schools—what we call secondary schools— begins to correct this inadequacy of elementary education. It begins to see things and events as parts of processes, and to understand their significance by tracing them back into their causes and forward into their results. While elementary education begins with isolated things, and finds shallow relations, secondary education deals with the deeper and more essential relations of things and events. It studies forces and laws, and the mode and manner in which things are fashioned and events accomplished. To turn off from occupation with dead results and to come to the investigation of the living process of production is a great step. Where the pupil in the elementary school studies arithmetic and solves problems in particular numbers, the secondary pupil studies algebra and solves problems in general terms. Each algebraic formula is a rule for the performance of an indefinite number of arithmetical examples. In geometry, the secondary pupil learns necessary relations of spatial forms. In general history, he studies the collisions of one nation with another, and learns to interpret all the events in the light of the principle involved in the struggle. In science, he learns the forms and relations of Nature's phenomena. In the study of foreign languages he notes the variations of words to indicate relations of syntax; he investigates the structure of language, in which is revealed the degree of consciousness of the people who made that language.

(c) But secondary education does not connect in any adequate manner the intellect and the will. It does not convert intellectual perceptions into rules of action. This is left for higher education. A principle of action is always a summing up of a series. Things and events have been inventoried and relations have been canvassed. Now the result must be summed up: " In view of all these data, a reasonable course of action is this or that " (see § 242). The conclusion must be reached, and then the will can act. If we act without summing up the results of inventory and reflection, our act will be a lame one. It is the glory of higher education that it lays chief stress on the comparative method of study; that it makes philosophy its leading discipline; that it gives an ethical bent to all its branches of study. Higher education seeks as its first goal the unity of human learning. Then in its second stage it specializes. It first studies each branch in the light of all others. It studies each branch in its history. A definition of science, already offered in preceding chapters, is, that it unites facts in such a way that each fact throws light on all facts and all facts throw light on each fact. The best definition of that part of higher education that is found in the college is, that it teaches the unity of human learning. It shows how all branches form a connected whole, and what each contributes to the explanation of the others. This has well been called the course in philosophy. After the course in philosophy comes the selection of a specialty; for there is not much danger of distorted views when one has seen the vision of the whole system of human learning. Higher education can not possibly be given to the person of immature age. A college that gave the degree of bachelor of arts to students of eighteen years would give only a secondary course of education after all; for it would find itself forced to use the methods of instruction that characterize the secondary school. The serious tone of mind, the earnest attitude which inquires for the significance of a study to the problem of life, can not be expected in the normally developed student from fourteen to eighteen years of age.

(d) The youth of proper age to enter on higher education has already experienced much of human life, and has arrived at the point where he begins to feel the necessity for a regulative principle, or a principle that shall guide him in deciding the endless questions which press upon him for settlement. Taking the youth at this epoch, when he begins to inquire for a principle, the college gives him a compend of human experience. It shows him the verdict of the earliest and latest great thinkers upon the meaning of the world. It gives him the net result of human opinion as to the trend of history. It gathers into one focus the results of the vast labours of specialists in natural science, history, jurisprudence, philology, political science, and moral philosophy. If the bachelor of arts is not acquainted with more than the elements of these multifarious branches of human learning, yet he is all the more impressed by their bearing upon the conduct of life. He sees their function in the totality, although he may not be an expert in the methods of investigation in any one of them.

(e) For the reason that higher education makes the ethical insight its first object, its graduates generally hold the place in the community at large of spiritual monitors. They exercise a directive power altogether disproportionate to their number.* They lead in the three learned professions, and they lead in the management of education of all kinds. They do much to correct the one-sided tendencies of elementary education, and to furnish the wholesome centripetal forces that hold in check the extravagances of the numerous self-educated people who have gone off in special directions after leaving the elementary school.

(f) The person who has had merely an elementary schooling has laid stress on the mechanical means of culture—on the arts of reading, writing, computing, and the like. He has trained his mind for the acquirement of isolated details. But he has not been disciplined in comparative studies. He has not learned how to compare each fact with other facts, and still less how to compare each science with other sciences. He has not inquired as to the trend of his science as a whole, nor has he asked as to its imperfections which need correction from the standpoint of other sciences. He has not yet entertained the question as to its bearing on the conduct of life. He has not yet learned the difference between knowledge and wisdom, or, what is better, the method of converting knowledge into wisdom; for it is the best description of the higher course of study to say that its aim is to convert knowledge into wisdom—to show how to discern the bearing of all departments of knowledge upon each. It is

---

* Dr. Charles F. Thwing, President of Western Reserve College (Ohio), found the following ratio by counting the college graduates that were of distinction enough to secure a place in Appletons' Cyclopædia of Biography: Out of the aggregate of 15,138 biographies given, there were 5,322 belonging to college graduates—a result showing that one out of every forty graduates and one out of ten thousand non-graduates of the entire population reached the degree of distinction in question. The proportion is in favour of the college men in the ratio of two hundred and fifty to one.

evident that the individual who has received only an elementary education is at great disadvantage as compared with the person who has received a higher education in the college or university, making all allowances for the imperfections of existing institutions. The individual is prone to move on in the same direction and in the same channel which he has taken under the guidance of his teacher. Very few persons change their methods after they leave school. Hence the importance of reaching the influence of the method of higher education before one closes his school career.

(*g*) All the influences of the university, its distinguished professors, its venerable reputation, the organization of the students and professors as an institutional whole, combined with the isolation of the student from the strong ties of the home and the home community—all these taken together are able to effect this change in method when brought to bear upon a youth for four years. He acquires an attitude of mind which may be best described as critical and comparative. It is at the same time conservative: he has learned to expect that an existing institution may have deeper grounds for its being than appear at first sight; while, on the other hand, the mind trained in elementary and secondary methods is easily surprised and captivated by superficial considerations, and has small power of resistance against shallow critical views. It is easily swept away by a specious argument for reform. It is true that the duller commonplace intellect that has received only an elementary education is apt to follow use and wont and not question the established order. It is the brighter class of minds, that stop with the elementary school, which become agitators in the bad sense of the term. The commonplace intellect has no adaptability, or at least small power of readjustment, in view of new circumstances. The disuse of hand labour and the adoption of machine labour, for instance, finds the common workman unable to substitute brain labour for hand labour, and he remains in the path of poverty, wending his way to the almshouse. Our numer-

GENERAL COURSE OF STUDY.

CLASS OF SCHOOL.	TOPICS RELATING TO NATURE.		TOPICS RELATING TO MAN, OR "THE HUMANITIES."		
	Inorganic.	Organic or cyclic.	Theoretical (intellect).	Practical (will).	Æsthetical (feeling and phantasy).
Elementary school.	Arithmetic. Oral lessons in natural philosophy.	Geography. Oral lessons in natural history.	Grammar. (Reading, writing, parsing, and analyzing.)	History (of United States).	Reading selections from English and American literature. Drawing and vocal music.
Secondary school.	Algebra. Geometry. Plane trigonometry. Natural philosophy. Chemistry.	Physical geography. Astronomy (descriptive). Botany or zoölogy. Physiology.	Latin. Greek. French or German. Mental and moral philosophy.	History (universal). Constitution of the United States.	History of English literature. Shakespeare or some standard author (one or more whole works read). Rhetoricals (declamation and composition). Drawing and vocal music. Study of works of art in painting, sculpture, and architecture.
College course for A. B. degree.	Analytical geometry. Spherical trigonometry. Differential and integral calculus. Physics. Chemistry. Astronomy. (Etc., elective.)	Anatomy and physiology. Botany. Zoology. Meteorology. Geology. Ethnology. (Etc., elective.)	Latin. Greek. French or German. Comparative philology. Logic. History of philosophy. Plato or Aristotle. Kant or Hegel.	Philosophy of history. Political economy and sociology. Civil and common law. Constitutional history. Natural theology and philosophy of religion.	Philosophy of art. History of literature. Rhetoric. The great masters compared in some of their greatest works: Homer, Sophocles, Dante, Shakespeare, Goethe, Phidias, Praxiteles, Skopas, Michael Angelo, Raphael, Mozart, Beethoven, etc.

REMARK.—It is understood that many topics named in the above can be replaced by other topics, which have the same psychological rank as studies.

ous self-educated men, of whom we are proud, are quite apt to be persons who have never advanced beyond elementary methods. Very often they are men of great accumulations in the way of isolated scraps of information, having memory pouches unduly developed. They lay stress on some insignificant phase of human affairs. They advocate with great vigour the importance of some local centre, some partial human interest, as the chief object of all life. They remind us of an astronomer who opposes the heliocentric theory, and favours the claim of some planet or satellite as the true centre. Notwithstanding, we admire the brave men who, deprived of leisure for school education, continue through life their struggle to master the world of learning. With the increase of books, and especially of the class of books which reveal the method of scientific investigation, the student needs less oral instruction.

(*h*) The general conspectus on page 340 shows how the branches of study are to be arranged so as to retain at all times the five co-ordinate divisions required by psychology for symmetrical culture of the mind.

CHAPTER XXXVII.

The Psychology of Quantity.

§ 213. THERE are two extremes in the course of study, mathematics and literature. The former deals with everything in a mechanical aspect, while the latter deals with human life in its highest forms.

In this and the next chapter I attempt to show briefly the psychological basis of these extremes.

§ 214. All school studies that deal with mathematics and physics necessarily involve a use of the
category of quantity. What is the first origin of
this category of quantity? Quantity is opposed to
quality as well as to self-activity (that is, to the form
of external perception and to the form of internal
perception, see Chapters II and III), and yet it presupposes both and participates in both. In the category of quality each thing is limited by an environment different in kind from itself. In quantity
each unit of number, extension, or degree has an
environment of the same kind. Its other is like
itself, whereas in quality everything is regarded as
different from the others. Thus, while quality is
the category of difference, quantity is the category
of indifference. We can not count objects except
in so far as we abstract from their difference. We
can count one, two, three oxen, but we can not
say that one ox, one sheep, and one tree are three
oxen, or three sheep, or three trees; but we can
say that they are three things, three objects, three
existences, or three units of any general class that
includes them all. We must abstract from their
quality and go back to a common class indifferent
to their special characteristics in order to count them.
So, too, of all extensive magnitude. We must regard

the mass as made up of similar units of extension. It must be homogeneous, in short, or we can not measure it as one extension. Take together a cubic yard of wood and the same amount of sand, and we do not have two cubic yards of sand or of wood; but we do have two cubic yards of material substance or two cubic yards of volume. There must be some common genus or species, and repetition of the same individual in order to have quantity at all.

(a) The reason why it requires a higher activity of thought to think quantity and understand mathematics than it does to perceive quality (or things and environments) lies right in this point. The thought of quantity is a double thought. It first thinks quality and then negates it or thinks it away. In other words, it abstracts from quality. It first thinks thing and environment (quality), and then thinks both as the same in kind or as repetitions of the same. A thing becomes a unit when it is repeated so that it is within an environment of duplicates of itself.

(b) Take the idea of quality and rise out of it to quantity. First consider one thing opposed to an environment different from it. Then consider the environment as another thing, opposed again to its environment, which again is another thing. At once we have a congeries of things limiting each other, but not qualitatively. We have reached quantity, and have mutual exclusion of parts; but also complete continuity of parts, because all are repetitions of the same, and extension or number is present. In quantity we have repetitions of the same unit, and then again the sum or the whole is a unit because all are homogeneous.

§ 215. Quantity is a ratio of the two units, the constituent units being the first, and the whole or sum which they make being the second unit. The difficulties in the study of mathematics increase just in proportion to the explicitness of this ratio—that is to say, the higher mathematics deals more with the ratio and less with the terms of the ratio, while elementary mathematics deals more with the terms of this ratio. Elementary arithmetic begins with numeration, or counting, in which the unit of the sum is merely stated in terms of the constituent unit.

(a) Seventeen (17) is a whole unit or unity composed of seventeen repetitions of the constituent unit. In addition we find the sum or unity of different numbers or sums by counting them together, and use remembered countings to facilitate the process. In subtraction we find a constituent sum from a higher sum, retracing the process of addition. In multiplication the constituent sums are identical, and hence they resemble the constituent units. The process of obtaining the result is facilitated by remembered multiplications or repetitions of sums—the multiplication table. Division is the facilitated process of repeated subtractions in order to ascertain the constituent sums. Involution and evolution, dealing with powers and roots, are forms of multiplication or division in which the sum is both constituent unit and unity; or, in other words, the factors are both the same number, and we have a sort of self-relation reached in quantity.

(b) It has been pointed out by Hegel (who invented this analysis of the idea of quantity) that science continually finds in Nature this preference for self-related numbers. The law of gravity, for example, shows us a ratio between the square of the time and the distance fallen; a ratio between the cubes of the planetary years and the squares of the orbits of revolution. In fact, space is three dimensional—or in some sort a third power of a line.

§ 216. This ratio between the unit of the sum and the elemental or constituent unit is not explicitly emphasized in the most elemental processes of arithmetic—addition, subtraction, multiplication, and division. But in common fractions it is made explicit by using two numbers to express the quantity.

(a) Seven eighths is neither 7 nor 8, but their ratio. The denominator 8 gives us the constituent unit (one eighth), and 7 gives us the unity of the sum, or aggregate. The child finds that it requires a double act of the mind to think quantity at all, for he has to start with quality and then abstract from it or think it away. But he has to double this mental act again to think a fraction. He thinks the simple number 8, and then 7; then he combines them in one thought, and his result is the thought of this fraction, seven eighths. The operations called ratio and proportion—the old-fashioned " Rule of Three "—belong to the same degree of complexity as common fractions. Hence the " Rule of Three " was the place where the clumsy wits of the pupil proved inadequate.

> " ' The Rule of Three ' doth puzzle me,
> And fractions make me mad."

(b) In every primary school there will be single pupils in each class that seem to lack the strength of mind to think quantity in the form of ratio. They will get on through simple addition and simple division, but they can not deal with fractions, because these involve the double or triple thought of two terms as united to form a result. I have noticed that minds which show brilliancy on the lower plane of unrelated numbers sometimes encounter a hard limit on entering the study of the ratio or the fraction, and break down. Again, there is a very large percentage that halt on the bridge over from arithmetic to algebra. They can think particular numbers, but not the general conditions expressed by formulæ.

(c) Decimal fractions involve one step of difficulty higher than common fractions. They have the same elements of ratio with the added difficulty that the denominator, instead of being expressed by a simple number, is itself a ratio, and must be calculated mentally by the pupil from the number of decimal places occupied in expressing the numerator. Hence in decimal fractions we have a double ratio to think—a further step of complexity.

(d) An excellent arithmetic was once made for use in normal schools; it showed the algebraic basis of each process. A mistake was made by the author, however, when he attempted to introduce the same methods into an arithmetic for mere elementary pupils. He placed decimal fractions before vulgar fractions—a correct process in the normal school, where notation and numeration are taught in view of the whole theory of the decimal system, but confusing enough to the pupil learning arithmetic for the first time. Here the author showed his ignorance of the psychology of quantity.

(e) To comprehend a ratio requires more than twice as much intellectual effort as to understand a simple term. In three fourths (¾) we have to think first 3, and then 4, and then their relation—3 as modified by 4, and 4 as modified by 3—just as above shown in the example of seven eighths. Three divided by four, therefore, requires three steps that must be retained all together. In the lowest mind a new subject crowds out the old one; it can not hold two ideas at once. So the simplest mathematical mind can hold 3 or 4, but not three fourths. Now, if a vulgar fraction or a ratio is hard to think, when both the terms are stated explicitly and written out in full, it is still more difficult to handle a fraction where only the numerator is given, and you are obliged to make a mental calculation to deduce the denominator. A decimal fraction demands the complex thought required to think a ratio *plus* another more complex process of calculation to determine the denominator. Hence the teachers who undertook the use of the arithmetic mentioned did not succeed until they had inserted the subject of vulgar fractions as a step in teaching decimals, by writing out the denominators of the decimals, in all cases, until the pupils had become familiar with the process, and could supply the suppressed term mentally.

(*f*) The general theory of a subject is a clew to the psychology of learning it. A knowledge of algebra answers to reveal the psychology of the greater part of the processes of arithmetic, and especially that of the construction of the rules; but to know the fundamental order of subjects requires the philosophy of quantity itself. The philosophy of arithmetic shows three steps of comprehension: the first, the grasping of simple numbers; the second, the grasping of the ratios of the first order, such as fractions and the "Rule of Three"; the third, the grasping the ratios based on involution and evolution—ratios expressed by powers. The last step is the hardest to understand, because there is, first, a relation of the simple number to itself—its product as multiplier and multiplicand to produce a power; and, secondly, the index which shows how many times the operation is performed, or the power to which the number is raised.

(*g*) In the case of logarithms, all simple numbers are regarded as powers of a basal number, and only their indices are employed, the terms of the ratio being entirely suppressed.

(*h*) Arithmetic rises into difficult regions of thought through making the ratio of the two orders of units (involved in all quantity) its object. Algebra drops out the definite expression of the two orders of units between which the ratio exists, and deals with ratios altogether. It treats of the functions of quantity, and elaborates these only, leaving to arithmetic the business of evaluating them in numbers. The complexity of such mathematical

25

thought is obvious. The expression of this ratio becomes still more explicit in fluxions and the differential calculus. In the calculus the term vanishes as having a distinct value, and the ratio becomes all in all. Inasmuch as this is the true expression for quantity in its innermost idea, we see how it is that the calculus furnishes a wonderful key for the explanation of the movements in Nature. Ratio is the essence of quantity. In the Calculus this is treated adequately.*

§ 217. The general form under which we behold objects in sense-perception is that of thing and environment. This is called the category of quality, as we have already seen. To the question that asks, What kind? or regarding the *qualities*, we answer by describing the differences of the thing from its environment. We mention its boundaries, its contrasts, and its reciprocal relations. In the category of quality there is (*a*) affirmation (of the thing), (*b*) negation (of the environment), and (*c*) limitation (of the thing by the environment).

(*a*) We have already seen that it is impossible to perceive self-activity by this category of quality or by external perception, which invariably uses this category in

---

* One of the most valuable articles on the philosophy of mathematics to be found in any language is that of Prof. George H. Howison, of the University of California (The Mutual Relations of the Departments of Mathematics, Journal of Speculative Philosophy for April, 1872, vol. v, pp. 144-179).

all its knowing. All that we thus perceive has the form of external limitation and dependence; and limitation and dependence make an object finite.

(*b*) In contrast to this is the category of internal perception, which beholds some example or specimen of self-activity—a feeling, an idea, or a volition. We have called (§ 9) the object of external perception phenomenon, and the object of internal perception noumenon. By " phenomenon " we mean something that is not a complete being existing for itself, but something dependent on another not only for its origin, but for its present existence. It is only a *manifestation* or *appearance* of some energy that has produced it and sustains it.

(*c*) A noumenon, on the other hand, is sufficient for itself; it is an original cause, a source of energy, an essence that manifests its own nature in what it produces. It is a self-activity. Introspection perceives self-activity as feeling, willing, and thinking. It perceives that which is sufficient for itself, and does not require another being as the source of its movements and functions. It, itself, is a producer of such effects; feelings, volitions, and thoughts are forms of its self-activity. A self is a noumenon, or independent being—a being that exists by itself and not merely in relation to something else. But a phenomenon exists only in relation to something else, and is wholly dependent; it is a show or appearance.

(*d*) There is a realm lying between these two forms of existence—the realm of the quantitative. Quantity is a very important category, because it lies midway between the form of external perception and that of internal perception, and participates in both.

(*e*) It is remarked by an acute thinker that the great significance of Pythagoras in the history of philosophy lies in the fact that he takes number as his principle, and that number lies one remove above sense-perception. It is one step of withdrawal from what is most external and superficial (the category of quality), and likewise one step of advance toward what is deepest and most substantial, the category of self-activity.

§ 218. The idea of quantity is one of the most important in psychology. It is an instrument by which man becomes lord of Nature. Man divides and conquers—that is to say, he enumerates and measures, and adapts his means to the work to be accomplished, all by the idea of quantity.

(*a*) He moves mountains and fills up the valleys by first estimating the number of cubic yards (or tip-cart loads) it is necessary to transport, and marshals against this quantity of earth the quantity of hands and machines necessary to produce the result in the quantum of time required. Man makes machines by aid of his quantitative idea. The very word "mechanical" denotes what is quantitative as opposed to what is self-active (see my Hegel's Logic, pp. 242-280).

(*b*) In studying physiological psychology we see a connection of self-active mind with its manifestation in the form of quantity; not quantity in its first aspect, that of extension, but as degree of intensity. All science of Nature, in fact, is, in the first place, an effort to get behind the qualitative aspects of external things to the quantitative conditions. The characteristics of accuracy and precision, which make science exact, are derived from quantity.

CHAPTER XXXVIII.

The Psychology of Art and Literature.

§ 219. THE psychology of the beautiful in art and literature has three aspects: (*a*) That of the sensuous elements, regularity, symmetry, and harmony, as symbolizing the activities of the soul; (*b*) the several arts, beginning with architecture, as progressively realizing more and more adequate forms of manifestation of human freedom; (*c*) the correspondence of epochs of art with the three great epochs of civilization—Oriental, classic, and modern.

(*a*) There is the theory that the primary function of art is amusement. What makes this degrading theory plausible is the fact that there is sensuous enjoyment in the contemplation of works of art. But if we analyze this effect we shall trace even it to something higher than sensuous sources.

(*b*) One of the good definitions of art describes it as a means of manifesting the Divine in material form for the apprehension of the senses and the reason. This definition makes art one of the three highest products of the soul. The three highest activities of the soul deal with the beautiful, the good, and the true. Religion deals with the revelation of the Divine as the good. Art deals with its manifestation as the beautiful, and the truth in science and philosophy deals with the definition of the Divine for pure thought. The beautiful must contain two factors—first, a material factor, as stone and other building materials for architecture; stone, bronze, and other material for sculpture; canvas, pigments, etc., for painting; air vibrations produced by the agency of strings and columns of air in wind instruments, etc., for music; mental pictures of sensuous objects created in the mind through the words of the poet. Besides this natural side in art there is the other side—namely, the disposition of the material in such a way as to suggest spiritual activity, the feelings and passions of the mind, the motives of its actions, etc. It is this union of the spiritual with the material that makes art.

(c) Inasmuch as matter has for its general characteristic inertness and receptivity of external impressions and complete absence of self-determination, what is material, as such, can not manifest mind, can not manifest intellect and will, because these are forms of self-activity. Material things become works of art when they are so disposed that they seem to manifest self-determination, or self-activity of a living soul, within them. It is evident, therefore, that the highest work of art will take on human form because the human body expresses most readily in its countenance, in its attitudes and gestures, the feelings, thoughts, and volitions of the soul.

(d) Art turns the world of externality pure and simple into a world of internality made perceptible to the senses of seeing and hearing. It shapes bronze, and wood, and marble into temples and statues. It brings out by light, shade, colour, and perspective on surfaces the paintings and drawings that represent rational and moral beings. It produces sounds, arranged in a tonic system, and can by this means express feelings in a more direct manner than by the plastic arts. Finally, it makes the words of language its art material, and reaches poetic expression, the highest of the arts, because of greater compass than all the others and more adequate in its manifestation of reason.

§ 220. I. *Sensuous Elements. Regularity.*—
Regularity is recurrence of the same—mere repeti-

tion. A rude people scarcely reaches a higher stage of art. Their desire for amusement is gratified by a string of beads or a fringe of some sort. It is a love of rhythm. The human form divine does not seem beautiful to the savage. It is not regular enough to suit his taste. He must accordingly make it beautiful by regular ornaments, or by deforming it in some way; by tattooing it, for example.

(*a*) Why does regularity please? Why does recurrence or repetition gratify the taste of the child or savage? The answer to this question is to be found in the generalization that the soul delights to behold itself, and that human nature is "mimetic," as Aristotle called it, signifying symbol-making. Man desires to know himself and to reveal himself, in order that he may comprehend himself; hence he is an art-producing animal. Whatever suggests to him his deep, underlying spiritual nature gives him a strange pleasure. The nature of consciousness is partly revealed in types and symbols of the rudest art. Chinese music, like the music of very young children, delights in monotonous repetitions that almost drive frantic any one with a cultivated ear. But all rhythm is a symbol of the first and most obvious fact of conscious intelligence or reason. Consciousness is the knowing of the self by the self. There are subject and object, and the activity of recognition. From subject to object there are distinction and difference, but with recognition sameness or identity is perceived, and the distinction or difference is retracted. What is this simple rhythm from difference to identity but regularity? It is, we answer, regularity, and it is much more than this. But the child or savage delights in monotonous repetition alone, not possessing the slightest insight into the cause of his delight. His delight is, however, explicable through this fact of the identity in form between the rhythm of his soul-activity and the sense-perception by which he perceives regularity. The sun-myth arises through the same feeling. Wherever there is repetition, especially in the form of return-to-itself, there comes this conscious or unconscious satisfaction at beholding it (see § 205).

§ 221. II. *The Sensuous Elements. Symmetry.* —Regularity expresses only the empirical perception of the nature of self-consciousness and reason. There is, as we have seen, a subject opposed to itself as object. Opposition or antithesis is, however, not simple repetition, but with a difference. The identity is therefore one of symmetry, instead of regularity. Symmetry contains and expresses identity under difference. We can not put the left-hand glove on our right hand. The two hands correspond, but are not repetitions of the same. It is a mark of higher æsthetic culture to prefer symmetry to regularity. It indicates a deeper feeling of the nature of the divine.

Nations that have reached this stage show their taste by emphasizing the symmetry in the human form by ornaments and symmetrical arrangement of clothing. They correct the lack of symmetry in the human form in the images of their gods. The face is on the front side of the head, but the god shall have a face on the back of his head, too, to complete the symmetry. The arms directed to the front of the body must also correspond to another pair of arms directed in the opposite direction. Perhaps perfect symmetry is still more exacting in its requirements, and demands faces with arms to match on the right and left sides of the body. To us the idols of the ancient Mexicans and Central Americans seem hideous; but it was the taste for symmetry that produced them.

§ 222. III. *The Sensuous Elements. Harmony.* —Harmony is the object of the highest culture of taste. Regularity and symmetry are so mechanical in their nature that they afford only remote symbols of reason in its concreteness. They furnish only the elements of art, and must be subordinated to a higher principle. Harmony is free from the mechanical suggestions of the lower principles, but it posessses in a greater degree the qualities which gave them their charm. Just as symmetry exhibits identity under a deeper difference than regularity, so harmony, again, presents us a still deeper unity underlying wider difference. The unity of harmony is not a unity of sameness, nor of correspondence merely, but a unity of adaptation to end or purpose. Harmony is the expression of freedom, and of subordination of matter to the soul. Mere symmetry suggests external constraint; but in art there must be freedom expressed. Regularity is still more suggestive of mechanical necessity. Harmony boldly discards regularity and symmetry, retaining them only in subordinate details, and makes all subservient to the expression of a conscious purpose. The divine is conceived as spiritual intelligence elevated above its material expression so far that the latter is only a means to an end.

(a) The Apollo Belvedere has no symmetry of arrangement in its limbs, and yet the disposition of each limb suggests a different disposition of another, in order to accomplish some conscious act upon which the mind of the god is bent. All is different, and yet all is united in harmony for the realization of one purpose. Here the human form, with its lack of regularity and symmetry, becomes beautiful. Harmony is a higher symbolic expression of the divine than were the previous elements. The human body is adapted to the expression of conscious will, and this is freedom. The perfect subordination of the body to the will is gracefulness. It is this which constitutes the beauty of classic art: to have every muscle under perfect obedience to the will—unconscious obedience—so that the slightest inclination or desire of the soul, if made an act of the will, finds expression in the body.

(b) When the soul is not at ease in the body, but is conscious of it as something separate, gracefulness departs, and awkwardness takes its place. The awkward person does not know what to do with his hands and arms; he can not think just how he would carry his body or fix the muscles of his face. He chews a stick or bites a cigar in order to have something to do with the facial muscles, or twirls a cane or twists his watch-chain, folds his arms before or behind, or even thrusts his hands into his pockets, in order to have some use for them which will restore his feeling of ease in his body. The soul is at ease in the body only when it is using it as a means of expression or action.

(c) Harmony is this agreement of the inner and outer, of the will and the body, of the idea and its expression, so that the external leads us directly to the internal of which it is the expression. Gracefulness then results, and gracefulness is the characteristic of classic or Greek art. Not only its statues, but its architecture and architectural ornament, exhibit gracefulness or freedom.

§ 223. Some writers hold the doctrine that art is the mere representation of Nature; but this can not be a true definition, because Nature presents the ugly as well as the beautiful, and to represent the ugly, of course, does not convert it into the beautiful. A picture of the front of the Parthenon is beautiful because the Parthenon itself is beautiful. A picture of the Vale of Tempe, if taken from the right point of view, is beautiful. There are many landscapes that are beautiful, but very few landscapes that are beautiful from all points of view. Nature in its prose reality is very seldom beautiful. The artist must select his point of view, and must remove from his picture certain objects which, though real, mar the presentation of the main features.

(a) Those who look upon Nature as the source of the beautiful, think of the landscape with its interesting variety of objects, its mountains and vales and winding streams, forests and meadows, the sky and the ocean. There is a sense of freedom which comes to us as we leave the city and pass into the country. In the city we have a burden of care constantly on our minds, because we must be mindful of our human environment. We have complicated relations with our fellow-men, and there is an unremitting pressure of duty. Constant attention to etiquette is necessary, in order to save ourselves from conflicts in which we embarrass our fellow-men and hinder our own work. When we come to the country, and are alone with trees, mountains, meadow brooks, and other inanimate objects, we have a sense of relief from duty and from the worry which a network of relations brings to us. This is not a sense of the beautiful; it is rather a charming sense of relief. The charming and the agreeable are sometimes the beautiful and sometimes not, and in the case of the enjoyment of the green fields and the wild luxuriance of Nature we do not have the sense of the beautiful so much as the sense of relief and freedom from care.

(b) Regularity, symmetry, and harmony are degrees of the full realization of the art idea. Regularity obeys a hidden principle; symmetry presents identity under a deeper difference than regularity; harmony shows the subordination of regularity and symmetry to a more complete expression of the soul. A string of beads shows regularity, the mere dead repetition of the same form, but even this dead repetition is a manifestation of identity and a suggestion of a common origin of the individuals in one process. Right and left hands are symmetrical, but not regular. There is correspondence instead of repetition, and this represents the mind more adequately than mere regularity. The mind is an eternal vibration of subject and object. This is manifested in mere regularity; but subject is opposed to object, and this opposition is represented in symmetry. But the essential activity of the mind is much deeper than this. The mind, as will, modifies the object so as to make it conform to the subject. The mind, as intellect, thinks out the explanation of the object, and finds it a manifestation of divine reason. Harmony, or the sway of material objects by the indwelling soul, which uses it as an instrument and expression of itself, is the highest means of art.

(c) With these principles in view, we are prepared to answer the question whether Nature presents the beautiful in as high a form as art. It is obvious that inorganic nature by itself considered does not take on forms that represent freedom. Its forms are derived from without, and do not express the desires, purposes, or volitions of mind. When inorganic nature is used as material, and the artist gives it the human form as a statue or group, or makes it expressive of human thought, it may become beautiful.

§ 224. *Symbolic Art.*—There are three great historical epochs of art and poetry, corresponding to the three great stages of advancement of the nations of, the world into conscious freedom. For the art and literature of a people reflect its degree of enlightenment, and are, in fact, next to religion, the chief means by which its civilization is preserved. We accordingly have, as the lowest stage, the art of nations that have reached only the freedom of the social world without reflecting it in the individual. The citizen is buried beneath a mass of customs and usages, laws and prescriptions, which he has had no hand in making and yet can not refuse to obey. This form of civilization is only a little above a condition of slavery for its citizens. Its art, accordingly, does not create forms of free movement, but represents by appropriate symbols the crushing out of individuality. Such is the art of the great nations of Egypt, East India, Persia, and western Asia.

(*a*) It has been described by Hegel, whose Æsthetik * is by far the most satisfactory philosophy of art, as *symbolic art*. Its works of art *adumbrate* or *hint at* what they do not adequately express (see § 191).

(*b*) The Hindu worshipped an abstract unity devoid of all form, which he called Brahma. His idea of the divine is defined as the negation not only of everything in Nature, but also everything human. Nothing that has form, shape, properties, or qualities—nothing, in short, that can be distinguished from anything else—can be divine according to the thought of the Hindu. This is pantheism. It worships a negative might which destroys everything. If it admits that the world of finite things arises from Brahma as creator, it hastens to tell us that the creation is only a dream, and that all creatures will vanish when the dream fades. There can be no hope for any individuality, according to this belief. Any art that grows up under such a religion will manifest only the nothingness of individuality and the impossibility of its salvation. Instead of beauty as the attribute of divinity, the Yogi studied to mortify the flesh; to shrivel up the body; to paralyze rather than develop his muscles. Instead of gymnastic festivals, he resorted to the severest penances, such as holding his arm over his head until it wasted away. If he could produce numbness in his body,

---

* Hegel's Æsthetik has been followed in this chapter, though at some distance. I have found it for thirty years a source of suggestive ideas that throw light on art, literature, and civilization. (See vols. i, ii, and iii of Journal of Speculative Philosophy for complete translation of Bénard's French analysis of the entire work, by James A. Martling. Also vols. v, vi, vii, and xi, xii, xiii, for complete translation of Hegel on Symbolic, Classic, and Romantic Art, by William M. Bryant; the part on Chivalry [in v, vi, vii] by Sue A. Longwell. Also see B. Bosanquet's translation of the Introduction of Hegel [London, 1886], and also Mr. Bosanquet's other writings in elucidation of Hegel's theory of art.)

so that all feeling disappeared, he attained holiness. His divine was not divine-human, but inhuman rather.

(c) Persian art adored light as the divine; it also adored the bodies that give light—the sun, moon, and stars—also fire; also whatever is purifying, especially water. The Persian religion conceives two deities—a god of light and goodness, and a god of darkness and evil. The struggle between these two gods fills the universe, and makes all existence a contest. The art of the Persian portrays this struggle, and does not let pure human individuality step forth for itself.

(d) In Assyria and Chaldea we have the worship of the sun rather than of pure light. Hence there were artificial hills or towers constructed, with ascending inclined planes on the outside rising to the flat top, crowned with a temple dedicated to Bel, or the sun god. Images partly human, partly animal, represented the divine. The lion, the eagle, the quadruped and bird, the human face, these were united to make the symbol of a divine being who could not be manifested in a purely human form. Their famous purple-dyed garments showed the visible struggle between light and darkness and the victory of light.

(e) The Egyptian religion, though it surpassed the Persian in that it conceived the divine as much more near human life, still resorted to animal forms to obtain the peculiarly divine attributes. There were the sacred bulls Apis and Mnevis, the goat Mendes, sacred hawks and the ibis, and such divinities as Isis-Hathor, with a cow's head; Touaris, with a crocodile's head; Thoth, with the head of an ibis; Horus, with the head of a hawk; but Ammon, Ptah, and Osiris, with human heads and bodies. Thus we see that the Egyptian wavered between the purely human and the animal form as the image of the divine. So long as it is possible for a religion to permit the representation of the divine by an animal form, that religion has not yet conceived God as pure self-consciousness or reason. Its art can not arrive at gracefulness. As a consequence of this defect, however, it can not account for the origin and destiny of the world in such a way as to explain the problem of the human soul. It is an insoluble enigma, whose type is a sphinx.

(f) The Sphinx is the rude rock out of which it rises, symbolizing inorganic nature; then the lion's body, typifying by the king of beasts the highest of organic beings below man; then the human face, looking up inquiringly to the heavens. Its question seems to be: " Thus far: what next? " Does the human break the continuity of the circle of Nature, within which there goes on a perpetual revolution of birth, growth, and decay, or does the human perish with the animal and plant and lose his individuality? How can his individuality be preserved without the body? The Egyptian's highest thought was this enigma. He combined the affirmative and negative elements of this problem, conceiving that man survives death, but will have a resurrection and need his particular body again, which therefore must be preserved by embalming it. The body of Osiris had to be embalmed by Isis. The sacred animals, bulls and others, were embalmed upon death.

(g) The Egyptian laid all stress on death. In his art he celebrated death as the vestibule to the next world and the life with Osiris. Art does not get beyond the symbolic phase with him. As in the hieroglyphic the picture of a thing is employed at first to represent the thing, and by and by it becomes a conventional sign for a word, so the works of art at first represent men and gods, and afterward become conventional symbols to signify the ideas of the Egyptian religion. The great question to be determined is this: What destiny does it promise the individual, and what kind of life does it command him to lead? The Egyptian symbolizes his divine by the processes of Nature, that represent birth, growth, death, and resurrection, and hence conceives life as belonging to it. The course of the sun—its rising and setting, its noonday splendour and its nightly eclipse; the succession of the seasons—the germination, growth, and death of plants; the flooding and subsidence of the Nile—these and other phenomena are taken as symbols expressing the Egyptian conception of the divine living being. Finally, it rises out of the pictured representations by symbols, and tells the myth of Osiris killed by his brother Typhon, and of his descent to the silent realm of the under-world, and of his there reigning king, and of his resurrection. East Indian art, on the contrary, dealt with symbols that were not analogous to human life. They reverenced mountains and rivers, the storm winds and great natural forces that were destructive to the individuality of man, but also reverenced life in animals. They founded asylums for aged cows, but not for decrepit humanity.

§ 225. *Classic Art.*—The highest form of art is reached by the so-called classic nations—Greece and Rome. They arrived at the expression of freedom in the body—freedom in its pose and freedom in its action. This is properly called gracefulness. The limbs of the body are obedient to the will of the soul. When the limbs are in the way, when the soul does not know what to do with them, we have awkwardness as a result, and not gracefulness. Greek art seizes for its theme some moment of life when all the limbs are required to express the purpose of the soul, as, for instance, in the Apollo Belvedere. If it takes for its theme a sitting figure—the Olympian Zeus—it poses the body in such a way that we see the full control of the will over the limbs. The sitting Zeus could rise instantly and hurl his thunderbolt. The "classic repose" of which we hear is ever a graceful repose—graceful because the whole body is pervaded and controlled by the soul.

26 ·

(*a*) The Greek religion made beauty the essential feature of the idea of the divine, and hence his art is created as an act of worship of the beautiful. It represents the supreme attainment of the world in pure beauty, because it is pure beauty and nothing beyond. Christianity reaches beyond beauty to holiness. Other heathen religions fall short of the Greek ideal, and lack an essential element which the Greek religion possessed. The Greeks believed that the divine is at the same time human; and human not in the sense that the essence of man, his purified intellect and will, is divine, but human in the corporeal sense as well. The gods of Olympus possess appetites and passions like men; they have bodies, and live in a special place. They form a society, or large patriarchal family.

(*b*) The manifestation of the divine is celestial beauty. Moreover, the human being may by becoming beautiful become divine. Hence the Greek religion centres about gymnastic games. These are the Olympian, the Isthmian, the Nemean, and the Pythian games. Exercises that shall give the soul sovereignty over the body and develop it into beauty, are religious in this sense. Every village has its games for physical development; these are attended by the people, who become in time judges of perfection in human form, just as a community that attends frequent horse-races produces men that know critically the good points of a horse. It is known who is the best man at wrestling, boxing, throwing the discus, the spear, or javelin; at running, at leaping, or at the chariot or horseback races. Then, at less frequent intervals, there is the contest at games between neighbouring villages. The successful hero carries off the crown of wild olive branches. Nearly every year there is a great national assembly of Greeks, and a contest open to all. The Olympian festival at Olympia and the Isthmian festival near Corinth are held the same summer; then at Argolis, in the winter of the second year afterward, is the Nemean festival; the Pythian festival near Delphi, and a second Isthmian festival, occur in the spring of the third year; and, again, there is a second Nemean festival in the summer of the fourth year of the Olympiad. The entire people, composed of independent states, united by ties of religion, assemble to celebrate this faith in the beautiful, and honour their successful youth. The results carried the national taste for the beautiful, as seen in the human body, to the highest degree.

(c) The next step after the development of the personal work of art in the shape of beautiful youth, by means of the national games and the cultivation of the taste of the entire people through the spectacle of these games, is the art of sculpture, by which these forms of beauty, realized in the athletes and existing in the minds of the people as ideals of correct taste, shall be fixed in stone and set up in the temples for worship. Thus Greek art was born. The statues at first were of gods and demigods exclusively. Those which have come down to us cause our astonishment at their perfection of form. It is not their resemblance to living bodies, not their anatomical exactness that interests us, not their so-called "truth to Nature," but their gracefulness and serenity, their "classic repose." Whether the statues represent gods and heroes in action, or in sitting and reclining postures, there is this "repose," which means indwelling vital activity, and not mere rest as opposed to movement. In the greatest activity there are considerate purpose and perfect self-control manifested. The repose is of the soul, and not a physical repose. Even sitting and reclining figures—for example, the so-called Theseus from the Parthenon, the torso of the Belvedere—are filled with activity, so that the repose is one of voluntary self-restraint, and not the repose of the absence of vital energy. They are gracefulness itself. (See Hegel's Philosophy of History, under Greece.)

§ 226. *Romantic Art.*—The third stage of art is Christian art, or, as Hegel calls it, romantic art, which at first is occupied in showing the superiority of the soul to the body, and for this purpose selects for its subjects examples of steadfastness under severe trial—martyrs, and especially the sufferings of Christ. It goes so far in this as to set itself in opposition to classic art, and sometimes indicates its contempt for gracefulness in order to accentuate its preference for inward freedom and spiritual elevation. It portrays freedom *from* the body, while Greek art shows freedom *in* the body. In the later development of Christian art we see the attempt to represent gracefulness without losing the expression of the predominance of the inner life of the soul over its corporeal life.

(*a*) In Fra Angelico's paintings we see Christian martyrs with tortured bodies, but meekness and peace in their faces—a peace that passeth understanding, for they are at one with the Divine. There is no longer the expression of the desires of the body, but only the religious longing for spiritual perfection. Classic art showed us the soul in the body, and with bodily desires and passions, but purified by subordination to social restraints. Christian art shows, in this first stage, the opposite of Greek art—not freedom in the body, but the renunciation of the body.

(*b*) Then there is a second and later phase of romantic art, represented by such artists as Raphael, Murillo, Da Vinci, Michael Angelo, Correggio, Holbein, and Rubens. Gracefulness has been more or less restored by these, but not the classic repose of the Greeks; for there remains, even in the latest forms of Christian or romantic art, the portrayal of a longing or aspiration of the soul for something beyond what it has achieved.

§ 227. Classic or Greek and Roman art is the perfect realization of the union of the material and spiritual; hence the highest type of art as art. Christian art, representing as it does the struggle of the soul against its physical environment, is a form of art that looks toward religion. It is therefore a transition from art to a higher form of the realization of reason—namely, religion.

(*a*) Art is not a mere transitory phase of human culture; it belongs to all subsequent ages of human history after it has once come into being. Moreover, the classic form of art will more and more come to be admired in all the future Christian ages, because it portrays freedom in the form of gracefulness. The earliest Christian ages could not admire Greek art without falling back into sensuality. They had not yet attained a persistent hold of the spiritual.

(*b*) When the Christian idea had been evolved in history to a point where natural science could be pursued in a free and untrammelled manner, then came the age of inventions, labour-saving and knowledge-extending inventions, that enable us to conquer Nature and emancipate ourselves from that drudgery which had been necessary for the sake of food, clothing, and shelter. In the presence of this development of power over Nature we desire to see a reflection of our material freedom, and we accordingly gratify ourselves by reproducing Greek art with its graceful forms. The perennial image of free control of bodily forms pleases us as it did the Greeks, but it does not excite in us a feeling of worship, as it did in them; for we worship a transcendent God, one who can not be fully revealed in graceful forms, like Zeus and Apollo, but who requires also science, religion, and philosophy for his revelation. For the Christian civilization needs not merely piety of sense-perception, which is art, but piety of the heart and piety of the intellect. We have varied our spiritual wants, and we have a place for art in our lives as a reflection of our freedom.

§ 228. *The Several Arts.*—The several fine arts are, in an ascending scale, architecture, sculpture, painting, music, and poetry. Dancing, landscape gardening, engraving, elocution, dramatic art, and rhetoric are accessory to one or more of the five great departments of art, rather than separate departments.

§ 229. *Architecture.*—The silent lessons of architecture—the impressiveness of its masses, its harmonious proportions, its suggestion of great natural powers overcome by spiritual might—these effects are obvious. Art portrays what has an end of its own, and to be art of a very high character it must show that the beautiful object exists for itself, and does not exist for the sake of other objects—not even for morals or religion. But, of course, the highest art will be found in harmony with both morals and religion.

(*a*) The architecture of India and Egypt belongs to symbolic art. The human is struggling against the natural, but is not able to subdue it and achieve freedom. The highest achievement of Egyptian architecture appears in the pillars or columns of its temple crowned with the lotus, for in the lotus capitals there is an approximation toward gracefulness.

(*b*) Greek architecture is much superior in its expression of freedom. Its Doric, Ionic, and Corinthian columns fully achieve gracefulness. In a solid wall for the support of the roof the manifestation of the forces which are struggling against the power of gravity are not so adequate as when the support is a pillar or column. The column being isolated, the effects of gravity are exhibited in the yielding of its capital—its expansion as in the Doric capital, or the graceful yielding curves as appearing in the Ionic volute, or the bending of the acanthus leaves in the Corinthian capital. Gravity is manifested on the one hand, but the Greek capital shows how easy and gracefully the supporting column resists the downward force.

(c) The Roman arch is converted into a dome by carrying out its principle on all sides, instead of laterally alone. The arch is a ready suggestion, symbolically, of the Roman national principle. Each stone in the arch is relatively a keystone to all the rest. All depends on each and each on all. Each Roman citizen felt and acted as if he were the keystone to his nation. The dome suggests the sky over all, and hence toleration. Under the dome of the Roman Pantheon the gods of all nations were set up and worshipped. The dome is an appropriate symbol for the state or nation. Each patriotic citizen consecrates his life for the life of the social whole, and each is in turn supported and protected by the rest, like a keystone.

(d) Romantic architecture comes to its highest completeness in such Gothic structures as the cathedrals of France and the abbeys of England, but especially in the Cologne Cathedral and that of Amiens, and the Sainte-Chapelle of Paris. It celebrates the Divine not as something originating in matter and lifted up away from matter by its self-activity, but it expresses rather the complete nugatoriness of matter except as supported by spirit; for, instead of expressing the effects of weight or gravity in its slender columns, it expresses rather the support of what is below by what is above. The columns seem visibly to pull instead of to push or thrust. It is the heavens that support the earth. It seems as if the

cathedral floor is fastened to the columns, and these pull
up and sustain the floor by fastening it to the roof. All
the lines point upward and seem to worship what is
above. The Christian religion is expressed in the Gothic
cathedral, which has been called a petrified prayer. The
Roman dome expresses the universal sway of civil law—
a sky of justice, which extends over all. The Greek temple
shows freedom in matter. It crowns a hill, like a blossom
which has ascended from the surface of the earth to
manifest a deep inner self-activity of matter itself.

§ 230. *Sculpture.*—The statuary of Egypt and
the Orient does not express freedom; it abounds in
stiff and ungraceful lines; but the statuary of the
Greeks is the supreme achievement of a people whose
religion was a worship of the beautiful. In the highest period of its perfection it represents so much
dignity of character, so much rationality and clear
consciousness of purpose in its figures of the gods,
that the Divine itself seems to be present in material
form. Christianity has not been able to express its
distinctive ideals in sculpture. It finds painting a
far more adequate means. Painting can express sentiment by means of colour; it can show subjective
feelings and subtle reactions occasioned by the situation in which the theme of the work of art is placed.
Modern sculpture is often defective through the fact
that an attempt is made to express sentiment rather
than action. The highest sculpture exhibits the serenity of the soul even in the presence of danger.

§ 231. *Painting.*—The proper subjects of painting are to be found especially in the Christian religion, and in the situations of modern life that appeal intensely to our ethical emotions. Greek painting, except what has been preserved for us in the frescoes of buried cities, is known to us only through descriptions. From the evidences before us, it is safe to say that painting did not find with the ancients its appropriate themes. The subjects of Christian painting are divine love and tenderness, as seen in the Madonnas; the soul, supported by its faith in the Divine, manifesting its constancy even when enduring the bodily tortures of martyrdom; the Divine, gracious and forgiving even in the crucifixion scene; the Transfiguration, reflecting the light of the soul when seeing pure truth; the Last Supper, exhibiting the emotions of the good when betrayed by the bad; the Last Judgment, showing the return of the deed upon the doer; not so much action as reaction, not so much the deed, as the emotion aroused in the depths of the soul by the presence of injustice and hate.

§ 232. *Music.*—Music has the form of time, while architecture, sculpture, and painting have the form of space; hence it can express all the steps in the genesis of the situation which it portrays, and is not confined to a single moment, like the other arts.

The group of statuary, the Laokoon, for instance, must seize the highest moment of the action and present it. In this highest moment we can see what has happened before, and what is likely to happen in the time that follows.

(a) Goethe has discussed this admirably in his essay on the Laokoon. It will not do for the sculptor to attempt to present us in his work of art the entire completion or working out of the theme; he must seize it in the middle, where the spectators can easily read the past series of actions and motives and forebode what is to succeed. Painting is not so closely confined to a point of time as sculpture. Painting can idealize space through perspective, light and shade, colour, clearness and obscurity. While actual size, actual length of line, is necessary in architecture, in painting it can be represented by perspective. Not only the largest temple of the world, but even Mont Blanc, could be painted on a piece of ivory which could be covered with one's thumb.

(b) Painting, moreover, by reason of the fact that it can present to us sentiment through the aid of colour, finds the limitation of its theme to a single moment of time less important. But music can take up the whole series of actions and reactions which are presupposed by a serious situation of the soul, and can carry these all through to the final *dénouement*.

(c) The material side of music is found in the structure and peculiarities of the several musical instruments: vibration by means of strings, columns of air in wind instruments, and, above all, by the vocal chords of the human being. A tone is a repetition of the same wave length. One tone can produce with another one which has an agreement with it partial or complete chords and concords; with another tone not agreeing with it, it produces a discord. There is a natural order of tones, partly discordant and partly concordant with the key-note, which forms the scale. It includes what is called an octave. An aria starts from the fundamental tone of a scale, or from its third or fifth, and, by departing from the fundamental tone or from those kindred with it, expresses its alienations and collisions. Finally, it returns to the fundamental tone or one of its close kindred, and the problem is solved.

(d) There is also counterpoint, which, like persons in a drama, expresses a concordant or opposing aria to the chief one. With these resources music excels all the plastic arts in its ability to portray problems and collisions of human life and their solution. Emotional disturbances and the restoration of harmony naturally take on this form of expression. But there is the music of sensuous pleasure, and opposed to it the music of moral action. The Italian boat song or the Scotch reel may express the former, and a sonata or symphony of Beethoven will express moral action. Architecture has been called frozen music. Neither architecture nor music deals directly with the shapes of rational creatures or with the image of the human form divine; they are confined to proportions and symmetries.

§ 233. *Poetry.*—Poetry is the form of art that unites in itself all the others. It is closely allied to music—the time art—and through the imagination it can reproduce each and all of the space arts. It can do more than this: it can, through its appeal directly to imagination, transcend the time limitations of music, and the space limitations of architecture, sculpture, and painting. There is the poetry of national collisions, or epic poetry, the poetry of the individual, or lyric poetry, and the poetry of society, or the drama, which takes the form of comedy or tragedy. Comedy shows us a collision which has arisen between the individual and some social ideal, in which the discomfiture of the individual is not so deep as to destroy him. The social organism in which man lives is such as to convert his negative deeds into self-refuting or self-annihilating deeds. This occasions laughter when the individual is not seriously injured by his irrational deed. Tragedy, on the other hand, shows us a serious attack upon the social whole and the recoil of the deed upon the doer, so that he perishes through the reaction of his deed. Tragedy, however, requires as a necessary condition that the individual who perishes shall have a rational side to his deed. A mere villain is not sufficient for a tragic character; there must be some justification for him.

(*a*) The greatest poets are Homer, Dante, Shakespeare, and Goethe, and these artists are in the truest sense educators of mankind. The types of character exhibited in their literary works of art, such as Achilles, Agamemnon, Ulysses, Macbeth, Hamlet, Wilhelm Meister, and Faust, have helped and will always help all mankind to self-knowledge, by showing them how feelings become convictions and how convictions become deeds, and how deeds react upon the doer through the great organisms of human society.

(*b*) The world-wisdom of a people is largely derived from its national poets, not as a moral philosophy, but as vicarious experience. Aristotle said that the drama purifies the spectator by showing him how his feelings and convictions will result when carried out. Without making the experience himself, he profits by participating in the world of experience depicted for him by the poet. It is more or less in human nature to recoil against direct advice, especially moral advice. We do not like to have its application made personal; but. in the work of art we see the moral energies of society acting upon ideal personages, and the lesson to the spectator is more impressive and more wholesome, because it is accepted by him in his freedom, and not imposed upon him by external authority.

§ 234. All that man does contributes to a revelation of human nature in its entirety, but art and literature lead all other branches of human learning in their capacity to manifest and illustrate the desires and aspirations, the thoughts and deeds of mankind. In the presence of the conflict of moral ideals, the struggle of passion against what is rational, the attacks of sin and crime on the divine order of the world, all that is deepest in human character is manifested. Art and literature portray these serious collisions, and like the mountain upheavals that break and tilt up the strata of the crust of the earth, and reveal to the geologist the sequence of the formations from the most primitive to the most recent, so these artistic situations reveal to all men the successive strata in the evolution of human emotions, ideas, and actions. Thereby the single individual comes to know the springs of action of his fellow-men.

CHAPTER XXXIX.

The Psychology of Science and Philosophy.

§ 235. SCIENCE is the systematized results of observation. Each fact in the world is placed in the light of all the other facts. All facts are made to help explain each fact. But each fact represents only one of the many possible states of existence which a thing may have. When one state of existence is real, the others are mere possibilities, or, as they are called, "potentialities." Thus water may exist as liquid, or vapour, or ice, but when it is ice the liquid and vapour states are mere potentialities. Science collects about each subject all its phases of existence under different conditions; it teaches the student to look at a thing as a whole, and see in it not only what is visible before his senses, but what also is not realized and remains dormant or potential.*

(*a*) The scientifically educated labourer, therefore, is of a higher type than the mere " hand-labourer," because he has learned to see in each thing its possibilities. He sees each thing in the perspective of its history. In the

---

* Compare with this § 201, (*a*) and (*b*), above.

educated labourer we have a hand belonging to a brain that directs, or that can intelligently comprehend a detailed statement of an ideal to be worked out: the labourer and the " boss " are united in one man. There are different degrees of educated capacity, due to the degree in which this power of seeing invisible potentialities or ideals is developed. The lowest humanity needs constant direction, and works only under the eye of an overseer; it can work with advantage only at simple processes; by repetition it acquires skill at a simple manipulation.

(b) The incessant repetition of one muscular act deadens into habit, and less and less brain work goes to its performance. When a process is reduced to simple steps, however, it is easy to invent some sort of machine that can perform it as well as, or better than, the human drudge. Accordingly, division of labour gives occasion to labour-saving machinery. The human drudge can not compete with the machine, and is thrown out of employment and goes to the almshouse or perhaps starves. If he could only be educated and learn to see ideals, he could have a place as manager of the machine. The machine requires an alert intellect to direct and control it, but a mere " hand " can not serve its purpose. The higher development of man produced by science therefore acts as a goad to spur on the lower orders of humanity to become educated intellectually. Moreover, education in science enables the labourer to acquire easily an insight into the construction and management of machines. This makes it possible for him to change his vocation readily. There is a greater and greater resemblance of each process of human labour to every other now that an age of machinery has arrived. The differences of manipulation are growing less, because the machine is assuming the hand-work, and leaving only the brain-work for the labourer. Hence there opens before labour a great prospect of freedom in the future. Each person can choose a new vocation, and succeed in it without long and tedious apprenticeship, provided that he is educated in general science.

§ 236. There are three stages in the development of science: First, there is the observation of things and facts—the scientists map out and inventory the objects in each department of Nature; secondly, the interrelations are investigated, and this leads to a knowledge of forces and influences which produce or modify those objects that have been inventoried in the first stage of science. This is the dynamic stage, the discovery of forces and laws connecting each fact with all other facts, and each province of Nature with all other provinces of Nature. The goal of this second stage of science is to make each fact in Nature throw light on all the other facts, and thus to illuminate each by all. Out of this arises the system of the whole, and the third stage of science is reached. Science in its third and final stage learns to know everything in Nature as a part of a process which it studies in the history of its development. When it comes to see each thing in the perspective of its evolution, it knows it and comprehends it.

(a) Science is said to be founded on facts of observation. Do facts have to be transformed into truths, or are they truths already? The direct fall of an apple from the tree is a fact to the swine that run to devour it; but the thoughtful man, Isaac Newton, sitting under the tree, sees involved in one fact the fall of the apple and the shaking of the tree by the wind, the wind occasioned by the movement of the sun to the equinox, and this again occasioned by the inclination of the earth's axis to the plane of the ecliptic, its revolution round the sun, etc.; he sees, too, the moon through the branches of the tree from which the apple has fallen; the fall of the apple is one fact with the fall of the moon in its orbit: he sees the law of universal gravitation in the fall of the apple.

(b) A fact is a relative synthesis—an *arbitrary* synthesis, we may say. It is a fragment of a larger whole of things and events. Since it is determined by all that exists in the universe as the totality of conditions, we can not seize any fact in its entire compass except by thinking the universe.

(c) A fact in its narrower compass may be easily seized; but the exposition of a fact in its widest relations is " a mere ingenious arrangement of words " to the one who is not equal to the task of rethinking those relations. Aristotle's works, taken as a whole, are an attempt to seize the facts of the world in their entirety—each fact in its entirety; and he finds that the entirety of each fact—each fact grasped in all its conditioning relations— is the entirety of all facts; in short, the ultimate fact is one, and that, namely, what Plato calls the Self-moved One.

§ 237. Philosophy investigates the ultimate presuppositions of existence. It seeks a first principle of all. Accordingly, it sets out from any given fact, thing, or event, and begins at once to eliminate from it what is accidental or contingent and drop it out of consideration. It does not begin with an inventory, but goes at once to a first principle, and tries with this to explain the inventory furnished it by experience. All sciences deal in unity. They unite phenomena in a

27

principle. If they have become genuine sciences, they find for a principle a definite causal energy, which unfolds or acts according to laws. These laws express the nature or constitution of that causal energy. A science that rests on mere classification has not yet arrived at a true scientific form, because it has not yet shown how its general principle produces its details and applications. Such an imperfect science reaches merely subjective unities—mere aggregates of things or events more or less independent of each other. The word process names the important idea in science. All the material of a science should be united in one process. To constitute a process, it is clear that there must be an active cause, and its operation according to a fixed method.

In a certain way, too, all science discusses presuppositions, and philosophy is not the only knowledge of presuppositions. Given a thing or event, science presupposes that it exists as a link in a chain of causality, and therefore sets itself to discover its antecedents and consequences; in short, to find its place in some process. This investigation on the part of science aims to learn the history of the thing or event. Its history reveals its former states and transmutations—in other words, the activity of the energy or cause by which it has come to be. The true method of science is the historical one—the method of discovering one by one the antecedent stages of things or events, and learning by this means the nature of the principle that reveals itself in the process.

§ 238. Natural science points toward philosophy as a sort of science of science; for that there is a general scientific method implies that all the sciences are related one to another through some universal condition, belong to processes, and have their explanation in principles. This underlying condition in which all objects find their unity is time and space, and all sciences presuppose the possibility of a science of time and space (mathematics and its applications).

§ 239. Ultimate science, or philosophy, finds causality to be transcendent, and discovers absolute or independent causality to be mind or reason—self-conscious, absolute personality (see Chapters VI and VII). Such ultimate science shows the place of things or events in the system of the universe, and reveals their origin and destiny. It explains things and events through the self-revelation of the absolute mind. Philosophy does not inventory anything whatever; it explains only what is furnished it; something being given in a definite manner, philosophy will discover one by one its presuppositions, and find its place and function in the absolute system.

(a) If the thing or event is not so far defined by one of the special sciences that it can be referred to some one of their principles, then only a very vague utterance about it can be made by philosophy. If it is only a thing or event, and it is not said whether it is animal, vegetable, or mineral, or some activity of one of them, then only the vague dictum can be pronounced that it arises somewhere in the creative process of the absolute, or, as religion states it, " it has arisen in the wisdom of God's providence," and we are sure in advance of all examination of the thing or event that it has a place and a purpose. If the thing or event is defined as falling within some science—say, for example, a plant, or some activity of it, as falling within botany—we can speak more definitely, and predicate of it what philosophy and science have discovered in regard to the place and function of vegetation in the world.

(*b*) For the reason that philosophy does not inventory any facts or events, but assumes them as thus inventoried by other sciences, it can not be accused of " affecting omniscience." It is, in fact, a special department of human knowledge, and requires special study and investigation just as other departments.

§ 240. The principle of specialization is conceived as opposed to that of philosophy. We are told that specialization is the principle of all progress; that philosophy deals with ultimate unities, and therefore can make no progress; that all progress comes through inventorying anew some minute province; that division or subdivision is best, because the minuter the field the more completely and exhaustively it may
. be inventoried.

Philosophy, it is said, is the enemy to this specializing and inventorying; it is content with any results that are handed to it, and manages to deal quite as well with imaginary things and events as with real ones. But as philosophy does not attempt any inventory, it is not a substitute for any one or for all of the special sciences. It

presupposes them as complementary to it; they give it its
objects to explain by the ultimate first principle.

§ 241. All philosophies imply the same first principle, although they do not all find it. Every philosophy sets up a first principle as the origin of all,
the cause of all, and the ultimate destiny of all. Let
such principle be called X. Then X is assumed as
originating all that exists or has existed or will exist,
through its own activity, and hence X is a self-activity; and self-activity is recognised by us in life and
mind.

(a) According to the current evolutionary view, all
nature is a struggle for survival of forms. The inorganic
forms go down before the organic forms. Of the organic
forms, the plant serves the animal and yields to him.
The animal in turn yields to man. Man, in fact, conquers
all nature. Here the law of survival of the fittest comes
to mean the survival of individuals that have most intelligence. All nature, it would seem, is a process for originating individuality and developing it into rational being.
Looked at theologically, this is satisfactory. Nature is the
creation of souls. It implies, of course, the supremacy
of mind, since all its lower processes exist for the production of spiritual beings—they depend on mind, so to
speak, and demonstrate the substantiality of mind. Mind
is the final cause and purpose of nature. This again implies that mind creates nature to reflect it. God creates
nature, and through nature creates spiritual beings who
participate in his blessedness. Hence nature presupposes
a God of grace and good will toward his creatures.

(b) Although this is satisfactory as a world-view, and
it harmonizes with the view taken in religion, it does not
follow that the methods of science study have a spiritual-

izing tendency, and, in fact, the opposite is the case. The method of external observation is sharply in contrast with the method of internal observation or introspection. When we look within we behold self-activity, as feeling, thinking, and willing; when we look out upon the material world with our sense-perception, we seem to see that everything is under fate, or external necessity. Everything, in short, is regarded as having an environment of outside conditions or relations upon which it depends: the totality of its conditions completely controls it, makes it what it is, and necessitates all its changes. Fate or necessity prevails universally according to such a view. The category of quality, according to philosophy, is that form of thinking which looks upon everything as related to other things—everything as dependent on an environment. This, we see, is precisely the attitude of external observation, and external observation prevails in the practical work of the natural sciences.

§ 242. To pass from the intellect to the will requires a philosophic activity; for philosophy is the form of thinking which is exercised or employed whenever one closes a train of reflection and resolves to act. Deliberation belongs to the intellect; it holds action in suspense until it shall get a complete survey of the subject. Such a survey implies an inventory and an act of systematizing. But by the nature of the case an inventory of an objective sphere can never be completed, by reason of the infinitude of its details. Each detail can be subdivided again and again.

If the will waited and held back its action until absolutely all the data were in, it would never act at all. The deed would be "sicklied o'er with the pale cast of thought." What is necessary is this: The inventory must be stopped, and all the facts must be assumed to be in hand. Then they must be summed up and their trend and bearing ascertained. This being done, the will is now in readiness to act; action assumes that the inventory is completed, and that the ultimate bearing of the data is known. Hence all practical action suspends the scientific or discursive form of thought, closes the case, so to speak, and puts on the philosophical attitude, assuming its survey to be a complete and absolute one.

(a) Every science, therefore, must put on a philosophic form before it becomes useful in practical life. If this sounds strange to any one, let him consider that a science (and let each one conceive here his own favourite special science—history, sociology, etc.) seeks first to make an exhaustive inventory of the facts within its field of investigation, and, secondly, to discover the laws of evolution of those facts. By the principle of evolution we come to see exactly how each fact is related to every other as antecedent or subsequent in the stage of development.

(b) Thus a science in its second stage unites facts into a system, so that each fact throws light on all other facts in its province, and is in turn illuminated by them. Such illumination of one detail by the rest brings out the principle of the whole system. The whole comes to be revealed in each part—not the whole as an aggregate, but the whole as a principle—the spirit that unites the details and makes them into an organism. Referring again to Kant's distinction between organic and inorganic, " In an organism each part is both means and end to all the others "; each part of the body—like the hand, for example—exists for the sake of all the other parts of the body, and so, too, all the other parts contribute in their turn to its production and sustenance.

(c) Science struggles toward a knowledge of the principle that animates the whole province, thus tending toward that kind of knowledge which we may term philosophical. In its third stage science becomes philosophical in very truth, for it seeks to discover the relation of each special science to every other, and to become the science of science. Each science, in that case, becomes an individual detail employed to throw light on every other science, and in turn to receive illumination by the concentrated light of all these others. Philosophy differs from science only by this comprehensiveness; it seeks to show the validity of a first principle of all things, whereas science in its second stage seeks only the principle of its subordinate province, and not the supreme principle of the world as a whole. But science in its third stage—comparative science—science that combines one science with another—is not different from philosophy.

(d) The actually working scientific man has to resist the tendency to philosophize. If he wishes to serve the cause of all science, he must single out some new province of investigation and proceed to inventory its facts and individual items. He must continually resort to the first stage of scientific work—the stage of mere inventory and verification—Antæus touching the earth, as it were. But confine himself as he may to the mere inventory of his chosen province, he proceeds insensibly into the second stage of scientific thought, and can not help seeing more and more in each of his facts the light which the other facts throw upon it. Upon completing an exhaustive inventory of the facts in his province, each part becomes luminous, because it is seen to be organically related to the rest. Goethe, as before noted, symbolizes this result of inductive science by the figure of Homunculus in the second part of his Faust. Limited to a small province, symbolized by the bottle, the entire province may be exhaustively inventoried, and then the facts be organically related, so that each is alike means and end for all the rest—a sort of a living organism, as it were—and this living organism is symbolized by Homunculus, who, as Goethe tells us, is continually longing to burst his bottle —that is, he wishes to transcend his narrow province of knowledge and attain to philosophic knowledge that sees one principle in everything. Poetic insight sees the same unity, and this is symbolized by Eros.

§ 243. Philosophy seeks to discover the bearing of all the conditioning circumstances on a situation. It is evident that the ultimate ground of action must always be a moral one, therefore, because the motive, express or implied, must always be some relation to the purpose that rules in the universe, its ultimate fact. Such relations are defined in only two ways— by religion or by philosophy.

Higher instruction differs from lower instruction chiefly in this: Lower instruction concerns more the inventory of things and events, and hence has less to do with inquiring into their unity. As pointed out elsewhere, its studies are comparative. Higher instruction deals more with the practical relation of all species of knowledge to man, as individual will and as will of the social whole. Such relation, it is admitted, is ethical. Now, since the doctrine of the ethical rests on the nature of the first principle, and philosophy is the investigation of that principle, it follows that philosophy, express or implied, must be the basis of higher education.

§ 244. The spirit of the first stage of scientific investigation is opposed to the practical, because it devotes itself to inventorying. Wisely to act, we must stop our inventory and assume that all our facts are in; we must close the case without taking further testimony, and, in view of what is already known, do our deed.

(a) All considerate action demands this general survey over the whole inventory and a distinct withdrawal of the mind from the investigation of fresh details. There must be a resolve to stop inventorying and close the case. " In view of so much investigation as has been completed, it seems wise to act thus and so "—and then we *act*.

(*b*) After the deed is done, we open our case once more and proceed with our inventorying until it becomes necessary to act again; for the course of experience is a continual process of inventory. This is true of all practical provinces. In medicine, we must try to heal with such remedies as we have discovered, and not wait until we have completed our science of healing. In politics, we must act in the light of such parts of history as have been inventoried, and not pause for the whole to be completed. Practical action, the human will, must close its inventory and take its general survey, and act on its generalization as if the insight were complete.

(*c*) It is quite as important that as soon as the necessity for action is past we should again open our investigations and proceed with our inventory. The inventory of the existing details of a province is something that can never be completed. If we delayed all practical action until this is complete, we should never act at all.

(*d*) Moreover, if we delayed our general survey—i. e., the philosophic attitude—until the inventory were complete, we should never take a general survey. But as practical steps must be taken and deeds be done, it is perpetually necessary to introduce the philosophical attitude of mind—that attitude which lets go its hold on some particular detail and, metaphorically, stands back so as to take a general survey of the whole in its proportions.

§ 245. So long, therefore, as the human will may act, as well as the intellect perceive, there is a necessary province of philosophical activity, and no practical man can escape it. If the practical man despises the philosophical aspect, his contempt is apt to appear in the one-sidedness and self-contradictory character of his deeds; for his contempt will cause neglect and carelessness in his general survey—he will not sum up the case judicially, but will give undue weight to some items of his inventory.

(*a*) The moral quality of deeds involves one's theory of the first principle of the universe. Inasmuch as every deed must be considered in its moral aspect before it can be called considerate, we see how completely the philosophic phase of the mind mediates between science and practice.

(*b*) We must take notice again here that this is not a question of specializing or not specializing in our work. The person who confines his attention to the inventorying of some very limited sphere of investigation—say, the dative case, or the history of the Juke family, or the course of a particular tornado—does not specialize his activity any more than the person who devotes his attention to the origin of the moral law, the ethnical trend of the Anglo-Saxon mind, or the fundamental moving principle in all human history. In the latter case, the person looks at the general form, and trains his mind to abstract from all other phases of detail. Neglecting content, he looks at form. Neglecting the temporary and local variation, he studies the large variations that fill entire epochs and whole continents. Each method of observation specializes and neglects the province of the other.

§ 246. The psychology of the history of philosophy is contained in the doctrine of the five intentions of the mind.* In every act of knowing there are

---

* See the Journal of Speculative Philosophy, vol. x, July, 1876, pp. 225-231.

present the object and the ego; the former may be
a sense-object (first intention), or a class of objects—
i. e., the object-producing cause (second intention);
or the first principle, as creator of the totality of being
in time and space (third intention); or the method of
proving the first principle (fourth intention); or the
totality of method, the first principle presupposed by
all method (the fifth intention).

I. In the most rudimentary form of knowing—
namely, in sense-perception—there is a union of the
two factors which form the extremes of cognition;
these are the pure ego and the sense-object. The
latter is particularity, immediately conditioned as
here and now perceived; the former is the self which
perceives, the universal subject of all activity of perceiving. The present now is a point in time, and
has no duration except through the synthetical addition of past and future times, which are not, but
either were or else will be. Thus the perception of
a permanent, say, a relation of any sort, can not take
place without attention on the part of the subject
who perceives to itself—that is to say, to the ego, or
self, which is the universal or permanent factor in
sense-perception. Thus the perception of relations is
accomplished by turning the attention from the sense-
object to the self: it is an act of reflection or bend-

ing back of the self to the self. The self turns from the content of perception and considers its form.

Since permanence is necessary in the subject in order that it may perceive any relation, it follows that self-perception enters all knowing. This explains the rôle of self-consciousness in cognition. From the emptiest act of knowing "this is now and here," up to the richest "God creates the totality to have it become a reflection of him through its own self-activity and independence," all predication is possible only through the withdrawal of the mind out of the limiting conditions of the particular here and now by means of attention to its own activity—the self as universal or transcendent, and at the same time as particular; for the ego is universal, because it fills each particular moment—is wholly present in each, and because it is transcendent or wholly outside each moment. It can exist quite as well after the moment has elapsed or been thrust aside by another moment. It is equally at home in all heres as in all nows, and likewise transcends them all.

§ 247. II. In the second intention, the cognition of general classes—which we have explained as the cognition of the individual object as a member of a species or class, and shown that this involves the ascent from thing to producing cause, the general being, the-collective-aggregate-of-causal-conditions-which-produce-this-object-and-others-like-it—the mind turns its attention on the activity that creates the particular; seeing it as objective process, it has climbed up from the particular toward the pure ego, or self, which forms the abstract or transcendent extreme of cognition. Just as the particular moments are grasped together through the determining cause that produces them, so, too, the multiplicity of determining causes perceived by the second intention are seen by the third intention to form one total, for they are in a process of interaction, and hence they have their negative unity or transcendent principle. The perception of this is the third intention.

Aristotle, in his Categories (V), speaks of two forms of being (οὐσίαι), or substances, the first being individual objects of sense, and the second being species, classes (or generic energies). If the distinction of first and second intentions of the mind is correctly attributed to Avicenna, it is evident that he attempted to find the psychological coefficients of Aristotle's two kinds 'of substances, the first intention perceiving individual things and the second their classes.

§ 248. III. The unity of universals or classes, or rather of their producing causes, is found by the third intention in a first cause or first principle. To posit a first principle for the world of things and events is to ascend above experience to a transcendent origin. And yet the beginnings of philosophy show us many thinkers who select some one object of second intention and make it the highest. Inasmuch, however, as the first principle is conceived as the origin of all that exists, it is the origin of very many things that are different from it in appearance.

Hence the system of philosophy is bound to explain how the first principle through its activity determines itself into other shapes or appearances. Suppose that the first principle assumed be called matter: then matter is the ultimate principle, the whence and whither of all; it is thus a universal, which is the sole origin of all particular existences, and also their final goal. Hence matter is conceived to be self-active, giving rise to the things and events of the world by the action of its energy within itself; for matter must contain potentially all that will come from it. It must be creative, causing them to arise, and destructive in so far as it replaces them by others, transforming the old into the new. It is therefore transcendent, or in a higher order of being than that which changes, begins, and ceases—higher, in short, than objects of first or second intention. Such a self-active being must possess a pure ego, or self, and also have the energy known as self-determination, or life.

Hence, as already shown in § 241, if we take X as the general symbol of the first principle, we shall be obliged to define it as a self-active being, living and intelligent.

§ 249. IV. The fourth intention turns away from the result—namely, the first principle—and notes carefully the method of proving it. It breaks the connection between the mind and truth, between the thinker and his theism, by criticising some step or steps in his method. The first stage of philosophy (third intention) was dogmatism; the second stage (fourth intention) is scepticism.

The third intention looked at the one first principle as origin of the many processes of the second intention and of the many facts of the first intention. But there was a psychologic coefficient—namely, the process of arriving at the first principle, the method of inquiry and demonstration. The fourth intention now considers this psychologic coefficient and criticises it; it compares the method with its result, and points out its inadequacies, seeming or real. Since the first stage of philosophy reasons objectively from effects or dependent beings to first or original causes (independent beings), it assumes the validity of its ideas of cause, phenomena and noumena, dependence and independence, subjective and objective. It arrives at an ontological proof of the existence of God. But there is possible also a psychological proof of God. The ontological proof finds the presuppositions of being through the principle of cause. So, too, a psychological proof may find the presuppositions of cognition to be an absolute reason. But at first psychology begins with pointing out the difficulties in knowing any objective being whatever. How can we pass over the gulf from the me to the not-me? The one and the many contradict each other, and hence what seems to us a world of being is an illusion. These were the earliest suggestions. Then came the nominalists, who attacked the second intention: universals are mere names or subjective classes; only individuals exist. Then came Hume with his denial of the validity of causality: instead of causality we have merely invariable sequence. Ontology could be certain still of its first principle, but only through its faith in causality. It could not answer any of the arguments of scepticism. The ancient scepticism showed that the existence of finite being is impossible, and that, even if it existed, the knowing of it is impossible. Modern scepticism finds our knowing subjective and inadequate for the knowing of any objective being. Both species of scepticism rest on difficulties in psychology, on mental incapacities; for even the objection that finite being is impossible, because it is a self-contradiction, is at bottom the psychological difficulty of conceiving dependent being (see § 143). The scepticism of Hume gave the impulse to Kant's studies. The Critique of Pure Reason made a systematic investigation of the psychology of cognition, and expounded one set of principles—those on which dogmatism had built its ontological proof—and another set of principles that had furnished the basis of scepticism. These were left standing in the form of an antinomy by Kant. The mind can prove two positions—one in accordance with dogmatism and the other with scepticism. By a criticism of the practical reason, Kant proves that the dogmatic conclusion must be believed and acted upon, although it can not be rescued from the antinomy of the pure reason. Kant's labour was so thorough and exhaustive that it was easy for his followers to escape altogether from the scepticism of the fourth intention. Schelling and Hegel accomplished this, but Fichte and Kant remained firmly on the negative or critical basis of the fourth intention.

§ 250. V. The fifth intention sees method as a totality: method is completed in a system. What the third intention does with the principle of causality and objective being—namely, sees the world to presuppose a divine first principle—the fifth intention does with psychology and the theory of cognition—it sees that the fact of consciousness presupposes an absolute ego or person. It sees that the underlying

28

presupposition even of scepticism is a personal first principle. Scepticism perceives philosophic method only in glimpses. The critical philosophy of Kant and Fichte, putting together systematically the frag- ments, arrives at a whole, and establishes the result that psychology presupposes the same first principle that ontology does. Give scepticism the rein, make it as thorough as possible, and the result is a sub- jective idealism, which affirms that the mind can not know anything but its own forms or ideas (see sec- ond part of Fichte's Vocation of Man for his most popular presentation of the view which is called solipsism). If that is so, face the conclusion, and we have the result that none of our categories apply to things-in-themselves. Time and space, qual- ity and quantity, causality and existence, are all subjective. But even then we have the world left precisely as experience had given it to us before. The difference is, that we know it to be subjec- tive now, and we thought it to be an objective thing-in-itself before. But we have still to divide our subjective world into a seeming subjective and a seeming objective world. But such a division proves to us that we have not thoroughly learned our doctrine of subjectivity; for we see now that we are still using one of our categories as objectively valid—namely, that of *objectivity*, or *thing-in-itself*; for unless our idea of objectivity is valid, there is no world-in-itself over against the one as subject, and we include both objectivity and subjectivity within mind or reason. But if it is valid, then our cognition must be objective in respect at least to that category. And if one, why are not all the categories objective? But we have remaining our seeming objective world of experience, though the objective world-in-itself has vanished. We now turn the doctrine round and enunciate it thus: I find within my reason both a subjective world and an objective world. Reason is then the absolute. I perceive now that I had been mistaken as to the extent of my personality. It is not a small affair, like my body in space; it in some way transcends space and time, for I am in some way participating in the absolute reason, and include somehow the entire world of subjectivity and the entire world of objectivity as found in my experience. This is the conclusion to which we arrive on the basis of a thoroughgoing critical scepticism. And this is the fifth intention of the mind; for it sees that reason is absolute person, including subject and object, both real. It sees that the individual ego is transcendent of subjective as well as objective limitations, and hence both free and immortal. To be unfree, it must be in space and not transcendent; it must be in a chain of causation and not self-active. To be mortal, it must be in time, and its ego must be like a flowing stream in which all moves, even its banks. But such a flowing stream could not be conscious nor an ego, for the act of cognition rests on self-identity. Without this absolutely permanent self-identity there could be no second intention of the mind. There could not even be a first intention; for the two extremes of each act of consciousness (see § 246) include an absolutely flitting present moment with an absolutely universal ego, abiding fixed in the flowing stream of present moments.

(a) Fichte's writings show an attempt to unite Kant's two critiques, the Pure and the Practical Reasons, with a stubborn resolution to retain the critical attitude of his master, and deny objectivity to the categories of the mind. He was engaged throughout his life in making new expositions, each one of which was a step toward the fifth intention—toward the insight into objectivity of reason. This is especially evident in his Way to a Blessed Life,* the last of some eleven different expositions, in which he gradually approaches the true ontological consequences of his system.† But he never quite sees that complete

---

* See William Smith's translation (Kegan Paul, London, fourth edition, 1889, Lectures III and IV, pp. 331-364 of vol. ii); see also Outlines of the Doctrine of Knowledge (in same volume).

† See my preface to the English edition of Kroeger's translation of Fichte's Science of Knowledge (Kegan Paul, London, p. xviii).

subjective idealism contradicts itself; that when you have the subjective purely by itself, it polarizes at once into subjective and objective worlds, and solipsism is converted into cosmothetic idealism; or, in other words, on shutting up the ego within itself, it finds a complete objective world identical with the one from which it has been excluded by scepticism. Schelling pondered over the significance of polarity, and at the time (1803) when he reached the doctrine that man and Nature are the two poles of existence, and absolute reason the indifference point uniting the two poles, we find the culmination of his thinking.

(b) Hegel, in his Phenomenology, or Voyage of Discovery, shows that he solved the Kantian dualism through the Practical Reason. The ethical form (justice and loving-kindness) is the necessary form for absolute being. If a self-active being were not ethical, it would reduce itself to a zero; for its self-objectivation by means of creative acts would by injustice and cruelty turn to naught, and hence its own consciousness of itself would grow dim and disappear altogether. According to Hegel, the moral is the necessary form in which freedom must exist if it exist at all. Hence in perceiving morality as the substance of the Divine being (the Old Testament idea of righteousness and goodness as essential attributes of Jehovah), man perceives the nature of absolute being, and thus arrives at absolute knowledge.

(c) This was Hegel's Voyage of Discovery, to pass from immediate sense-perception to the knowledge of true being. He had now before him the problem to be treated in a work which he called Logic—namely, to show how all the categories of the mind, all its general ideas, presuppose the ethical ideal.* It should begin with empty

---

* See The Science of Thought, by Prof. C. C. Everett, for an independent survey of this deduction of the categories of the mind in such a logic, and a critical interpretation of the labors of Hegel in this direction. (Boston: De Wolfe, Fiske & Co., new edition, enlarged, 1890.)

being, and end with ethical personality as the absolute. He is sure in advance that all ideas of the mind are fragments or imperfect definitions of ethical personality. Hegel's entire system is an exposition of the fifth intention of the mind, the insight into the union of the subjective and objective in pure thought, or the validity of philosophy. He appears greatest in his treatment of history. Civil history, the history of philosophy, of religion, art, and jurisprudence, all show the progress from Orientalism, in which man is unconscious of the divine-human in the absolute, to Occidentalism, in which the principle of ethical freedom gets realized progressively in all institutions.

THE END.